Surnames in Ireland

Seán E. Quinn
B.A. (Hons.), H. Dip. in Ed., M. Litt., Barrister-at-Law.

Irish Genealogy Press
2000

Published in 2000 by Irish Genealogy Press,
15 Rathclaren, Killarney, Bray, Co. Wicklow, Ireland.

Quinn, Seán Eoghan

Surnames in Ireland

ISBN 1 871509 39 4 Pck

Cover : Author's birthplace, Clonglash, Inishowen, Donegal

Printed by Colour Books Ltd., Baldoyle, Co. Dublin, Ireland.

To the memory

of

my father

**Daniel Joseph
(Joe)**

1925 - 1988

Preface

My Father sowed the seed of my interest in surnames, and I have been unable to rid myself of this hereditary affliction. As we drove from Dublin to Donegal every summer during the late fifties and sixties, he would comment upon the surnames written on the shops and other business premises in the towns through which we passed. He was naturally enough particularly interested in the surname "Quinn", and pointed out in Longford for example that they were of the *Muintir Ghiollagáin* of *Anghaile*, and nothing to do with ourselves as we were of the *Cineál Eoghain* (of *Magh Itha* to be precise). In parts of Ulster he would note and pass comment upon the number of plantation surnames, these surnames were numerous in east Donegal, where his paternal grandfather had been born.

In my own case I subsequently took History in my primary degree and later taught the subject. I have relentlessly pursued my interest in both Genealogy and in the origin and meaning of Surnames which my father passed on to me. I would refer the reader to my *An Introduction to Irish Ancestry* (now in its second edition), and *Trace Your Irish Ancestors* (third edition in course of preparation). Another work that I should mention is *The Surname Quinn: A history of the various septs and branches of the Quinns* (also in course of preparation)

As stated in the Introduction my intention is to make as much information as possible available about the largest number of surnames. The result is that approximately seven hundred out of a possible four thousand surnames in Ireland are dealt with. Furthermore in a work of a general nature such as this it is not possible to do justice to each surname. Perhaps some readers may be encouraged to take up the cause with respect to their own particular surname, or a surname which is of interest to them.

This work has been in gestation for the best part of ten years and has turned out differently to what I anticipated. If this book generates the interest which I hope it does, I will be happy to hear from those who come across it.

Seán Ó Cuinn / Seán E. Quinn

13th November 2000

seanequinn@ireland.com

Contents

Preface

Glossary

Ancient territories

Chapter 1	Introduction	1
Chapter 2	Evolution of Irish surnames	4
Chapter 3	Anglicisation of Irish surnames	6
Chapter 4	Surname groups	10
Chapter 5	Distribution and frequency of surnames	13
	Hundred most numerous surnames	17
Chapter 6	Surnames in England, Wales and Scotland	18
	Hundred most numerous surnames in England and Wales	22
	Hundred most numerous surnames in Scotland	23
Chapter 7	Surnames in the United States	24
	Most numerous Irish surnames in United States	25
	Thousand most numerous surnames in United States	30
Main text	**Surnames in Ireland**	37

Ancient territories

The following ancient territories in existence from earliest times are mentioned frequently in the main text. The Danes arrived between the ninth and twelfth centuries. They founded Dublin in 852, and their chief towns were Dublin, Wexford, Waterford, Cork and Limerick.

Anaghaile (Annaly) This comprised Longford. This was the territory of ó Fearghail, ó Cuinn.

Breifne (Breffny) This comprised Cavan and western Leitrim. This was the territory of ó Raghallaigh.

Corcu Lóighdhe This comprised south west Cork. This was the territory of ó Ceallaigh, ó Ceallacháin.

Dál Riada This comprised north Antrim. The ó Loingsigh were driven from here after the Cambro Norman invasion.

Déise (Decies) This comprised west Waterford.

Deas Mhumhan (Desmond) This comprised part of Cork and Kerry. The ó Súilleabháin established themselves in the west of Desmond. The Mac Carthaigh were Kings of Desmond.

Iar Connacht This comprised mainly Connemara.

Muscraidhe (Muskerry) This comprised central and north west Cork.

Orghialla (Oriel) This comprised Armagh, Monaghan and parts of south Down, Louth and Fermanagh.

Ur Mhumhan (Ormond) This comprised part of Kilkenny and north Tipperary. The ó Cinnéide became Lords of Ormond after being driven out of Clare.

Tir Chonaill This comprised west Donegal. This was the territory of ó Domhnaill, ó Baoighill, ó Gallchobhair. As the Mac Lochlainn declined in power the ó Dochartaigh a leading sept of the Cineál Chonaill became rulers of Inishowen.

Tir Eoghain This comprised Tyrone and the barony of Loughshinlon in Derry. This was the territory of the ó Néill. The original territory was Inis Eoghain the chief sept of which was the Mac Lochlainn.

Thuas Mhumhan (Thomand) This comprised Clare and Limerick. This was the territory of the Dál gCais septs such as ó Briain,

Uí Mhaine This comprised parts of Galway, Mayo and Roscommon. This had been the territory ó Muireadhaigh.

Glossary

Barony A territorial division imposed on Ireland by the Normans, sometimes co-extensive with, or composed of a number of the ancient Gaelic Tuath. There are 273 baronies and from the sixteenth century they were used as an administrative unit.

Brian Bóirmhe High-king of Ireland lived from 926 to 1014, reigned from 1002 until his death at the Battle of Clontarf. He was chief of the Dál gCais of Thuas Mhumhan (Thomond).

Cambro-Normans Those Normans who having settled in Wales accepted the invitation of Diarmuid MacMurchadha to come to Ireland. In course of time it was stated that their descendants became more Irish than the Irish themselves (*Hiberniores Hibernicis ipsis*).

Clann A large tribal unit in Gaelic society which bore the name of a common ancestor. The septs later emerged out of the clanns.

County Ireland began to be shired by the English government from the thirteenth century, and the process ended with Wicklow in 1606. These became the principal administrative units of local government.

Diocese These are administrative divisions of the Church, presided over by a Bishop. Many of these boundaries date from the twelfth century, and reflect secular boundaries of that time.

Elizabeth I Queen of England from 1558, lived from 1533 to 1603. Known to the Irish as "Bloody Bess".

Erenagh (*aircinnech*) The head of a church or abbey, who was a lay lord and whose family held such office for generations.

Galloglass Mercenary soldiers usually from Scotland.

Niall Naoi-Ghiallach Historical high king of Tara who may have died around 454. It was said that he held hostages from each of the five provinces, as well as from the Scots, the Saxons, the Britons, and the Franks. His descendants known as the Uí Néill were most powerful for 600 years, they divided into a northern and southern branch.

Normans William Duke of Normandy invaded England in 1066, with the defeat of King Harold, William became King.

Pale, The The area around Dublin under control of the English government. It varied in extent through time.

Parish An area over which a local church exercised jurisdiction. Churches may have been administered by particular families. There are 2,445 civil parishes in total.

Plantation Beginning in the sixteenth century parts of Ireland were settled with English and later Scots settlers.

Sept The extended family unit in Gaelic society which adopted and bore a hereditary surname based upon the personal name of a common ancestor, and who occupied the same territory.

Strongbow Richard fitz Gilbert de Clare, lord of Strigoil and earl of Pembroke, landed in Ireland in 1170 at the invitation of Diarmuid MacMurchadha. He later established himself in Leinster.

Townland The smallest administrative division which relate to ancient Gaelic divisions. There are approximately 62,000 townlands.

Chapter One

Introduction

The intention in writing this book on surnames in Ireland is to make
available as much information as possible about as many surnames as
possible. Such information includes original Gaelic form (where
applicable); meaning; English variants; identification of septs, or
branches who bore such surname (where applicable); territory of
origin; position of surname amongst most numerous in Ireland,
England and Wales, Scotland, and United States; counties in which
principally found in Ireland; and estimated number of bearers in
Ireland and United States.

Basis of inclusion
All surnames in Ireland (which would easily exceed four thousand)
are not included in this work, and neither are all Irish surnames
properly so called. It was necessary to decide on what basis surnames
should be included. The criterion was that any surname that had
approximately 1,000 bearers in 1890 was included. In addition the
most numerous surnames in each of the counties at that time are also
included. These criteria subject to very few exceptions (surnames
borne by my own ancestors) dictated inclusion. This has meant the
inclusion of many English and Scottish surnames because they
satisfied the criteria. The inclusion of the less numerous surnames
would have increased the size of the book considerably.

Surnames and Genealogy
In Ireland the relationship between surnames and genealogy is
stronger than in other countries. However the reader should be careful
to distinguish between the two, and an absolute blood relationship
between the bearers of any particular surname would have to be
grounded upon a fully documented pedigree. A question which may
be asked is : Are all those who bear a common surname descendant of
a common ancestor? The answer in most cases is no. With respect to
the bearers of Irish surnames of a particular sept, the answer is a more
probable yes. However one must be cautious about this.

Surnames landscape
The surname landscape in Ireland is not homogeneous, it is strongly
influenced by our neighbours England and Scotland. In Ireland, in
addition to surnames whose origin is Gaelic Irish, there are English
surnames and Scottish surnames, and Irish surnames whose origin is
Cambro-Norman, English, Welsh and Scottish. In addition there are
other surnames of different origins. This issue is considered further in
Chapter Four. A knowledge of Irish history would aid in an
understanding of these influences, and readers unfamiliar with the
history of Ireland should refer to the topic.

Sources of information

An account on the source of the particular information on each surname follows. It is not absolute as given the number of surnames involved, information obviously came from other sources. There are for example books which refer to surnames in particular counties to which reference was made. It would be remiss not to mention in particular: *Sloinnte Gaedheal is Gall* (Irish Names and Surnames) (1923) by Patrick Woulfe; and *Special Report on Surnames in Ireland* (1909) by Robert E. Matheson.

The English version of a surname is given first and this is the order in which the surnames are arranged. Where there are two or more such variants, and this is often the case, the most common variant dictates the order irrespective of alphabetical order. Sometimes there is simply the addition of a letter or a change in one letter which gives rise to the variant. Reference is made to Matheson with respect to such variants. The Gaelic version (if there is one) follows and this is usually in accord with Woulfe. In addition a modern Gaelic form is sometimes given and this is taken from *An Sloinnteoir Gaelige agus An tAinmneoir* by Ó Droighneáin. The suggested modern Gaelic form is not included in all cases.

The vast majority of the surnames included are based upon personal names. Thus such personal names dictate the meaning. With regard to Gaelic personal names Woulfe's view is checked with *Gaelic Personal Names* by Ó Corráin and Maguire. With regard to English names the source is *Dictionary of English Christian Names* by Withycombe. In most other cases of derivation the view of Woulfe is given.

For the origin of Gaelic surnames my principal source is Woulfe whose view is cross check with anything else that has been available. For English surnames *A Dictionary of English Surnames* by Reaney and Wilson, and for Scottish surnames *The Surnames of Scotland* by Black.

With reference to the territorial origin the principal source is Woulfe, and reference is also made to *Onomasticon Goedelicum* by Hogan. A problem here is that the Annals will indicate that a particular sept occupied a particular area during the twelfth to fourteenth century, yet by the nineteenth century their descendants were gone and this cannot be explained. In the case of Scottish surnames the reference is Black.

In the past hundred years there has been a major shift in the population of Ireland from west to east. This movement in population distorts the natural distribution of our surnames. Matheson based his work on the birth index of 1890, a date long preceding current movements in population. It is most likely that the 1890 distribution has held fast for at least three hundred years (this is to leave aside the movement of population to Belfast in the nineteenth century), and is an appropriate distribution for a work of this kind. Accordingly the information here is taken entirely from Matheson.

The frequency of a Surname in England and Wales in 1853, and for Scotland in 1863 is taken from Matheson. The current frequency for England and Wales, and for Scotland is taken from the websites to which reference is made in Chapter Six.

The source of the frequency of particular surnames in the United States is the United States Census Bureau. In the summer of 1990, immediately following the 1990 Decennial Census, the Census Bureau conducted a large scale survey to measure undercount in the 1990 Census. The actual number of person records making up the sample was 6,290,251 individuals, this figure was approximately one fortieth of the population. The Census Bureau has placed information from this survey on its web site: www.census.gov/genealogy/names. There is a list of 88,799 surnames in order of rank, together with the frequency in percent of each surname.The documentation and methodology issued by the Census Bureau cautions that the sample upon which the frequency list is based intentionally over-sampled both Afro-Americans and Hispanic-Americans. Notwithstanding the limitations of such a survey, it is a valuable source as to the frequency of surnames in the United States. The exact manner as to how the estimate figures were worked out is illustrated in Chapter Seven.

Select Bibliography

Bardsley, Charles Waering English Surnames (London, 1915)
Barry, John J. The Study of Family History in Ireland (O'Donnell Lecture 1967)
Black, George F. The Surnames of Scotland (New York, 1946)
ó Corráin, Donnchadh and Maguire, Fidelma Gaelic Personal Names (Dublin 1981)
ó Droighneáin, Muiris An Sloinnteoir Gaelige agus An tAinmneoir (1982)
Ekwall, Eilert English Place-Names (Oxford, 1960)
MacGiolla-Domhnaigh Some Anglicised Surnames in Ireland (Some Ulster Surnames) (1923)
Hanks, Patrick and Hodges Flavia A Dictionary of Surnames (New York, 1988)
Hogan, Edmund Onomasticon Goedelicum (Dublin, 1923)
Hook, J. N. Family Names (New York, 1982)
MacLysaght, Edward The Surnames of Ireland (Dublin. 1980)
Matheson, Robert E. Surnames and Christian Names in Ireland (Dublin, 1901)
Matheson, Robert E. Special Report on Surnames in Ireland (Dublin, 1909)
Morgan T .J. and Morgan Prys Welsh Surnames (Cardiff, 1985)
ó Murchadha, Diarmuid Family Names of County Cork (Dublin, 1985)
Murphy, Hilary Families of Co. Wexford (Wexford, 1986)
Quilliam, Leslie Surnames of the Manks (Isle of Man, 1989)
Reaney, P .H. and Wilson R. M. A Dictionary of English Surnames (London, 1991)
Withycombe, E. G. Dictionary of English Christian Names (Oxford, 1977)
Woulfe, Patrick Irish Names and Surnames (1923)
Index to the Townlands and Towns, Parishes, and Baronies of Ireland (Dublin, 1861)

Chapter Two

Evolution of Irish Surnames

In Ireland the system of hereditary surnames began earlier than in most other European countries. Irish surnames evolved over many hundreds of years, and developed out of a more ancient system of clann name. The Irish septs which grew out of these clanns came to be identified by their surname. The bearers of a particular surname occupied a particular territorial unit. Notwithstanding the many confiscations of land in Ireland's history, the bearers of any particular Irish surname in most case still inhabit those areas their ancestors occupied prior to such confiscations.

Clann names
The clann names were formed from the name of distinguished ancestors, and descendants occupied particular areas. It is important to remember that the history of these clanns evolved over at least five centuries, from the fifth or sixth century to the eleventh century.
Uí Néill, descendants of Niall of the Nine Hostages in Meath and west Ulster; these divided into the **Northern Uí Néill** and the **Southern Uí Néill**. The Uí Neill by the seventh and eight centuries dominated the northern half of Ireland, which was known as Leth Cuinn (Conn's Half). The Northern Uí Néill claimed descent from Conall Gulban, Enda, and Eoghan, and ruled Aileach. The Southern Uí Néill claimed descent from Coirpre, Lóegaire, Fiachu, Maine, and Conall Cremthainne, and ruled Tethbae, Mide and Brega.
Uí Briúin, descendants of Niall's brother Brian. They ruled in Connacht and subsequently a sub-branch the **Uí Briúin Bréifne** expanded into what is now Leitrim and Cavan (Breffny).
Uí Fiachrach, descendants of Fiachrach, also a brother of Niall; these divided into the the **Uí Fiachrach Muaidhe** in north Mayo and Sligo and the **Uí Fiachrach Aidhne** in south Galway.
Uí Maine, descendants of Maine Mór in Connacht.
Dál Cais, descendants of Cormac Cas in Munster.
Eoghanacht, descendants of Eoghan Mór in Munster.

The Tuath
As time passed perhaps during the seventh or eight centuries, the clanns split into distinctive smaller groups, who inhabited their own particular kingdoms. These small kingdoms were known as *Tuath* and there were probably 150 of them in existence at any given time. Each *Tuath* had its own *Rí* (king). Any increase in the number of *Tuath* brought about an increase in the number of dynastic families. Every Irish *Rí* was elected from within the royal *fine* of his own *Tuath*, usually from the *derbfhine*. These were the descendants in the male line from a common great-grandfather. Practically all such *Rí* were subject to the overlordship of another *Rí*, at the top of the pyramid was the *Ard-Rí*. However too much must not be read into the possible authority of an Irish medieval High Kingship.

4

Septs
Gaelic society further evolved between the eleventh and twelfth centuries. Those who were descendants of a common ancestor, and inhabited the same locality came to be known as septs. The area of land controlled by a sept was know as a ballybetagh (and may have been co-extensive with the later parish), which was composed of sixteen ballyboes. A ballyboe was an area of land which could support a number of families, the modern equivalent is a townland. The overlord (himself being the chief of a sept) of a number of septs perhaps would have had the lordship of an area the size of a barony. Above such an overlord would have been another overlord the status of *ó Neill* or *ó Domhnaill.* The sept system was adopted by those who arrived during the Cambro-Norman invasion (see Chapter Four). The members of these septs were designated by a common surname.

What is not readily understood, when we look at how numerous many Irish surnames are, is that the bearers of a particular surname may be descendant of distinctly different septs. Also it often happened that sub-septs were formed, and quite different surnames were adopted by the descendants of a common ancestor.

Commenting upon how numerous were the members of some septs, Dubhaltach MacFirbhisigh wrote in 1650 "For it is a usual thing in the case of great princes, when their children and their families multiply, that their clients and followers are squeezed out, wither away and are wasted". Eoin MacNeill suggested that a reason for this was the Law of Debad which had the effect of passing an increased amount of land to an overlord in the absence of direct heirs. The septs were an important part of the organisation of Gaelic society.

In Gaelic Ireland the bonds which cemented society were the duties and rights attached to blood relationship. The sept system did not survive the colonisation of Ireland during the seventeenth century. It could not do so in the absence of the Brehon Law or the Gaelic leadership.

Patronymic and hereditary surnames
Before surnames becoming fixed and hereditary, individuals were designated other than by their own personal name. From an early period a personal name derived from a father (patronymic) or male ancestor came to be used to particularize the individual. Irish patronymics surnames were formed by prefixing 'Mac' (son of) to the genitive case of the fathers name, or 'Ua' or 'ó' (grandson of) to that of the grandfather. The Annals are full of such designations. The practise of forming surnames with 'Ua' or 'ó' had ceased before the Cambro-Norman invasion. 'Mac' surnames are generally of a later date than 'ó' surnames. In time the patronymic, which before was purely personal and changed with each generation gradually became fixed like the clann names centuries before, and began to assume the permanent and hereditary character of a family surname. The period at which this change began can only be determined approximately. The eleventh and twelfth centuries must be assigned as the period within which Irish patronymic surnames became fixed and hereditary.

Chapter Three

Anglicisation of Irish Surnames

Irish surnames, be they of Gaelic or of Cambro-Norman origin, have been greatly corrupted in their anglicisation. Woulfe enumerates various ways in which Irish surnames have been anglicised, and the matter will be discussed under those heads.

Phonetically

The anglicisation of most Irish surnames seems to have begun in the late sixteenth century. The anglicisation seems to have been the work of the officials of the English Government in Ireland. The surname was written down more or less as it was pronounced, without any regard to the Irish spelling. This method was used almost exclusively when surnames were first anglicised.

For example :

O'Brien for *ó Briain*
O'Callaghan for *ó Ceallacháin*
O'Donoghue for *ó Donnachadha*
O'Flanagan for *ó Flannagáin*
O'Neill for *ó Néill*

The same surname often gives several very different anglicised forms owing to dialectical variations and the vagaries of the phonetic system employed to represent them.

For example :
ó Cobhthaigh became, Coffey, Cowie, Cowhey, Cowhig, etc.,
ó Dubhthaigh became, Duffy, Dowie, Dooey, Duhig, etc..

On the other hand, very different surnames have been given the same anglicised form.

For example :
Coffey for *ó Cobhthaigh, ó Cathbhadha, ó Cathbhuadhaigh, ó Cathmhogha.*

In many instances the anglicised form has in the course of time been contracted.

For example :
O'Hare for O'Hehir,
O'Kane for O'Cahan.

Sometimes only a part of the original form has been retained.

For example : Ryan for O'Mulryan.

Surname have been further mutilated by dropping the prefix *Mac* or ó, and *Mac* when retained is improperly written, Mc or M'. This is particularly bad in the case of the anglicisation of Gaelic surnames in Scotland, where Mac surnames are not followed by a capital letter but are written as one word.

For example :
Macdonald rather than MacDonald (*Mac Dhomhnuill*),
Mac(k)intosh rather than MacIntosh (*Mac an Toisich*),
Mackenzie rather than MacKenzie (*Mac Coinnich*),
Macgrory rather than MacGrory (*Mac Ruaidhrí*).

Translation
During the eighteenth and nineteenth centuries, many rejected the phonetic rendering of their surname and adopted an English surname which was suppose to be a translation of their Irish surname. These translation are in many cases incorrect.

For example :

Badger for *ó Bruic*
Banks for *ó Bruacháin*
Barnacle for *ó Cadhain*
Blessing for *ó Maoilbheannachta*
Bonner for *ó Cnáimhsí*
Bridgeman for *ó Droichid*
Ryder for *ó Marcaigh*
Salmon and Fisher for *ó Bradáin*
Carpenter and Freeman for *Mac an tSaoir*
King for *Mac Conraoi*
Forde for *Mac Conshnámha*
Johnson for *Mac Seáin*.

The translated form sometimes takes an English termination.

For example :

ó Draighneáin translated Thornton.
ó Gaoithín translated Wyndham.

Attraction
A rare surname is often attracted to, and confounded with a more numerous surname of similar sound existing in the same locality. The surname instead of assuming a proper anglicised form, assumes the anglicised form of the more numerous surname.

For example :

	anglicised	attracted to
ó Bláthmhaic,	Blawick, Blowick,	Blake,
ó Braoin,	O'Breen, Breen,	O'Brien,
ó Duibhdhíorma,	O'Dughierma, Dooyearma,	MacDermott,
ó hEochagáin,	O'Hoghegan,	Mageoghegan,
ó Maoil Sheachlainn,	O'Melaghlin,	MacLoughlin.

7

Assimilation
The custom of assimilating Irish to foreign names is old in Ireland. Irish scholars writing in the Middle Ages, instead of latinising Irish names, simply substituted for them well known Latin names, such as Eugenius for *Eoghan*.This practice was extended to surnames during the seventeenth century. According to John O'Donovan the principal cause of this change, was the ridicule thrown upon Irish surnames by English magistrates and lawyers who were ignorant of the Irish language, and an anxiety on the part of the people to rid themselves of undersireable surnames.

For example :

      Broderick for *ó Bruadair*,
      Carleton for *ó Cairealláin*,
      Harrington for *ó hArrachtáin*, and *ó hIongardail*,
      Reddington for *ó Roideacháin*,
      Summerville for *ó Somacháin*.

In a few instances the assimilation is to a French surname.

For example :

      De Lapp for *ó Lapáin*,
      De Moyleyns for *ó Maoláin*,
      D'Ermott for *ó Duibhdhíorma*.

Substitution
In these case the similarity between the Irish surname and its English equivalent is remote and often there is no connection.

For example :

      Clifford for *ó Clúmháin*,
      Fenton for *ó Fiannachta*,
      Loftus for *ó Lachtnáin*,
      Neville for *ó Niadh*,
      Newcombre for *ó Niadhóg*.

It also happens when the Mac or ó is dropped the natural phonetic rendering of an Irish surname has the same form as an English surname.

For example ;

      Barry for *ó Beargha*,
      Ward for *Mac an Bháird*,
      Buckley for *ó Buachalla*.

Legislative provisions
There were statutory provisions introduced to encourage the anglicisation process. By a Statute of 1366, it was provided that "every Englishman do use the English language and be named by an English name, leaving off entirely the manner of naming used by the

Irish" and in 1465 a law was passed enacting "that every Irishman that dwells betwixtor amongst Englishmen in the County of Dublin, Myeth, Vriell, and Kildare . . . shall take to him an English surname of one town, as Sutton, Vhester, Trym, Skryne, Corke, Kinsale; or colour, as white, blacke, browne,; or arte or science, as smith or carpenter; or office, as cooke, butler...".

Corruption of Ó Cuinn

My own surname is a good example to take of how a Gaelic surname has been corrupted over the centuries of English administration. 'Quinn' is an anglicised corruption of the Gaelic surname 'ó Cuinn' (see the main text), and the variations of the surname that have emerged over the years illustrate the anglicising process.

Over a period of five hundred years one comes across Ua Cuinn, O'Coyne, O'Quyane, O'Quin, Quin and finally Quinn as well as other unmentionable corruptions. In the Calendar of State Papers for the period the sept is referred to as O'Quins, Quins, O'Quynnes. One man is referred to as Neale O'Quyn, O'Quin, O'Quinn, O'Quyne, O'Quynn, O'Quynne, Quyn (rather than as Niall ó Cuinn).

In the State Papers for the mid seventeenth century the prefix O' is dropped and the name is represented by Quin, Quiny, Quine, Quynne. From the end of the seventeenth century until the end of the eighteenth century, O'Quin is the most common form in the documents although other corruptions can still be found, though to a lesser extent than the immediately preceding period, examples of these are: Quin, Quayne, O'Quyne.

With the nineteenth century the prefix O' came finally to be dropped in English, 'Quin' was now the most common form of the surname but before the middle of the century it had been surpassed by 'Quinn'. From an examination of Griffith's Land Valuation circa 1850's it is obvious that 'Quinn' had surpassed 'Quin' by at least two to one. The practise of adding the extra "n" continued right up to the end of the century.

As has already been noted the vast majority of the Irish people in the past were unable to read or write, but when a situation arose, where it was necessary for the surname to be written down, it was written down in a contemporary form. On the other hand literate people were certainly not going to be told how to spell their own surname, and would write it as they would have understood how their forebears had done with only one 'n'.

My grandfather born in 1891 was registered as 'John Quinn', his father born in 1866 was registered as 'James Quin'. In my own case though registered as 'John Quinn' (being called after my grandfather), I am known as 'Seán Quinn', though in many official documents I am 'Seán ó Cuinn'.

Chapter Four

Surname groups

The Irish population is a mixture of a number of different national and cultural surname groups of which the Gaelic Irish is the most predominant. The additional groups identified by Matheson follow.

Danish surnames
The Danes came to Ireland between the ninth and twelfth centuries and established themselves on the eastern and southern coast. They founded the Kingdom of Dublin in 852, and their chief towns were Dublin, Wexford, Waterford, Cork and Limerick. Surnames traceable to Danish origin are: Betagh; Coppinger; Dowdall; Dromgoole or Drumgoole, Gould, Harold, Palmer, Plunkett, Skiddy, Sweetman (Swedeman) and Trant. It is accepted that many families of Danish origin took Irish surnames, prefixing O and Mac, so that their descent cannot now be ascertained without difficulty.

Cambro-Norman surnames
The Cambro-Norman invasion resulted in a second graft to our Gaelic surnames and there are many examples of such surnames in the main text. Examples given by Matheson are: Barry, Bellew, Bermingham, Burke, Carew, Clare, Cogan, Dalton, Darcy, De Courcy, Delamere, Dillon, FitzEustace, Fitzgerald, Fitzhenry, Fitzmaurice, Fitzsimons, Fitzstephen, Gernon, Grace, Hussey, Keating, Lacy, Le Poer, Marshall, Montmorency, Mortimer, Nangle, Nugent, Petit, Prendergast, Purcell, Roche, Staunton, Taafe, Talbot, Tuite, Tyrrell, Verdon, Vesey.

Adoption of Irish durnames
MacDermott, in his annotations to the Annals of Ireland by the Four Masters, refers to the fact that many of these families adopted Irish surnames: "The de Burgos or Burkes, of Connaught, took the name of MacWilliam, and some of them that of MacPhilip; the de Angulos or Nangles, of Meath and Mayo, changed the name to MacCostello; the de Exeters, of Mayo, to MacJordan; the Barretts of Mayo to MacWattin; the Stauntons of Mayo to M'Aveeley; ... the de Berminghams of Connaught and other places to MacFeorais, or Peorais; ... the Fitzsimmons of the King's County, to MacRuddery; ... the Poers of Kilkenny and Waterford to MacShere; the Butlers to MacPierce; the Fitzgeralds to MacThomas and MacMaurice; the de Courcys of Cork to MacPatrick; the Barrys, of Cork to MacAdam; and many others. in like manner.".

English surnames
Large numbers of English came to Ireland between the twelfth and eighteenth centuries, thus the large number of English surnames at present in Ireland. In addition there was the legislative provisions of 1366 and 1465 referred to in Chapter Three. Matheson gives the following examples of English surnames: Adams; Andrews; Arnold;

10

Ashe; Atkinson; Baker; Barr; Barton; Bates; Bennett; Berry; Bingham; Bolton; Bradshaw; Brooks; Canning; Carlisle; Carter; Christy; Cooper; Cox; Crowe; Downes; Edwards; English; Field; Fisher; Freeman; Goodwin; Hall; Harper; Harris; Harrison; Hawthorne; Henry; Hewitt; Hill; Holmes; Hopkins; Hunt; Hunter; Jackson; Jenkins; Johnson; Kidd; King Lamb; Lane; Little; Long; Mitchell; Morton; Nash; Osborne; Pearson; Richardson; Roberts; Robinson; Salmon; Shaw; Short; Simpson; Small; Somers; Swan; Taylor; Thornton; Turner; Walker; Wall; Waters; Watson; Webb; Webster; West; White; Woods; and Wright. Many of these surnames are considered in the text as they are numerous in particular counties, and exceed the estimated 1,000 bearers.

Cornish surnames

Cornish surnames are also to be found in Ireland. Wicklow and Wexford have many examples of such surnames. The Cornish surnames referred to by Matheson are: Jagoe, Lanyon, Pascoe, Pender, Pendred, Penrose, Tredennick, Tresilian, Trevelyan, and Vivian.

Welsh surnames

Welsh surnames are also to be found in Ireland, particularly in Wicklow and Wexford. Apart from Walsh and it's Gaelic form Breathnach which are referred to in the main text the following surnames are to be found: Howell, Lawless, Lillis, Lynagh, Lynnott, and Merrick. A Welsh colony established itself in the baronies of Forth and Bargy in Wexford at the time of the Cambro-Norman invasion, and retained its exclusiveness up until a hundred and fifty years ago. Surnames to be found there included Cod; Hore; Quiney; Rossiter; Sinnott; Stafford; Stephen; Walsh; and Whitty, these surnames were numerous in the town of Wexford.

Scottish surnames

Scottish surnames are also to be found in Ireland, particularly in Ulster. Prior to the Plantation of Ulster there was Scottish settlement in east Ulster (Antrim and Down). With the the Plantation of six of the Ulster counties, Scottish settlement in Ireland increased dramatically and the abundance of surnames from Scotland is clear from the text.

Manx surnames

Matheson points out similarities between the development of surnames in Ireland and the Isle of Man. The Isle of Man passed through similar phases of occupancy: first it was inhabited by the Gaels; then there was a period of Scandinavian domination; to be followed by English domination. Many native Manx surnames have the same derivation as Gaelic surnames. Examples being Cannell as the Gaelic MacConaill; Kermode as the Gaelic Mac Diarmada; and Mylchreest as the Gaelic Mac Giolla Chriosd.

French Huguenot surnames

The Parliament of Ireland in 1674 passed an Act granting letters of naturalization to Protestant refugees predominantly from France who were known as Huguenots. Colonies were established in Dublin, Kilkenny, Portarlington, Waterford, Cork and Lisburn, and they started the manufacture of silk, gloves, lace, cloth, and linen. Examples of Hugenot surnames are: Barre, Blacquiere, Boileau, Chaigneau, Du Bedat, Champion, Chenevix, Corcellis, Crommelin, Delacherois, Drelincourt, Dubourdieu, Du Cros, Fleury, Gaussen, Logier, Guerin, Hazard (Hassard), La Touche, Le Fevre, Lefroy, Lefanu, Maturin, Perrin, Saurin, Trench, Des Vignolles.

German Palatinate surnames

In the eighteenth century there was migration to Ireland from the Palatinate of the Rhine in Germany. These German refugees settled principally in Limerick around 1709, and their seperate culture remained intact up until a hundred years ago. Palatinate surnames to be found in and around: Court, Matrix, Ballingran, Killiheen, and Adare in Limerick were: Baker, Bovanizer, Bowen, Doube, Delmege, Gillard, Latchford, Ligier, Millar, Lodwig, Modlar, Pyper, Reynard, Ruttle, Shire, Stark, and Switzer.

Jewish surnames

Jewish surnames in Europe may be classified as either Ashkenazic (Yiddish speaking Jews and their descendants), or Sefardic (the Jews of the Iberian Peninsula and their descendants), but this division is not always absolute. There is a further division into Western Ashkenazic referring to speakers of Western Yiddish, and Eastern Askenazic referring to speakers of Easter Yiddish. The boundary between them being the old Geman-Polish border. Eastern Yiddish is further subdivided into North-Eastern, Central, and South-Eastern.

In the years 1881 to 1890 the Jewish population of Ireland which had resided in the cities were added to by the arrival of Russian and Polish Jews (North-Eastern Ashkenazic). Many of these settled in the south side of Dublin, and formed a Jewish Quarter.

Examples of Jewish settler surnames given by Matheson are: Coplan, Fridberg, Greenberg, Hesselberg, Maisell, Matufsky, Rabinovitch, Rossin, Statzumsky, Stuppel, Wachman, Wdedeclefoky, Weeeiner, and Winstock.

Chapter Five

Distribution and Frequency of Surnames

The principal surnames for each county is listed, they are in order of the numerical strength in which they occur. The figure after the surname is the number of entries in the birth index for 1890. The estimated number of persons of each surname can be ascertained by multiplying the figure by the average birth rate, which for that year was 1 in 44.8 persons.

Although 'Murphy' is the most numerous surname in the country at large, it does not occupy the leading position in many of the counties. In Leinster in the counties of Wexford and Carlow 'Murphy' is first. In the counties of Dublin. Louth and Wicklow. 'Byrne' is first, whereas in Kildare and Offaly 'Kelly' is first. In Longford and Meath, 'Reilly' is first, in Kilkenny, Brennan, in Laois 'Dunne', and in Westmeath 'Lynch'. In Munster, 'Sullivan' is the predominant surname in Cork and Kerry, followed in Cork by 'Murphy'. 'Ryan' heads the list in Limerick and Tipperary, while 'McMahon' is the leading surname in Clare, and 'Power' in Waterford. In Ulster 'Murphy' is the first surname in Armagh only. In Antrim 'Smith' is first, in Cavan, 'Reilly', in Donegal, 'Gallagher', in Down 'Thompson', in Fermanagh 'Maguire', in Derry, 'Doherty', in Monaghan, 'Duffy', and in Tyrone 'Quinn'. In Connacht, 'Kelly' takes precedence in Galway, Roscommon, and Leitrim (along with Reynolds), Murphy does not occupy the principal position in any county. Walsh is first in Mayo, and Brennan in Sligo.

The table on page 17 lists one hundred of the most numerous surnames together with an estimate of the number of bearers in 1890.

Province of Leinster

Carlow
Murphy 41, Byrne 33, Doyle 32, Nolan 28, Neill 27, Brennan 24, Kelly 15, McDonald 15, Kavanagh 14, Whelan 12, Ryan 10.

Dublin
Byrne 301, Kelly 194, Doyle 162, Murphy 132, Smith 106, O'Brien 105, Kavanagh 97, Dunne 93, O'Neill 93, Reilly 93, Nolan 89, Connor 82, Walsh 77, Farrell 73, Carroll 71, Ryan 65, Moore 63, Cullen 62, Keogh 60, Murray 60, Whelan 59, Brady 52, Kennedy 51.

Kildare
Kelly 40, Murphy 34, Dunne 32, Byrne 28, Nolan 20, Connor 18, Smith 18, Farrell 15, Ryan 15, Moore 14, Carroll 13, Neill 13, Bolger 12, Doyle 12.

Kilkenny
Brennan 49, Walsh 45, Murphy 35, Ryan 34, Carroll 25, Byrne 22, Butler 22, Maher 21, Dunne 20, Phelan 18, Kelly 17, Neill 17, Power 17, Purcell 17, Brien 15, Shea 15, Delaney, 14, Dowling 14.

Laois (Queen's)
Dunne 34, Delaney 30, Conroy 19, Lalor 18, Phelan 18, Fitzpatrick 17, Ryan 13, Carroll 12, Whelan 12, Byrne 11, Kavanagh 11, Kennedy 11, Brennan 10, Kelly 10, Murphy 10.

Longford
Reilly 78, Farrell 36, Kiernan 24, Kelly 23, Donohoe 19, Murphy 14, Brady 13, Quinn 12, Smith 12.

Louth
Byrne 36, Kelly 30, Murphy 30, Smith 26, Clarke 23, Duffy 21, McArdle 20, Reilly 20, Carroll 19, Mathews 16, Martin 14, Donnelly 13, Farrell 13, Morgan 13, Rice 13, Hanratty 12, McCourt 12, McKenna 12, Boyle 11, Connor 11, Lynch 11, O'Hare 11.

Offaly (King's)
Kelly 34, Dunne 23, Daly 20, Egan 17, Molloy 16, Mooney 16, Carroll 12, Walsh 12, Kenny 11, Murray 11, Dempsey 10, Kennedy 10, Maher 10.

Meath
Reilly 53, Smith 30, Lynch 17, Brady 16, Farrell 14, Farrelly 14, Kelly 14, Brien 13, Daly 11, Maguire 11, Duffy 9, Dunne 9, Byrne 8, Connor 8, Mahon 7, Clarke 7, Martin 7, Mathews 7.

Westmeath
Lynch 14, Farrell 13, Reilly 12, Daly 11, Murray 10, Duffy 9, McCormick 9, Walsh 9, Dalton 8, Kelly 8, Smith 8, Byrne 7, Carey 7, Dunne 6, Flynn 6, Leavy 6, Murtagh 6, O'Neill 6.

Wexford
Murphy 137, Doyle 102, Walsh 56, Byrne 46, Cullen 34, Kavanagh 34, Brien 32, Roche 31, Kelly 30, Nolan 30, Redmond 30, Connor 28, Kehoe 28, Ryan 26, Bolger 25, Whelan 25.

Wicklow
Byrne 87, Doyle 53, Murphy 26, Kelly 25, Kavanagh 24, Nolan 21, Brien 18, Kehoe 16, Lawlor 15, Toole 14, Dunne 13, Farrell 11, Redmond 10.

Province of Munster
Clare
McMahon 74, McNamara 61, Moloney 50, O'Brien 47, McInerney 39, Kelly 38, Keane 33, Murphy 29, Griffin 27, Halloran 26, Ryan 23, Lynch 22, Clancey 21.

Cork
Sullivan 418, Murphy 390, McCarthy 277, Mahoney 193, Donovan 182, Walsh 143, O'Brien 139, Callaghan 134, Leary 134, Crowley 116, Collins 115, Driscoll 110, Connell 109, Barry 108, Cronin 102,

Buckley 100, Daly 97, Sheehan 97, Riordan 94, Kelleher 92, O'Connor 91, Hurley 86, Regan 85, O'Keeffe 84, Harrington 82, Fitzgerald 81, O'Neill 75.

Kerry
Sullivan 349, Connor 188, Shea 146, Murphy 95, McCarthy 88, Moriarty 74, Fitzgerald 72, Griffin 58, Connell 56, Brosnan 55, Foley 55, Leary 47, Clifford 45, Walsh 45, Cronin 43, Lynch 41, Mahoney 38, Daly 34.

Limerick
Ryan 91, O'Brien 78, Fitzgerald 58, Sullivan 50, Hayes 45, Walsh 45, Collins 40, O'Connell 39, Murphy 38, Moloney 38, O'Connor 37, Lynch 31, McNamara 31, O'Donnell 28, Ahern 25.

Tipperary
Ryan 277, Maher 74, O'Brien 74, Kennedy 70, Dwyer 64, Hogan 46, Hayes 38, Gleeson 38, Mc Grath 38, Walsh 38, Kelly 31, Lonergan 31.

Waterford
Power 125, Walsh 97, O'Brien 47, Murphy 35, Ryan 35, McGrath 31, Foley 30, Flynn 28, Morrissey 27, Kelly 26, Phelan 25, Sullivan 25, Whelan 23, McCarthy 22, Butler 21, Tobin 20.

Province of Ulster

Antrim
Smith 134, Johnston 126, Stewart 126, Wilson 119, Thompson 101, O'Neill 98, Campbell 96, Moore 96, Bell 90, Robinson 89, Millar 86, Brown 82, Boyd 81, Scott 66, Graham 64, Reid 63, Martin 61, Kerr 60, Hamilton 50.

Armagh
Murphy 50, Hughes 47, Wilson 45, Campbell 42, O'Hare 37, Smith 31, McCann 29, Donnelly 28, Watson 28, Quinn 26, Johnston 25, Kelly 25, Thompson 23.

Cavan
Reilly 137, Smith 108, Brady 85, Lynch 51, McCabe 36, Clarke 30, Farrelly 29, Maguire 26, Sheridan 26, Galligan 20, Fitzpatrick 19, Dolan 18, McGovern 18, Donohoe 17, Martin 15, McMahon 15.

Derry (Londonderry)
Doherty 80, McLaughlin 68, Kelly 50, Bradley 40, Brown 36, McCloskey 36, Campbell 33, Mullan 33, Smith 31, O'Neill 29, Kane 26, Moore 25, Gallagher 23.

Donegal
Gallagher 196, Doherty 160, Boyle 102, O'Donnell 102, McLaughlin 81, Sweeney 50, Ward 40, Kelly 37, McGinley 37, McFadden 33, McGowan 33, Duffy 33, Campbell 28.

Down
Thompson 55, Smith 53, Campbell 45, Patterson 41, Martin 35, Wilson 35, Graham 34, Johnston 34, Murray 33, Brown 31, Robinson 29, Hamilton 28, Bell 27, Scott 27, Boyd 25.

Fermanagh
Maguire 44, McManus 30, Dolan 23, McGovern 23, Johnston 22, McHugh 20, Cassidy 17, Wilson 15, Thompson 14, Elliott 13, Irvine 13, McLoughlin 12, Gallagher 11, Murphy 11, Reilly 11, Fitzpatrick 10, Flanagan 10.

Monaghan
Duffy 38, Connolly 36, McMahon 33, McKenna 32, Hughes 25, Murphy 24, McCabe 22, Martin 19, Smith 19, Keily 18, Quinn 18, Maguire 17, Murphy 17, Woods 14.

Tyrone
Quinn 40, Mullan 39, Kelly 38, Donnelly 34, Gallagher 34, McKenna 33, Campbell 32, Hughes 31, Wilson 30, McLaughlin 29, O'Neill 29, Doherty 27, Smith 25, Hamilton 23.

Province of Connaught
Galway
Kelly 119, Burke 89, Conneely 89, Joyce 85, McDonagh 80, Walsh 80, Fahy 63, Mannion 59, Flaherty 48, Murphy 47, Connolly 46, Keane 40, King 36, Forde 35, Connor 33, Lyons 30, Mullin 30, Egan 29, Kenny 27, Toole 25.

Leitrim
Kelly 30, Reynolds 30, Flynn 20, McLoughlin 20, McHugh 19, Rooney 18, McMorrow 18, McTernan 17, Keany 16, McGowan 16, Moran 16, Reilly 16, Maguire 15, Dolan 14, Beirne 13, Gallagher 13, McDermott 13, McGovern 13, McShary 13, Mulvey 13.

Mayo
Walsh 134, Gallagher 92, Kelly 89, Malley 78, Moran 77, Duffy 55, McHale 50, Gibbons 47, Joyce 46, Connor 45, Conway 40, Higgins 39, Murphy 39, Burke 36, Reilly 36, Durkan 35, Doherty 34, McHugh 34, Sweeney 33, Lyons 32.

Roscommon
Kelly 68, McDermott 45, Beirne 38, Regan 35, Flanagan 32, Connor 30, McDonagh 26, Quinn 25, Murray 24, Brennan 22, Higgins 22, Towey 22, Kenny 21, Flynn 20.

Sligo
Brennan 31, McLoughlin 28, Gallagher 26, Kelly 23, Harte 20, McGowan 18, Walsh 18, Kennedy 16, Durkan 15, Henry 15, Flynn 14, Gilmartin 14, Leonard 14, Scanlon 14, Connolly 13, O'Hara 13, Feeney 11, Stenson 11, Conway 10, Sheridan 10.

1	Murphy	62,600	51	Sweeney	12,500
2	Kelly	55,900	52	Hayes	12,300
3	Sullivan	43,600	53	Kavanagh	12,200
4	Walsh	41,700	54	Power	12,100
5	Smith	33,700	55	McGrath	11,900
6	O'Brien	33,400	56	Moran	11,800
7	Byrne	33,300	57	Brady	11,600
8	Ryan	32,000	58	Stewart	11,400
9	Connor	31,200	59	Casey	11,300
10	O'Neill	29,100	60	Foley	11,200
11	Reilly	29,000	61	Fitzpatrick	11,100
12	Doyle	23,000	62	Leary	11,000
13	McCarthy	22,300	63	McDonnell	11,000
14	Gallagher	21,800	64	McMahon	10,700
15	Doherty	20,800	65	Donnelly	10,700
16	Kennedy	19,900	66	Regan	10,500
17	Lynch	19,800	67	Donovan	9,900
18	Murray	19,600	68	Burns	9,800
19	Quinn	18,200	69	Flanagan	9,800
20	Moore	17,700	70	Mullan	9,800
21	McLaughlin	17,500	71	Barry	9,700
22	Carroll	17,400	72	Kane	9,700
23	Connolly	17,000	73	Robinson	9,700
24	Daly	17,000	74	Cunningham	9,600
25	Connell	16,600	75	Griffin	9,600
26	Wilson	16,300	76	Kenny	9,600
27	Dunne	16,300	77	Sheehan	9,600
28	Brennan	16,000	78	Ward	9,500
29	Burke	15,900	79	Whelan	9,500
30	Collins	15,700	80	Lyons	9,400
31	Campbell	15,600	81	Reid	9,200
32	Clarke	15,400	82	Graham	9,100
33	Johnston	15,200	83	Higgins	9,100
34	Hughes	14,900	84	Cullen	9,000
35	Farrell	14,700	85	Keane	9,000
36	Fitzgerald	14,700	86	King	9,000
37	Brown	14,600	87	Maher	9,000
38	Martin	14,600	88	McKenna	9,000
39	Maguire	14,400	89	Bell	8,800
40	Nolan	14,300	90	Scott	8,700
41	Flynn	14,300	91	Hogan	8,600
42	Thompson	14,200	92	Keeffe	8,600
43	Callaghan	14,000	93	Magee	8,600
44	O'Donnell	13,900	94	McNamara	8,600
45	Duffy	13,600	95	McDonald	8,500
46	Mahoney	13,500	96	McDermott	8,400
47	Boyle	13,000	97	Moloney	8,300
48	Healy	13,000	98	Rourke	8,300
49	Shea	13,000	99	Buckley	8,200
50	White	13,000	100	Dwyer	8,100

Chapter Six

Surnames in England, Wales, and Scotland

England

My principal source for English surnames is: A Dictionary of English Surnames by Reaney and Wilson. The meaning of English surnames as contained in the main text is in most cases based upon that work. The earliest hereditary surnames are found after the Norman Conquest of England, and are of Norman rather than native English origin. English surnames were effected not only by the Normans and Old English, but also by Scandinavian, Breton, and Celtic influence. During the thirteenth century surnames began to come into general use, and by the end of the fourteenth century practically all persons bore hereditary surnames.

English surnames may be classified as follows :
Local surnames.
Surnames of relationship.
Surnames of occupation or office.
Nicknames.
Within these groups there is considerable overlapping and an accurate classification is not possible. In the case of English surnames it is far less likely that families bearing the same surname are connected to one another.

Local
Local surnames are the largest group and derive from a place name. They indicate where the man held land, or the place from which he had come, or where he actually lived. In general these surnames derive from English, Scottish or French places and were originally preceded by the preposition de, at, by, in, etc. I consulted English Place-Names by Ekwall, with respect to such matters.

Relationship
The principal surnames of relationship were patronymic, where the surname was based upon the father's personal name. However there are also metronymics surnames based upon the mother's name, which are less common.

Occupation or office
Occupational surnames originally denoted the actual occupation followed by the individual. It is difficult to say when such surnames became hereditary. Among the Normans some offices of state were hereditary and gave rise to hereditary surnames. However surnames of occupation are common, and many surnames previously regarded as nicknames are really occupational.

Nicknames
"Nicknames arise spontaneously from some fortuitous chance.",

18

according to Reaney. Some nicknames describe physical attributes or peculiarities, others mental and moral characteristics, and sometimes they may be names of animals, being descriptive of appearance or disposition. Nicknames are common in medieval records, but few have give rise to modern surnames.

Wales

Hereditary surnames developed late in Wales. Surnames of Welsh origin developed in Ireland and England earlier than in Wales itself. The frequency of the surname Walsh in Ireland illustrates the 'Cambro-'' nature of the Norman Invasion, and the influence of a close neighbour upon Irish surnames. It was during the reign of Henry VIII that surnames became hereditary among the gentry, and this spread slowly among the ordinary people. It was not uncommon in the nineteenth century for a man to take his father's personal name as his surname. The result is that many Welsh surnames are based upon personal names that are not Welsh. In recent times some surnames have been 'cymricised' thus adding to the confusion of Welsh surnames.

Patronymic surnames
Patronymic surnames predominate in Wales and as already noted the period in which these became fixed and hereditary was much later than most of Europe. Since medieval times personal names were strongly influenced by the Bible, and as surnames were adopted after this time, they came to be based upon a small number of non-Welsh personal names.

Other derivations
Less common influences upon Welsh surnames were those related to personal characteristics and occupation. However surnames derived from place names are more common. This is because the land owning classes took the names of their estates as surnames.

Anglicised areas
Large parts of Wales became anglicised from the fourteenth century or earlier. This is particularly so in the south and the English border region. The result is that in these areas of Wales and the adjoining part of England there was an anglicised development of Welsh surnames. Surnames developed earlier in these areas and there is a greater variety of surnames. In addition there is a greater number of surnames that are not Welsh.

Double surnames
Double surnames have developed in Wales during the past hundred years. This is because of the small number of surnames and the need to distinguish individuals in a larger population. The surname of the mother was frequently adopted for this purpose. When descendants adopted the double surname and hyphenated it the result was a 'new'

surname. A separate list of surnames for Wales is not available. Notwithstanding that it is clear that the following surnames would predominate: Jones; Williams; Davies; Evans; Thomas; Lewis; Morgan; and as always Smith.

Table of hundred most numerous surnames in England and Wales
The table of the hundred most numerous surnames in England and Wales follows at page 22. Those surnames dealt with in the main text are highlighted in bold type. This is extracted from the official UK statistics website at: www.statistics.gov.uk/themes/compendia_reference/surnames.asp.

Scotland

The principal source for Scottish surnames is: The Surnames of Scotland, by George F. Black, and the reader will find reference to such work in the main text. Surnames in Scotland fall into two distinct groups, those of Gaelic origin in the Highlands and Islands, and those of English origin in the Lowlands and Borders.

Lowlands
Surnames were first adopted in the Lowlands by the Norman nobility, who were called after the lands they possessed. These are known as surnames of territorial origin. These surnames spread as tenants often took the name of their landlords, with whom they had no blood connection. A similar type surname were those of local origin which arise from residence in or near a particular town, the place name thus becoming the surname. A large number of Scottish surnames are deprived from the trade or office of the first bearers. Numerous offices were hereditary in feudal and in later times.

Highlands
In the Highlands of Scotland the surnames were originally Gaelic, and had the same meaning as in Ireland. However it was standard practice for people to adopt the surname of a powerful clan. A surname could spread and decline in number with the fortunes of a particular clan. Many Gaelic surnames were renounced as people adopted the surname of the local laird. Sometimes this was policy on the part of chiefs of clans and heads of landed families, to increase the number of followers bearing their own surname. In general hereditary surnames in the Highlands were adopted later, even as late as the first quarter of the eighteenth century there were examples of men being designated by their father's personal name.

Irish immigration
From earliest times there has been a connection between Ireland and Scotland, particularly between the North-east of Ireland and the West of Scotland. From the seventeenth century large numbers of Scots came to Ulster, many of their descendants subsequently moved on to what became the United States. Scotland has greatly influenced the

surname landscape in Ireland. However the traffic has moved in both directions, and from about 1820 there has been constant emigration from Ireland to the southwest of Scotland.

Table of hundred most numerous surnames in Scotland
The table of the hundred most numerous surnames in Scotland that follows at page 23, is derived from the birth, death and marriages registers for 1995. Those surnames dealt with in the main text are highlighted in bold type. This is taken from the GRO(Scotland) website: http://wood.ccta.gov.uk/grosweb/grosweb.nsf/pages/surnames.

Also Available:

An Introduction to
Irish
Ancestry

Second Edition
ISBN 1 871509 34 3

Seán E. Quinn

* **Ancestral Research**
* **Records**
* **Repositories**
* **Irish Surnames**
* **Family Record Sheets**
* **Ancestor Charts**
* **Websites**

www.irishgenealogyhomepage.com
seanequinn@ireland.com

Seán E. Quinn, 15 Rathclaren, Killarney, Bray, Co. Wicklow, IRELAND

1	SMITH	51	MITCHELL
2	JONES	52	KELLY
3	WILLIAMS	53	COOK
4	TAYLOR	54	CARTER
5	BROWN	55	RICHARDSON
6	DAVIES	56	BAILEY
7	EVANS	57	COLLINS
8	WILSON	58	BELL
9	THOMAS	59	SHAW
10	JOHNSON	60	MURPHY
11	ROBERTS	61	MILLER
12	ROBINSON	62	COX
13	THOMPSON	63	RICHARDS
14	WRIGHT	64	KHAN
15	WALKER	65	MARSHALL
16	WHITE	66	ANDERSON
17	EDWARDS	67	SIMPSON
18	HUGHES	68	ELLIS
19	GREEN	69	ADAMS
20	HALL	70	SINGH
21	LEWIS	71	BEGUM
22	HARRIS	72	WILKINSON
23	CLARKE	73	FOSTER
24	PATEL	74	CHAPMAN
25	JACKSON	75	POWELL
26	WOOD	76	WEBB
27	TURNER	77	ROGERS
28	MARTIN	78	GRAY
29	COOPER	79	MASON
30	HILL	80	ALI
31	WARD	81	HUNT
32	MORRIS	82	HUSSAIN
33	MOORE	83	CAMPBELL
34	CLARK	84	MATTHEWS
35	LEE	85	OWEN
36	KING	86	PALMER
37	BAKER	87	HOLMES
38	HARRISON	88	MILLS
39	MORGAN	89	BARNES
40	ALLEN	90	KNIGHT
41	JAMES	91	LLOYD
42	SCOTT	92	BUTLER
43	PHILLIPS	93	RUSSELL
44	WATSON	94	BARKER
45	DAVIS	95	FISHER
46	PARKER	96	STEVENS
47	PRICE	97	JENKINS
48	BENNETT	98	MURRAY
49	YOUNG	99	DIXON
50	GRIFFITHS	100	HARVEY

1	SMITH		51	MARSHALL
2	BROWN		52	STEVENSON
3	WILSON		53	WOOD
4	THOMSON		54	SUTHERLAND
5	ROBERTSON		55	CRAIG
6	CAMPBELL		56	WRIGHT
7	STEWART		57	MCKENZIE
8	ANDERSON		58	KENNEDY
9	MACDONALD		59	JONES
10	SCOTT		60	BURNS
11	REID		61	WHITE
12	MURRAY		62	MUIR
13	TAYLOR		63	MURPHY
14	CLARK		64	JOHNSTONE
15	MITCHELL		65	HUGHES
16	ROSS		66	WATT
17	WALKER		67	MCMILLAN
18	PATERSON		68	MCINTOSH
19	YOUNG		69	MILNE
20	WATSON		70	MUNRO
21	MORRISON		71	RITCHIE
22	MILLER		72	DICKSON
23	FRASER		73	BRUCE
24	DAVIDSON		74	KING
25	GRAY		75	CRAWFORD
26	MCDONALD		76	DOCHERTY
27	HENDERSON		77	MILLAR
28	JOHNSTON		78	CUNNINGHAM
29	HAMILTON		79	SINCLAIR
30	GRAHAM		80	WILLIAMSON
31	KERR		81	HILL
32	SIMPSON		82	MCGREGOR
33	MARTIN		83	MCKAY
34	FERGUSON		84	BOYLE
35	CAMERON		85	SHAW
36	DUNCAN		86	FLEMING
37	HUNTER		87	MOORE
38	KELLY		88	CHRISTIE
39	BELL		89	DOUGLAS
40	GRANT		90	DONALDSON
41	MACKENZIE		91	ALEXANDER
42	MACKAY		92	MACLEAN
43	ALLAN		93	FORBES
44	BLACK		94	MCINTYRE
45	MACLEOD		95	FINDLAY
46	MCLEAN		96	JAMIESON
47	RUSSELL		97	AITKEN
48	GIBSON		98	REILLY
49	WALLACE		99	THOMPSON
50	GORDON		100	HAY

Chapter Seven

Irish Surnames in the United States

Ever since St. Brendan the Navigator discovered America in the sixth century, the Irish have been crossing the Atlantic. The next Irish cleric to land in what is now the United States was Richard Arthur who was put ashore in 1597 by a Spanish ship in Florida.

Before the English began transporting the Irish as convicts to Australia, they had transported them to their colonies in North America. This began during the time of the Cromwellian Plantation, and in the year 1660 10,000 Irish children were shipped. The total so transported was estimated at between 60,000 and 100,000. The Irish were spread throughout the colonies, however the colony which attracted them most was Maryland. While the British were anxious to attract all settlers this did not stop the Irish being subjected to the Penal Laws in the New World. The Irish played an important part in the War of Independence. According to Hook on March 17, 1776, General George Washington ordered that the password for the night should be 'St. Patrick'.

In the nineteenth century approximately 8 million people left Ireland, the vast majority of whom went to the United States. In 1860 38.93% of the foreign born population in the United States was Irish. In 1870, 33.3% of the foreign born population in the United States was Irish. The Civil War brought an end to violent expressions of antipathy to the Irish immigrants, the Irish having distinguished themselves on both sides.

Surnames in the United States
There are well over a million different surnames in the United States. A small proportion of these surnames would be Irish. However a large proportion of Americans bear an Irish surname and are of Irish descent. Seventy-two of the hundred most numerous surnames in the United States are dealt with in this book. Together with a large proportion of the one thousand most numerous surnames in the United States, and Irish surnames from amongst the ten thousand most numerous surnames in the United States.

The surname landscape in the United States is not so much a melting pot, as a patchwork quilt. Irish surnames are amongst the most numerous in the States of Connecticut, Delaware, Maryland, Massachusetts, New Jersey, New York, and Pennsylvania. In addition the majority of those who bear Scottish surnames in the United States, are most likely the descendants of the Ulster-Scots.

In the same manner as Gaelic surnames were corrupted and anglicised in Ireland, in the United States many surnames became Americanised. In the United States this process was not as devastating with the Irish as with other nationalities, the Irish already had the 'advantage' of speaking English. Nevertheless there are many instances of Americanised corruption, to which reference is made in the main text.

United States Census Bureau Frequency List

There is reference in the main text to the frequency of particular surnames in the United States. The source of this information has been referred to in Chapter One. Given the information available how then would one go about estimating the number of bearers of a particular surname. Let us take Quinn (and its variants) as an example. First it is necessary to get a population figure, 275,000,000 is a rounding based upon the figure given at the present time on the web site of the U. S. Census Bureau. Quinn is number 402 in the list with .028 frequency in percent, O'Quinn is number 6,426 in the list with .002 frequency in percent, and Quin is number 15,374 in the list with .001 frequency in percent. This gives Quinn an estimated 77,000 (275,000,000 x .028%) bearers, O'Quinn an estimated 5,500 bearers, and Quin an estimated 2,500 bearers. This gives an estimated total figure of 85,000 for Quinn including variants.

Tables of surnames in United States

There are two tables of surnames following. The first is a table of Irish surnames, from the ten thousand plus most numerous surnames in the United States. The second is a table of the thousand most numerous surnames in the United States.

Table
of
Most numerous Irish surnames in United States

The following is a list of the most numerous Irish surnames in the United States (including surnames found in Ireland that are not exclusively Irish), which is taken from the list of the ten thousand plus most frequent surnames in the United States issued by the Census Bureau. The list is ranked in order of frequency with position noted.

On this page only the exclusively Irish surnames are highlighted in bold; other more numerous surnames in the United States are also included with their positions in Ireland (IRL); England and Wales (EW), and Scotland (S), also listed. Note that the first three surnames in Ireland are also the top three Irish surnames in the United States.

SMITH 1; 5 IRL; 1 EW; 1 S
JOHNSON 2; 23IRL; 10EW; 28S
BROWN 5; 37 IRL; 5 EW; 2 S
WILSON 8; 26 IRL; 8 EW; 3 S
MOORE 9; 20 IRL; 33 EW; 87 S
MARTIN 16; 38 IRL; 28EW;33S
MURPHY 59; 1IRL; 60EW;63S
WARD 66; 78 IRL; 31 EW
KELLY 74; 2 IRL; 52EW; 38S
HUGHES 88; 34IRL; 18EW; 65S
FORD 102; 116 EW
SULLIVAN 105; 3 IRL; 241EW

REYNOLDS 112; 113 EW
MURRAY 122; 18 IRL;98 EW;12 S
KENNEDY 137 16IRL;168EW;58S
GRANT 154; 136 EW; 40 S
CARROLL 176; 22 IRL;283 EW
BRADLEY 181; 124 EW
KELLEY 198
RYAN 203; 8 IRL; 135 EW
LYNCH 235; 17 IRL; 249 EW
BURKE 243; 29 IRL; 222 EW
BARRETT 280; 145 EW
O'BRIEN 281; 6 IRL; 130 EW

CURRY 313
LEONARD 324
WALSH 325
LYONS 326
CUMMINGS 336
McGEE 356
HIGGINS 370
MALONE 397
MOODY 401
QUINN 402
BLAKE 403
McCARTHY 409
FITZGERALD 417
DOYLE 419
WATERS 429
McBRIDE 433
McLAUGHLIN 440
MORAN 444
BRADY 448
McCORMICK 449
LAMB 477
HARRINGTON 478
CASEY 479
CLARKE 482
HOGAN 489
McGUIRE 494
FLYNN 520
O'CONNOR 530
GILMORE 538
O'NEAL 540
GALLAGHER 547
MATHEWS 552
SHIELDS 580
SAVAGE 582
CALLAHAN 621
CAREY 627
STAFFORD 628
ENGLISH 649
SWEENEY 650
CONWAY 654
FARRELL 658
LOWERY 659
SHANNON 679
NOBLE 691
FOLEY 692
WALLS 697
BARR 698
KERR 721
McCONNELL 722
FINLEY 734

McCULLOUGH 739
NOLAN 741
BRENNAN 744
KANE 746
JOYCE 748
BUCKLEY 749
HALEY 750
CROSBY 758
O'NEILL 768
BARRY 771
McINTYRE 782
MORIN 789
GILLESPIE 790
HURLEY 807
McNEIL 811
McFARLAND 816
MACDONALD 821
DILLON 825
FARLEY 826
HAYDEN 847
COFFEY 850
McCARTY 851
BONNER 855
FERRELL 859
MULLEN 869
O'DONNELL 875
DAUGHERTY 880
DUFFY 889
FITZPATRICK 890
DONOVAN 897
REILLY 901
MOONEY 904
McGOWAN 905
WYNN 909
KINNEY 921
BURKS 928
DELANEY 929
MADDEN 943
McFADDEN 949
CARNEY 956
O'NEIL 978
BOYLE 989
McMAHON 990
SHEA 1001
COWAN 1008
O'CONNELL 1013
GALVAN 1035
BOYCE 1046
CROWLEY 1057
MAHONEY 1071

CONNOR 1077
TRACY 1082
MAGEE 1097
FLANAGAN 1102
DONAHUE 1108
McGINNIS 1110
LYON 1117
McGRATH 1120
McGHEE 1132
MALONEY 1134
GRADY 1147
GIBBONS 1151
GRACE 1167
HICKEY 1173
GORMAN 1175
McCABE 1200
WELSH 1205
McDERMOTT 1212
BYRNE 1224
DOWNEY 1235
DOOLEY 1236
DEMPSEY 1253
LACY 1263
COURTNEY 1273
COSTELLO 1297
SHEEHAN 1302
DONNELLY 1312
DALY 1349
CONNOLLY 1350
DWYER 1368
FERRIS 1405
CURRAN 1435
DOHERTY 1467
McGRAW 1469
McMANUS 1478
CASSIDY 1505
DOLAN 1510
DALEY 1511
DEVINE 1522
DRISCOLL 1569
SHERIDAN 1572
REDMOND 1573
McNAMARA 1599
McMULLAN 1602
McKENNA 1603
McDONOUGH 1604
EGAN 1621
TIMMONS 1622
O'HARA 1623
KEEN 1624

26

FINN 1626
CLIFFORD 1630
HAGAN 1651
CAHILL 1673
LACEY 1682
CONNELLY 1683
DUGAN 1705
DARBY 1730
HEALY 1735
KEARNEY 1750
TOBIN 1761
KERNS 1771
KEENE 1778
CURRIE 1791
McNALLY 1795
MAHER 1798
KENNY 1799
CONNELL 1827
O'LEARY 1836
CULLEN 1859
CONNORS 1866
HARE 1885
WALDRON 1904
COLEY 1918
LEARY 1924
DORAN 1961
CORCORAN 1968
EARLY 1994
REAGAN 2000
CRONIN 2016
MALLOY 2030
ROCHE 2053
BOYLES 2065
REGAN 2067
FLAHERTY 2115
RING 2137
ENNIS 2148
ROONEY 2158
COREY 2201
LAWLER 2213
CONROY 2215
NUGENT 2233
McHUGH 2244
KEARNS 2270
FAY 2277
KILLIAN 2301
DOWLING 2305
LAUGHLIN 2325
UPTON 2371
REARDON 2372

O'ROURKE 2393
MAGUIRE 2407
MONAHAN 2411
McCORMACK 2412
MOFFETT 2418
KEATING 2420
GILCHRIST 2447
CAVANAUGH 2461
CLEARY 2478
McMAHAN 2493
O'KEFE 2499
GANNON 2501
MORRISSEY 2524
McCARTNEY 2629
GAVIN 2659
DOWD 2660
POWER 2665
CRAWLEY 2684
HARKINS 2695
GEARY 2703
MEEHAN 2729
NOLEN 2746
GAFFNEY 2759
HANNON 2792
McALISTER 2795
DUGGAN 2799
GROGAN 2820
MATTHEW 2827
O'MALLEY 2845
McNUTT 2846
McNULTY 2847
McGOVERN 2848
COONEY 2880
NEIL 2884
MULLIGAN 2892
FOY 2894
BEGLEY 2897
PHELAN 2914
DENNEY 2924
NAGLE 2931
REEDY 2937
McHENRY 2958
FARRINGTON 3009
BREEN 3011
DONOHUE 3024
CONDON 3042
CLANCY 3043
McDONNELL 3058
FANNING 3062
CARLIN 3073

O'TOOLE 3080
McNEELY 3106
NOONAN 3158
McINTIRE 3160
BYRNES 3169
COTTER 3199
MOFFITT 3206
DAILY3250
SCANLON 3257
EARLY 3283
DEVLIN 3284
MULLIN 3306
KEELING 3310
NEILL 3345
FLANNERY 3392
TIERNEY 3411
HEALEY 3466
STACK 3474
PLUNKETT 3480
COLLEY 3515
BOGAN 3518
LEAHY 3528
HANLON 3559
O'REILLY 3584
GLYNN 3591
GILLEN 3603
FALLON 3613
KEEGAN 3631
AGNEW 3657
GALVIN 3666
COYNE 3669
WYNNE 3674
RONEY 3683
SHAY 3699
STAGGS 3718
KEENEY 3767
REDDY 3776
LAWLESS 3825
FERRY 3839
O'SULLIVAN 3853
ASHE 3864
REDDEN 3873
McCAFFREY 3874
Fitzsimmons 3901
FAHEY 3902
DONNELL 3974
AHERN 3983
RAFFERTY 4018
FEENEY 4027
CURTIN 4029

27

DUNNE 4053
O'CONNER 4066
MORIARTY 4067
HORAN 4072
COSGROVE 4098
WHELAN 4144
FINNEGAN 4158
McALLISTER 4172
MACLEAN 4174
GILSON 4179
BOLAND 4207
SHARKEY 4216
SCULLY 4238
McReynolds 4263
BROGAN 4273
O'BRYAN 4283
O'SHEA 4326
McKEEVER 4329
McKEOWN 4357
LAFFERTY 4392
CONNERS 4400
SLATTERY 4410
COWLEY 4425
HYLAND 4445
McDADE 4489
HENNESSEY 4497
HILLARD 4513
SOMERVILLE 4524
ROUSSEL 4548
McKEON 4551
CALLAGHAN 4560
SHERRY 4620
McCLEARY 4644
MONAGHAN 4661
McCLARY 4664
FLANIGAN 4670
SHELLY 4711
PENDER 4716
FURLONG 4780
TRACEY 4790
SHANAHAN 4816
LOFTUS 4850
FANIN 4876
McMULLIN 4897
MADIGAN 4899
MILEY 4926
McGOUGH 4927
MARRA 4928
CARTY 5035
RIORDAN 5114

DESMOND 5129
TRAINOR 5141
MULLENS 5150
HENNESSY 5161
TULLY 5176
HAMILL 5273
HARNEY 5308
McGINTY 5363
McEVOY 5364
McDEVITT 5397
GALLAHER 5408
BOYLAN 5417
MULHOLLAND 5437
FORDE 5451
TOOLE 5470
O'BRIAN 5528
CONLON 5551
COAKLEY 5553
BIRMINGHAM 5559
McCAFFERTY 5609
GILLIGAN 5709
O'GRADY 5733
McHALE 5774
COWEN 5795
MULCAHY 5814
HEFFERNAN 5820
YOOMEY 5846
McKEAN 5903
McGINLEY 5947
McCLUSKEY 5948
NESTER 6023
MURPHEY 6025
McGARRY 6068
DORR 6085
MOLLOY 6165
CASSADY 6189
CUSICK 6233
BRIAN 6239
BRIEN 6278
TYRRELL 6374
HAGANS 6400
CALLEN 6408
O'QUINN 6426
McGLOTHLIN 6429
KERRIGAN 6433
HANRAHAN 6436
LAWLOR 6480
SEALY 6518
SCANLAN 6519
RIGNEY 6524

McCASLIN 6533
McARDLE 6534
BAILY 6565
TINNEY 6571
LENARD 6592
O'BRYANT 6635
BARRINGTON 6665
McMORRIS 6688
PRENDERGAST 6733
McGUINNESS 6745
LALLY 6858
DORE 6873
NEARY 6898
McANALLY 6905
HALLORAN 6917
EAGAN 6922
KEELEY 6961
BROPHY 6983
O'HARE 7008
KEAN 7017
HASSON 7024
GILLISPIE 7030
CURRIN 7037
NEALE 7070
MANION 7077
KAVANAGH 7087
DUFFEY 7097
McAULEY 7139
MALOY 7141
O'KELLEY 7187
MOFFATT 7189
McGLYNN 7193
McCOWAN 7194
GREELEY 7210
LAVELLE 7266
FRAWLEY 7279
DRENNAN 7284
CUMMING 7288
CAWLEY 7289
MUSGRAVE 7314
MURDOCH 7315
McCARY 7317
KAVANAUGH 7325
HALLEY 7330
BERGIN 7357
HARDEMAN 7404
FRIEL 7409
BANNON 7436
McCLEAN 7473
BRIDGEMAN 7496

TWOMEY 7505
MULVEY 7520
McSHANE 7522
McLOUGHLIN 7523
DUNLOP 7543
OMEARA 7586
McGARY 7590
McCOURT 7591
McCOLLOUGH 7592
MILFORD 7661
McCULLY 7664
CONLIN 7688
CARLEY 7692
MOYNIHAN 7736
McGANN 7739
McCREADY 7740
MANGAN 7819
LONEY 7822
COWANS 7846
CALLAN 7853
SHERWIN 7871
Shaugnasessy 7872
MOHAN 7887
McCARLEY
MALEY 7893
McMURRY 7955
MacFarlane 7961
KINSELLA 7966
CROTTY 7989
AHEARN 8011
MALLON 8093
DONEY 8065
KILEY 8127
GARRY 8140
YRAYNOR 8158
ROURKE 8171
MULVANEY 8179
HOULIHAN 8190
DRENNEN 8207
CANON 8214
TOLAND 8234
ROGAN 8252
MEENTIRE 8271
McAULIFFE 8272
FEELEY 8299
CAFFEY 8319
McKOWN 8366
McANDREW 8368
GORMLEY 8388
GILROY 8390

NAUGHTON 8451
SOMMERVILLE 8525
MULDOON 8545
KILLEN 8561
GIVEN 8572
DUNLEAVY 8576
DEVANEY 8580
COEN 8587
O'DAY 8624
MUNDAY 8626
GOWAN 8652
FINLAY 8653
CASSITY 8665
CALLIHAN 8667
SKELLY 8694
SEALEY 8696
MACNELL 8716
KIRWAN 8723
FINNELL 8741
EAMES 8746
DUNIGAN 8747
McNEESE 8810
LAVERY 8820
DOODY 8838
CAULEY 8848
O'LOUGHLIN 8898
McINERNY 8906
McGUIGAN 8907
HEDDEN 8921
DONOHOE 8946
CABE 8959
SCURRY 8988
ROANE 8993
McBRYDE 9003
HUGHS 9018
HEANEY 9021
CULLEY 9047
McNARY 9103
HORGAN 9120
HEADY 9125
HANNIGAN 9127
GILLES 9131
O'BANNON 9204
McNIEL 9212
McMANN 9213
McCRAE 9214
LUCY 9218
CONNALLY 9253
BIGLEY 9262
McCARRON 9310

LAVERTY 9314
GALLIGAN 9336
DEEGAN 9348
CORR 9351
McMASTERS 9421
McKEEHAN 9422
MARRON 9424
LANGAN 9430
KEOWN 9435
FEY 9452
COGAN 9460
SHEEHY 9501
NOLIN 9520
McGLONE 9528
McCAMMON 9529
MANUS 9533
LONERGAN 9537
KEEVER 9550
HOYE 9553
GALLION 9572
FERRIN 9576
DONEGAN 9580
COAN 9587
MILLETT 9661
McGOWEN 9663
CUSACK 9719
BOHANNAN 9741
SWEENY 9766
McSWEENEY 9800
McQUADE 9801
McCAY 9802
DINEEN 9849
BOYES 9863
VEASEY 9881
SHEARIN 9905
O'Shaughnessy 9923
OHALLORAN 9924
LOUGHLIN 9939
HEGARTY 9960
FORAN 9973
CURREY 9987
COLGAN 10111
DUNPHY 10239
DONAHOE 10240
FLANNIGAN 10359
CARRON 10380
MANAHAN 10462
KENNELLY 10480
McCARDLE 10596
DUNNIGAN 10638

Table
of
First thousand most numerous surnames in Unites States

The following is a list of the most frequent surnames in the United States. The list is in order of frequency and is taken from the United States Census Bureau website already referred to. Those surnames dealt with in the main text are highlighted in bold. It is unlikely that the majority of bearers of the highlighted surnames on this table are of Irish extraction, in view of the fact that many Irish surnames were anglicised to conform with common British surnames.

It is clear that there is duplication between this table and the table of most numerous Irish surnames in the United States. A comparison between this table and the tables for Ireland, England and Wales, and Scotland is interesting. A strong commonality of surnames between all the countries is to be noted.

1 **SMITH**	33 **HILL**	65 **HOWARD**
2 **JOHNSON**	34 **SCOTT**	66 **WARD**
3 **WILLIAMS**	35 **GREEN**	67 TORRES
4 **JONES**	36 **ADAMS**	68 **PETERSON**
5 **BROWN**	37 **BAKER**	69 **GRAY**
6 **DAVIS**	38 GONZALEZ	70 RAMIREZ
7 **MILLER**	39 **NELSON**	71 JAMES
8 **WILSON**	40 **CARTER**	72 **WATSON**
9 **MOORE**	41 **MITCHELL**	73 BROOKS
10 **TAYLOR**	42 PEREZ	74 **KELLY**
11 **ANDERSON**	43 **ROBERTS**	75 SANDERS
12 THOMAS	44 **TURNER**	76 **PRICE**
13 **JACKSON**	45 **PHILLIPS**	77 **BENNETT**
14 **WHITE**	46 **CAMPBELL**	78 **WOOD**
15 **HARRIS**	47 **PARKER**	79 **BARNES**
16 **MARTIN**	48 **EVANS**	80 **ROSS**
17 **THOMPSON**	49 **EDWARDS**	81 **HENDERSON**
18 GARCIA	50 **COLLINS**	82 **COLEMAN**
19 MARTINEZ	51 **STEWART**	83 JENKINS
20 **ROBINSON**	52 SANCHEZ	84 PERRY
21 **CLARK**	53 **MORRIS**	85 POWELL
22 RODRIGUEZ	54 **ROGERS**	86 **LONG**
23 **LEWIS**	55 REED	87 **PATTERSON**
24 **LEE**	56 **COOK**	88 **HUGHES**
25 **WALKER**	57 **MORGAN**	89 FLORES
26 **HALL**	58 **BELL**	90 WASHINGTON
27 **ALLEN**	59 **MURPHY**	91 **BUTLER**
28 **YOUNG**	60 **BAILEY**	92 SIMMONS
29 HERNANDEZ	61 RIVERA	93 **FOSTER**
30 **KING**	62 **COOPER**	94 GONZALES
31 **WRIGHT**	63 **RICHARDSON**	95 BRYANT
32 LOPEZ	64 **COX**	96 **ALEXANDER**

97 RUSSELL	**147 ROBERTSON**	197 PETERS
98 GRIFFIN	**148 HUNT**	**198 KELLEY**
99 DIAZ	**149 BLACK**	199 FRANKLIN
100 HAYES	150 DANIELS	200 LAWSON
101 MYERS	151 PALMER	201 FIELDS
102 FORD	**152 MILLS**	202 GUTIERREZ
103 HAMILTON	**153 NICHOLS**	**203 RYAN**
104 GRAHAM	**154 GRANT**	204 SCHMIDT
105 SULLIVAN	155 KNIGHT	**205 CARR**
106 WALLACE	**156 FERGUSON**	206 VASQUEZ
107 WOODS	157 ROSE	207 CASTILLO
108 COLE	158 STONE	208 WHEELER
109 WEST	159 HAWKINS	209 CHAPMAN
110 JORDAN	**160 DUNN**	210 OLIVER
111 OWENS	161 PERKINS	**211 Montgomery**
112 REYNOLDS	162 HUDSON	212 RICHARDS
113 FISHER	163 SPENCER	**213 WILLIAMSON**
114 ELLIS	164 GARDNER	**214 JOHNSTON**
115 HARRISON	**165 STEPHENS**	215 BANKS
116 GIBSON	166 PAYNE	216 MEYER
117 McDONALD	**167 PIERCE**	217 BISHOP
118 CRUZ	**168 BERRY**	**218 McCOY**
119 MARSHALL	**169 MATTHEWS**	219 HOWELL
120 ORTIZ	170 ARNOLD	220 ALVAREZ
121 GOMEZ	171 WAGNER	**221 MORRISON**
122 MURRAY	**172 WILLIS**	222 HANSEN
123 FREEMAN	173 RAY	223 FERNANDEZ
124 WELLS	174 WATKINS	224 GARZA
125 WEBB	175 OLSON	**225 HARVEY**
126 SIMPSON	**176 CARROLL**	**226 LITTLE**
127 STEVENS	**177 DUNCAN**	227 BURTON
128 TUCKER	178 SNYDER	228 STANLEY
129 PORTER	**179 HART**	229 NGUYEN
130 HUNTER	**180 Cunningham**	230 GEORGE
131 HICKS	**181 BRADLEY**	231 JACOBS
132 CRAWFORD	**182 LANE**	**232 REID**
133 HENRY	**183 ANDREWS**	233 KIM
134 BOYD	184 RUIZ	234 FULLER
135 MASON	**185 HARPER**	**235 LYNCH**
136 MORALES	**186 FOX**	236 DEAN
137 KENNEDY	**187 RILEY**	237 GILBERT
138 WARREN	**188 ARMSTRONG**	238 GARRETT
139 DIXON	189 CARPENTER	239 ROMERO
140 RAMOS	190 WEAVER	240 WELCH
141 REYES	**191 GREENE**	241 LARSON
142 BURNS	192 LAWRENCE	242 FRAZIER
143 GORDON	**193 ELLIOTT**	**243 BURKE**
144 SHAW	194 CHAVEZ	244 HANSON
145 HOLMES	195 SIMS	245 DAY
146 RICE	196 AUSTIN	246 MENDOZA

247 MORENO	298 PENA	349 CROSS
248 BOWMAN	299 BECK	350 GARNER
249 MEDINA	300 NEWMAN	351 MANN
250 FOWLER	301 HAYNES	352 MACK
251 BREWER	302 McDANIEL	353 MOSS
252 HOFFMAN	303 MENDEZ	**354 THORNTON**
253 CARLSON	304 BUSH	355 DENNIS
254 SILVA	305 VAUGHN	**356 McGEE**
255 PEARSON	306 PARKS	357 FARMER
256 HOLLAND	**307 DAWSON**	358 DELGADO
257 DOUGLAS	308 SANTIAGO	359 AGUILAR
258 FLEMING	309 NORRIS	360 VEGA
259 JENSEN	310 HARDY	361 GLOVER
260 VARGAS	311 LOVE	**362 MANNING**
261 BYRD	**312 STEELE**	363 COHEN
262 DAVIDSON	**313 CURRY**	364 HARMON
263 HOPKINS	314 POWERS	**365 RODGERS**
264 MAY	315 SCHULTZ	366 ROBBINS
265 TERRY	316 BARKER	367 NEWTON
266 HERRERA	317 GUZMAN	368 TODD
267 WADE	318 PAGE	**369 BLAIR**
268 SOTO	319 MUNOZ	**370 HIGGINS**
269 WALTERS	320 BALL	371 INGRAM
270 CURTIS	321 KELLER	372 REESE
271 NEAL	323 WEBER	**373 CANNON**
272 CALDWELL	**324 LEONARD**	374 STRICKLAND
273 LOWE	**325 WALSH**	375 TOWNSEND
274 JENNINGS	**326 LYONS**	376 POTTER
275 BARNETT	327 RAMSEY	377 GOODWIN
276 GRAVES	328 WOLFE	378 WALTON
277 JIMENEZ	329 SCHNEIDER	379 ROWE
278 HORTON	**330 MULLINS**	380 HAMPTON
279 SHELTON	331 BENSON	**382 PATTON**
280 BARRETT	332 SHARP	383 SWANSON
281 O'BRIEN	333 BOWEN	384 JOSEPH
282 CASTRO	334 DANIEL	386 GOODMAN
283 SUTTON	335 BARBER	387 MALDONADO
284 GREGORY	336 CUMMINGS	388 YATES
285 McKINNEY	337 HINES	389 BECKER
286 LUCAS	338 BALDWIN	390 ERICKSON
287 MILES	339 GRIFFITH	391 HODGES
289 RODRIQUEZ	340 VALDEZ	392 RIOS
290 CHAMBERS	341 HUBBARD	**393 CONNER**
291 HOLT	342 SALAZAR	394 ADKINS
292 LAMBERT	343 REEVES	**395 WEBSTER**
293 FLETCHER	344 WARNER	396 NORMAN
294 WATTS	**345 STEVENSON**	**397 MALONE**
295 BATES	346 BURGESS	398 HAMMOND
296 HALE	347 SANTOS	399 FLOWERS
297 RHODES	348 TATE	400 COBB

401 MOODY	451 BROCK	501 WILCOX
402 QUINN	452 POOLE	502 PITTS
403 BLAKE	453 FRANK	503 CONLEY
404 MAXWELL	**454 LOGAN**	504 MARQUEZ
405 POPE	455 OWEN	505 BURNETT
406 FLOYD	456 BASS	506 RICHARD
407 OSBORNE	457 MARSH	507 COCHRAN
408 PAUL	458 DRAKE	508 CHASE
409 McCARTHY	459 WONG	509 DAVENPORT
410 GUERRERO	460 JEFFERSON	510 HOOD
411 LINDSEY	461 PARK	511 GATES
412 ESTRADA	462 MORTON	512 CLAY
413 SANDOVAL	463 ABBOTT	513 AYALA
414 GIBBS	464 SPARKS	514 SAWYER
415 TYLER	465 PATRICK	515 ROMAN
416 GROSS	466 NORTON	516 VAZQUEZ
417 FITZGERALD	467 HUFF	517 DICKERSON
418 STOKES	468 CLAYTON	518 HODGE
419 DOYLE	469 MASSEY	519 ACOSTA
420 SHERMAN	470 LLOYD	**520 FLYNN**
421 SAUNDERS	471 FIGUEROA	521 ESPINOZA
422 WISE	**472 CARSON**	**522 NICHOLSON**
423 COLON	473 BOWERS	523 MONROE
424 GILL	474 ROBERSON	524 WOLF
425 ALVARADO	475 BARTON	**525 MORROW**
426 GREER	476 TRAN	**526 KIRK**
427 PADILLA	**477 LAMB**	527 RANDALL
428 SIMON	**478 HARRINGTON**	528 ANTHONY
429 WATERS	**479 CASEY**	529 WHITAKER
430 NUNEZ	480 BOONE	**530 O'CONNOR**
431 BALLARD	481 CORTEZ	531 SKINNER
432 SCHWARTZ	**482 CLARKE**	532 WARE
433 McBRIDE	483 MATHIS	533 MOLINA
434 HOUSTON	484 SINGLETON	534 KIRBY
435 CHRISTENSEN	485 WILKINS	535 HUFFMAN
436 KLEIN	486 CAIN	536 BRADFORD
437 PRATT	487 BRYAN	537 CHARLES
438 BRIGGS	488 UNDERWOOD	**538 GILMORE**
439 PARSONS	**489 HOGAN**	539 DOMINGUEZ
440 McLAUGHLIN	490 McKENZIE	**540 O'NEAL**
441 ZIMMERMAN	491 COLLIER	541 BRUCE
442 FRENCH	492 LUNA	542 LANG
443 BUCHANAN	493 PHELPS	543 COMBS
444 MORAN	**494 McGUIRE**	544 KRAMER
445 COPELAND	495 ALLISON	545 HEATH
446 ROY	496 BRIDGES	546 HANCOCK
447 PITTMAN	497 WILKERSON	**547 GALLAGHER**
448 BRADY	498 NASH	548 GAINES
449 McCORMICK	499 SUMMERS	549 SHAFFER
450 HOLLOWAY	500 ATKINS	550 SHORT

551 WIGGINS	601 DURAN	651 STRONG
552 MATHEWS	**602 HUTCHINSON**	652 PRINCE
553 McCLAIN	603 HESS	**653 McCLURE**
554 FISCHER	604 DORSEY	**654 CONWAY**
555 WALL	605 BULLOCK	655 WALTER
556 SMALL	606 ROBLES	656 ROTH
557 MELTON	607 BEARD	657 MAYNARD
558 HENSLEY	**608 DALTON**	**658 FARRELL**
559 BOND	609 AVILA	**659 LOWERY**
560 DYER	610 VANCE	660 HURST
561 CAMERON	611 RICH	**661 NIXON**
562 GRIMES	612 BLACKWELL	662 WEISS
563 CONTRERAS	613 YORK	663 TRUJILLO
564 CHRISTIAN	614 JOHNS	664 ELLISON
565 WYATT	615 BLANKENSHIP	**665 SLOAN**
566 BAXTER	616 TREVINO	666 JUAREZ
567 SNOW	617 SALINAS	667 WINTERS
568 MOSLEY	618 CAMPOS	**668 McLEAN**
569 SHEPHERD	619 PRUITT	669 RANDOLPH
570 LARSEN	620 MOSES	670 LEON
571 HOOVER	**621 CALLAHAN**	671 BOYER
572 BEASLEY	622 GOLDEN	672 VILLARREAL
573 GLENN	623 MONTOYA	673 McCALL
574 PETERSEN	624 HARDIN	674 GENTRY
575 WHITEHEAD	625 GUERRA	675 CARRILLO
576 MEYERS	**626 McDOWELL**	676 KENT
577 KEITH	**627 CAREY**	677 AYERS
578 GARRISON	**628 STAFFORD**	678 LARA
579 VINCENT	629 GALLEGOS	**679 SHANNON**
580 SHIELDS	630 HENSON	**680 SEXTON**
581 HORN	631 WILKINSON	681 PACE
582 SAVAGE	632 BOOKER	682 HULL
583 OLSEN	633 MERRITT	683 LEBLANC
584 SCHROEDER	634 MIRANDA	684 BROWNING
585 HARTMAN	**635 ATKINSON**	685 VELASQUEZ
586 WOODARD	**636 ORR**	686 LEACH
587 MUELLER	637 DECKER	687 CHANG
588 KEMP	638 HOBBS	688 HOUSE
589 DELEON	639 PRESTON	689 SELLERS
590 BOOTH	640 TANNER	690 HERRING
591 PATEL	641 KNOX	691 NOBLE
592 CALHOUN	642 PACHECO	**692 FOLEY**
593 WILEY	**643 STEPHENSON**	693 BARTLETT
594 EATON	644 GLASS	694 MERCADO
595 CLINE	645 ROJAS	695 LANDRY
596 NAVARRO	646 SERRANO	696 DURHAM
597 HARRELL	647 MARKS	**697 WALLS**
598 LESTER	648 HICKMAN	**698 BARR**
599 HUMPHREY	**649 ENGLISH**	**699 McKEE**
600 PARRISH	**650 SWEENEY**	700 BAUER

34

701 RIVERS	751 VALENTINE	801 BATTLE
702 EVERETT	752 MADDOX	802 SANTANA
703 BRADSHAW	753 RUSSO	803 CABRERA
704 PUGH	754 McKNIGHT	804 CERVANTES
705 VELEZ	755 BUCK	805 HOWE
706 RUSH	756 MOON	806 HINTON
707 ESTES	**757 McMILLAN**	**807 HURLEY**
708 DODSON	758 CROSBY	**808 SPENCE**
709 MORSE	759 BERG	809 ZAMORA
710 SHEPPARD	760 DOTSON	810 YANG
711 WEEKS	761 MAYS	**811 McNEIL**
712 CAMACHO	762 ROACH	812 SUAREZ
713 BEAN	763 CHURCH	813 CASE
714 BARRON	764 CHAN	814 PETTY
715 LIVINGSTON	765 RICHMOND	815 GOULD
716 MIDDLETON	766 MEADOWS	**816 McFARLAND**
717 SPEARS	767 FAULKNER	817 SAMPSON
718 BRANCH	**768 O'NEILL**	818 CARVER
719 BLEVINS	769 KNAPP	819 BRAY
720 CHEN	770 KLINE	820 ROSARIO
721 KERR	**771 BARRY**	**821 MacDONALD**
722 McCONNELL	772 OCHOA	822 STOUT
723 HATFIELD	773 JACOBSON	823 HESTER
724 HARDING	774 GAY	824 MELENDEZ
725 ASHLEY	775 AVERY	**825 DILLON**
726 SOLIS	776 HENDRICKS	**826 FARLEY**
727 HERMAN	777 HORNE	827 HOPPER
728 FROST	778 SHEPARD	828 GALLOWAY
729 GILES	779 HEBERT	829 POTTS
730 BLACKBURN	780 CHERRY	830 BERNARD
731 WILLIAM	781 CARDENAS	831 JOYNER
732 PENNINGTON	**782 McINTYRE**	832 STEIN
733 WOODWARD	783 WHITNEY	833 AGUIRRE
734 FINLEY	784 WALLER	834 OSBORN
735 McINTOSH	785 HOLMAN	835 MERCER
736 KOCH	**786 DONALDSON**	836 BENDER
737 BEST	787 CANTU	837 FRANCO
738 SOLOMON	788 TERRELL	838 ROWLAND
739 McCullough	789 MORIN	839 SYKES
740 DUDLEY	**790 GILLESPIE**	840 BENJAMIN
741 NOLAN	791 FUENTES	841 TRAVIS
742 BLANCHARD	792 TILLMAN	842 PICKETT
743 RIVAS	793 SANFORD	843 CRANE
744 BRENNAN	794 BENTLEY	844 SEARS
745 MEJIA	795 PECK	845 MAYO
746 KANE	796 KEY	846 DUNLAP
747 BENTON	797 SALAS	**847 HAYDEN**
748 JOYCE	798 ROLLINS	848 WILDER
749 BUCKLEY	799 GAMBLE	**849 McKAY**
750 HALEY	**800 DICKSON**	**850 COFFEY**

851 McCARTY	**901 REILLY**	951 GOOD
852 EWING	902 COMPTON	952 BYERS
853 COOLEY	903 RAYMOND	953 KIRKLAND
854 VAUGHAN	**904 MOONEY**	954 KIDD
855 BONNER	**905 McGOWAN**	955 WORKMAN
856 COTTON	906 CRAFT	**956 CARNEY**
857 HOLDER	907 CLEVELAND	957 DALE
858 STARK	908 CLEMONS	958 McLEOD
859 FERRELL	909 WYNN	959 HOLCOMB
860 CANTRELL	910 NIELSEN	960 ENGLAND
861 FULTON	**911 BAIRD**	961 FINCH
862 LYNN	912 STANTON	962 HEAD
863 LOTT	913 SNIDER	963 BURT
864 CALDERON	914 ROSALES	964 HENDRIX
865 ROSA	915 BRIGHT	965 SOSA
866 POLLARD	916 WITT	966 HANEY
867 HOOPER	**917 STUART**	967 FRANKS
868 BURCH	918 HAYS	968 SARGENT
869 MULLEN	919 HOLDEN	969 NIEVES
870 FRY	920 RUTLEDGE	970 DOWNS
871 RIDDLE	921 KINNEY	971 RASMUSSEN
872 LEVY	922 CLEMENTS	**972 BIRD**
873 DAVID	923 CASTANEDA	973 HEWITT
874 DUKE	924 SLATER	**974 LINDSAY**
875 O'DONNELL	925 HAHN	975 LE
876 GUY	926 EMERSON	976 FOREMAN
877 MICHAEL	927 CONRAD	977 VALENCIA
878 BRITT	928 BURKS	**978 O'NEIL**
879 FREDERICK	**929 DELANEY**	979 DELACRUZ
880 DAUGHERTY	930 PATE	980 VINSON
881 BERGER	931 LANCASTER	981 DEJESUS
882 DILLARD	932 SWEET	982 HYDE
883 ALSTON	933 JUSTICE	983 FORBES
884 JARVIS	934 TYSON	984 GILLIAM
885 FRYE	935 SHARPE	985 GUTHRIE
886 RIGGS	936 WHITFIELD	986 WOOTEN
887 CHANEY	937 TALLEY	987 HUBER
888 ODOM	938 MACIAS	988 BARLOW
889 DUFFY	**939 IRWIN**	**989 BOYLE**
890 FITZPATRICK	940 BURRIS	**990 McMAHON**
891 VALENZUELA	941 RATLIFF	991 BUCKNER
892 MERRILL	942 McCRAY	992 ROCHA
893 MAYER	**943 MADDEN**	993 PUCKETT
894 ALFORD	944 KAUFMAN	994 LANGLEY
895 McPHERSON	945 BEACH	995 KNOWLES
896 ACEVEDO	946 GOFF	**996 COOKE**
897 DONOVAN	947 CASH	997 VELAZQUEZ
898 BARRERA	948 BOLTON	998 WHITLEY
899 ALBERT	**949 McFADDEN**	999 NOEL
900 COTE	950 LEVINE	1,000 VANG

Adams
In most cases this surname is of either English or Scottish origin, derived from the personal name Adam, from the Hebrew 'red' from the colour of skin. In 1890 Adams was principally found in Antrim and Derry, and the estimated number of bearers was 3,450. In the United States Adams is the 36th most numerous surname with an estimated 478,500 bearers. In England and Wales in 1996 it was the 69th most numerous surname.

Agnew, ó Gnímh
A surname of Norman origin, from the Baronie d'Agneaux in the Bocages of Normandy. A branch of the family of d'Agneaux came to Ulster with John de Courcy and were granted the Lordship of Larne in Antrim. In Scotland in 1363 the Lochnaw family of the name were appointed hereditary sheriffs of Galloway by King David II. The ó Gnímh sept who were hereditary poets to the ó Neills of Clandeboy in Antrim, have so anglicised their surname. In 1890 Agnew was principally found in Antrim (25 births), Armagh and Down, and the estimated number of bearers was 1,750. In the United States Agnew is the 3,657th most numerous surname with an estimated 82,500 bearers.

Ahern, Aherne, Ahearn, ó hEachthigheirn
A Gaelic surname meaning descendant of *Eachthighearna*, meaning 'horse-lord'. A sept of Dál Cais who were chiefs of Ui Cearnaigh now the parish of Kilfinaghty in Clare. Woulfe states they were driven out by the MacNamaras around 1318. They were later to be found in east Cork. In 1890 Ahern was numerous in Limerick, it was also to be found in Cork. The estimated number of bearers was 5,465. In the United States Ahern is the 3,983rd most numerous surname, and Ahearn is the 8,011th most numerous surname making an estimated total of 85,250 bearers.

Alexander
A surname of Scottish origin, from the Greek meaning 'defender of man'. It was introduced into Scotland by Margaret, wife of King Malcolm Ceannmor in the eleventh century from the Hungarian Court. Subsequently three Kings of Scotland bore the personal name. It is numerous as a surname in the west of Scotland See MacAllister below. In 1890 Alexander was principally found in Antrim and Down, and the estimated number of bearers was 2,375. In the United States Alexander is the 96th most numerous surname with an estimated 233,750 bearers. In England and Wales in 1996 it was the 295th most numerous surname. In Scotland in 1995 it was the 91st most numerous surname.

Allen, Allan, MacAilon
An English surname which derives from the Old French *Alain*, Old Breton *Alan*, and was originally a German tribal name *Alemannus*, meaning 'all men'. Alan the name of a Welsh and Breton saint was brought to England by William, Duke of Normandy. It is also spelt as

Allan. A Scottish surname from the Gaelic *MacAilín*, from *ail*, meaning 'rock', subsequently *MacAllen*. In 1853 Allen was the thirty-eight most numerous surname in England and Wales. In 1863 it was the forty-second most numerous surname in Scotland. In Ireland in 1890 it was a scattered name and chiefly found in Antrim, Armagh and Dublin, and the estimated number of bearers was 7,300. In the United States Allen is the 27th most numerous surname with an estimated 547,250 bearers. In England and Wales in 1996 Allen was the 40th most numerous surname, and Allan was the 444th most numerous surname. In Scotland in 1995 Allan was the 43rd most numerous surname.

McAllister, McAlister, MacAlastair
A Gaelic surname that originated in Scotland, meaning son of Alexander. In the fourteenth century they were brought to east Ulster as gallowlass by the MacDonnells. In 1890 McAllister was principally found in Antrim, and the estimated number of bearers was 3,900 (all variants). In the United States McAllister is the 1.090th most numerous surname, McAlister is the 2,795th most numerous surname; and McCallister is the 4,172nd most numerous surname making an estimated total of 49,500 bearers.

Anderson
An English or Scottish surname meaning son of Andrew, Andrew is from the Greek meaning 'manly'. The apostle Andrew has been the patron saint of Scotland since the thirteenth century, the national flag of Scotland is the Saint Andrew's cross. In 1990 it was the ninth most numerous surname in Scotland. In Ireland in 1890 Anderson was principally found in Antrim, Dublin, Down and Derry, and the estimated number of bearers was 7,840. In the United States Anderson is the 11th most numerous surname with an estimated 855,250 bearers. In England and Wales in 1996 it was the 66th most numerous surname.

Andrews,
An English surname derived from the Greek meaning 'manly'. Andrew being the patron saint of Scotland has given rise to the surname there as well. In 1890 the surname was principally found in Antrim and Down, and the estimated number of bearers was 1,880. In the United States Andrews is the 183rd most numerous surname with an estimated 148,500 bearers. In England and Wales in 1996 it was the 109th most numerous surname.

McAneny, McEneaney, McEneany, Mac an éanaigh
A Gaelic surname a corruption of *Mac Conaonaigh*, meaning 'son of *Cú-aonaigh*' (hound of the fair). A sept of Monaghan who were seated in Clones. A sept who were a branch of the MacDonnells of Antrim, who Woulfe suggests are now probably represented in Tyrone. It has been mistranslated as Bird (*éan* being a bird), and as Rabbit (similarity to *coinín* being a rabbit) in Connacht. In 1890 McAneny

was principally found in Tyrone, McEneaney in Louth and McEneany in Monaghan, and the estimated number of bearers was 1,430.

McArdle, MacArdghail
A Gaelic surname meaning son of *Airdgal*, 'fierce or valorous'. A sept who were a branch of the *MacMathghamhána* (MacMahon's) of Orghialla (Oriel). The present County Louth was at one time known as English Oriel. In 1890 McArdle was numerous in Louth, it was also to be found in Monaghan and Armagh, and the estimated number of bearers was 2,464 (including variants). In the United States McArdle is the 6,534th most numerous surname with an estimated 5,500 bearers.

Armstrong
An English surname from the Borders, from the Old English *earm strong*, meaning strong in the arm. They were a numerous and warlike clan in Liddesdale. Sometimes an anglicisation of *ó Labhradha tréan*, which is more usually anglicised as Lavery (see below). In 1890 Armstrong was principally found in Antrim, Fermanagh, Cavan and Tyrone, and the estimated number of bearers was 6,300. In the United States Armstrong is the 188th most numerous surname with an estimated 145,750 bearers. In England and Wales in 1996 Armstrong was the 138th most numerous surname.

McAteer, Mac an tSaoir
A Gaelic surname meaning 'son of the craftsman' (*saor* for a mason, carpenter, freeman). Several septs. Also a Scottish surname (McIntyre) from Glen O in Lorn in Argyllshire. In 1890 McAteer was principally found in Armagh, Antrim and Donegal, and the estimated number of bearers was 1,610.

Atkinson
Both an English and a Scottish surname meaning son of Adkin (Adam), In 1890 Atkinson was principally found in Antrim, Armagh and Down, and the estimated number of bearers was 1,660. In the United States it is the 635th most numerous surname with an estimated 52,250 bearers. In England and Wales in 1996 it was the 123rd most numerous surname.

McAuley, McCauley, MacAmhlaoibh
A Gaelic surname meaning son of *Amhlaoibh*, an Irish form of the Norse *Olaf*. A sept of Fermanagh, a branch of the Maguires (see below) whose territory comprised tbe Barony of Clanawley. Also a Scottish surname of similar derivation whose seat was Ardincaple, in Dumbartonshire. In 1890 the surname was principally found in Antrim and Donegal and the estimated number of bearers for McAuley was 2,195, and for McCauley was 1,340. In the United States McAuley is the 7,139th most numerous surname with an estimated 5,500 bearers.

MacAuliffe, Mac Amhlaoibh
A Gaelic surname derived from *Amhlaoibh*, an Irish form of the
Norse *Olaf*. A sept who were a branch of the MacCarthys, whose
territory comprised the district lying between Newmarket and the
boundaries of Limerick and Kerry. A sept who were a branch of the
Maguires, whose territory comprised the Barony of Clanawley in
Fermanagh. A Scottish sept from Ardincaple in Dumbartonshire,
anglicised as McAulay (see above). In 1890 the surname was
principally found in Cork and the estimated number of bearers was
1,790. In the United States McAuliffe is the 8,272nd most numerous
surname with an estimated 2,750 bearers.

Bailey, Bailie, Bayley
A surname of both English and Scottish origin, derived from the Old
French *bailli*, meaning a person who was chief magistrate of a county
or barony. In Scotland the principal branches of this family were
those of Lamington, Jerviswood, Polkemmet, and Dochfour. In 1890
Bailey was principally found in Antrim and Wexford, Bailie was
principally found in Antrim and Down, and Bayley was principally
found in Tipperary and Dublin. The estimated number of bearers for
all variants was 3,130. In the United States Bailey is the 60th most
numerous surname with an estimated 312,650 bearers. In England
and Wales in 1996 it was the 56th most numerous surname.

Baird
A Scottish surname of territorial origin. A family *de Bard(e)* held
land in Lanarkshire. *Mac a' bhaird* (Macward) has also been so
anglicised. In 1890 Baird was principally found in Antrim and Down,
and the estimated number of bearers was 1,750. In the United States it
is the 911th most numerous surname with an estimated 35,750
bearers.

Baker
An English surname from the occupation of a baker. In 1890 was
principally found in Dublin and Antrim, and the estimated number of
bearers was 1,340. In the United States it is the 37th most numerous
surname with an estimated 470,250 bearers.

Barr, ó Barr
A Gaelic surname meaning descendant of *Barr*, short for *Fionnbharr*,
meaning 'fair-haired'. There were many saints of the name, including
St. Finnbarr of Moville whose feast day is 10th September. The
surname Barr is numerous in the Inishowen peninsula of Donegal,
particularly in the parishes of Lower Fahan, Muff and Moville. Barr is
also a Scottish surname of local origin from Barr in Ayrshire or Barr
in Renfrewshire, from whence it came to Ulster at the time of the
Plantation. In Ireland in 1890 the estimated number of persons
bearing the name was 2,700, and it was principally found in Antrim,
Derry and Down. In the United States Barr is the 698th most
numerous surname with an estimated 46,750 bearers.

40

Barrett, Baróid
A surname of Cambro-Norman origin meaning son of *Baraud*, a Norman form of the Teutonic *Berwald*. A sept of the name established itself in West Cork and a branch of these later settled in Mayo. In 1890 Barrett was principally found in Dublin, Cork, Kerry, Limerick, Galway and Mayo, and the estimated number of bearers was 6,540. In the United States it is the 280th most numerous surname with an estimated 107,250 bearers. In England and Wales in 1996 it was the 145th most numerous surname.

Barron, Baron, MacBarúin
A surname of Gaelic, Cambro-Norman, and Scottish origin. *MacBarúin* were a branch of the Ó Neill's. Baron was assumed as a surname by a branch of the Fitzgerald's from Kilkenny. In Scotland Baron usually meant one who held his lands from the king by military service. In other instances 'Barons' were landowners who had a certain amount of jurisdiction over the peoples on their lands. In 1890 Barron was principally found in Antrim, Donegal, Wexford and Waterford, and the estimated number of bearers was 1,920 (including variants). In the United States Barron is the 714th most numerous surname with an estimated 46,750 bearers.

Barry, de Barra
A surname of Cambro-Norman origin. Robert *de Barri* was amongst the Normans who landed at Bannow Bay in May 1169, he was a son of William de Barri of Monorbier Castle, Pembrokeshire in Wales. In 1179 Philip de Barry was granted the three cantreds of Ui Liatháin (Barrymore), Muscraighe-trí-maíghe (Orrery) and Cineál Aodha (Kinelea). The family divided into several branches, the chiefs of which were know as :
>   An Barrach Mór (the Great Barry);
>   An Barrach Ruadh (Red Barry);
>   An Barrach óg (Young Barry);
>   An Barrach Maol (Bald Barry); and
>   An Barrach Láidir (Strong Barry).
In 1229 Walter de Barri was granted land in Crosspatrick in the Barony of Shillelagh, Wicklow. Subsequently between 1247 and 1251 Raymond de Barry was lord of Ardamine (barony of Ballaghkeen, Wexford). *De Barri* became anglicised as Barry and Gaelicised as *de Barra*. It is difficult to distinguish the Cambro-Norman Barrys from Gaelic septs also anglicised as Barry : *ó Baire*, meaning descendant of *Barr*, short for *Fionnbharr*, meaning "fair-haired". A sept of the Corcu Lóighdhe who anciently possessed the peninsula of Muntervary in west Cork. *ó Beargha*; descendent of *beargha* meaning "spear-like". A sept who were lords of Ivecross, in the barony of Kenry, Limerick. In 1890 Barry was the seventy first most numerous surname, the estimated number of bearers was 9,700, and the surname was chiefly found in Cork, Limerick and Waterford; half of all entries were to be found in Cork (108 births). In the United States Barry is the 771st most numerous surname with an estimated 41,250 bearers. It

41

is numerous in the states of Connecticut, Massachusetts, and New York. In England and Wales in 1996 it was the 473rd most numerous surname.

Baxter
Both an English and a Scottish surname, from the occupation of *baxester* 'a woman that baked'. In 1890 Baxter was principally found in Antrim and the estimated number of bearers was 1,390. In the United States it is the 566th most numerous surname with an estimated 57,750 bearers. In England and Wales in 1996 it was the 257th most numerous surname.

Beattie, Beatty
A Scottish Border surname, from Bate or Baty, pet or diminutive form of Bartholomew. In 1890 Beattie was principally found in Antrim and Down and the estimated number of bearers was 2,730, Beatty was principally found in Dublin, Armagh and Tyrone and the estimated number of bearers was 1,610.

Beggs
A Scottish surname from the Gaelic *beag* meaning 'small'. Also an English surname which referred to a member of a thirteenth century religious sect. In 1890 Beggs was principally found in Antrim and Dublin, and the estimated number of bearers was 1,340.

Begley, ó Beaglaoich
A Gaelic surname meaning 'descendant of the little hero'. Originally a sept of Donegal, they went south with the MacSweeneys whom they served as gallowglasses. In 1890 Begley was principally found in Kerry and Donegal, and the estimated number of bearers was 1,750. In the United States it is the 2,897th most numerous surname with an estimated 11,000 bearers.

Behan, Beahan, ó Beacháin
A Gaelic surname meaning descendant of *Beachán*, a diminutive of *beach* meaning 'a bee' a name applied to a child. A sept of Laois-Offaly, originally a literary family, who have spread throughout Leinster. The surname has also been anglicised as; Beaghan, Behane, Beegan, Beane, Bean. In 1890 Behan was principally found in Dublin and Kildare, and the estimated number of bearers was 2,060.

Beirne, ó Beirn, ó Birn
A Gaelic surname meaning descendant of *Biorn* (from the Norse personal name *Bjorn*). A sept of Siol Muireadhaig who were stewards to *ó Conchobhair* (O'Connors). In the middle of the thirteenth century they superseded the *ó Manacháin* (O'Monaghans) as chiefs of Tir Bhriuin in Roscommon. Also *ó Birn* of Ui Fiachrach, who were seated north of Ballinrobe in Mayo. In 1890 Beirne was numerous in Roscommon and Leitrim, and the estimated number of bearers was 2,867.

42

Bell, MacGiollaMhaoil
The English or Scottish surname Bell has a number of derivations: descriptive *bel* being the Old French for 'beautiful' or in Old English it may have meant 'bellringer' or 'a dweller by a church or town bell'. It has been Gaelicised as *Mac Giolla Mhaoil*. It may also be of Cambro-Norman origin In Ireland. In 1863 Bell was the forty-seventh most common surname in Scotland, with an estimated 10,100 bearers. In Ireland in 1890 Bell was the eighty-ninth most numerous surname and the estimated number of bearers was 8,800. In that year the surname was chiefly found in Antrim, Down, Tyrone, Armagh and Dublin. In the United States it is the 58th most numerous surname with an estimated 321,750 bearers. In England and Wales in 1996 it was the 58th most numerous surname. In Scotland in 1995 it was the 39th most numerous surname.

Bennett
A surname of English, Scottish and Cambro-Norman origin. Bennett was a diminutive of Benedict (from the Latin for blessed), the fame of St. Benedict made the personal name popular. In 1890 Bennett was principally found in Cork, Dublin, Antrim, Armagh and Down, and the estimated number of bearers was 3,630. In the United States it is the 77th most numerous surname with an estimated 272,250 bearers. In England and Wales in 1996 it was the 48th most numerous surname.

Bergin, ó hAimheirgin
A Gaelic sept of Offaly from *Aimhirgin* meaning 'wonderous birth', they were chiefs of the barony of Geashill. The surname has been corrupted to *ó Meirgin* and *ó Beirgin*. In 1890 Bergin was principally found in Tipperary, Laois and Dublin, and the estimated number of bearers was 1,790. In the United States it is the 7,357th most numerous surname with an estimated 5,500 bearers.

Bermingham, Birmingham,
A surname of Anglo-Norman origin. The de Berminghams took part in the conquest of Connacht in the thirteenth century. They later spread to other parts of the country. Those descendant from Piers de Bermingham took the surname *Mac Fheorais*, subsequently anglicised as Corish (see below), they settled in south Wexford. In 1890 the surname was principally found in Dublin, Offaly and Cork, and the estimated number of bearers was 1,790. In the United States Birmingham is the 5,559th most numerous surname with an estimated 5,500 bearers.

Berry, Beary, ó Béara
A Gaelic sept of Offally who were of the same stock as the O'Connors and O'Dempseys, also a sept of Mayo. An English surname from the Old English for "fort". May have meant 'servant at the manor-house', or 'dweller by an enclosure near the fort'. In Scotland the surname was found in Fife. In 1890 Berry was principally found in

43

Antrim, Offally and Mayo, and the estimated number of bearers was 1,340. In the United States Berry is the 168th most numerous surname with an estimated 154,000 bearers. In England and Wales in 1996 it was the 157th most numerous surname.

Bingham, de Bingeham
An English Surname of local origin from the places so named. In 1890 Bingham was principally found in Down and Antrim, and the estimated number of bearers was 1,340.

Bird, see **McAneny** and **Henehan**

Bissett, see **McKeown**

Black, de Bláca
A surname of Cambro-Norman origin. *de Bláca* or *le Bláca* meaning 'black' descended from Richard Caddell, Sheriff of Connacht in 1303. One of the "Tribes of Galway". A branch settled in Kildare and spread to Wicklow, In 1890 Black was principally found in Antrim, Armagh, Tyrone and Down, and the estimated number of bearers was 5,200. In the United States it is the 149th most numerous surname with an estimated 173,250 bearers. In England and Wales in 1996 it was the 310th most numerous surname. In Scotland in 1995 it was the 44th most numerous surname.

Blair
A Scottish surname of territorial origin, from the places of the name. Derived from the Gaelic *blar* meaning 'a plain'. In 1890 Blair was principally found in Antrim, Derry and Tyrone, and the estimated number of bearers was 3,500. In the United States it is the 369th most numerous surname with an estimated 82,500 bearers.

Blake
The Blakes are one of the "Tribes of Galway", who descend from Richard Caddell, also called Blake who was Sheriff of Connacht in 1303. In the seventeenth century Blake supplanted Caddell. Also an English surname, where in some cases interchangeable with Black. In 1890 Blake was principally found in Cork, Galway, Clare, Antrim and Dublin, and the estimated number of bearers was 2,600. In the United States it is the 403rd most numerous surname with an estimated 77,000 bearers.

Bogue, see **Boyce**

Bohan(e), Boug(h)an, Bowen, Bohanan ó Buadhacháin
A Gaelic surname derived from *Buadhach* meaning 'victorious'. A scattered surname. In 1890 Bohan was principally found in Leitrim and Galway (Bohane in Cork), and the estimated number of bearers was 1,340. In the United States Bohannan is the 9,741st most numerous surname with an estimated 2,750 bearers.

44

Boland, ó Beólláin
A Gaelic surname meaning descendant of *Beóllán*, a rare personal name whose meaning is unclear. A sept in Sligo who were ecclesiastics and were erenaghs of the Columban church at Drumcliffe. A sept of the Ui Fiachrach in Sligo who were seated at Doonaltan in the Barony of Tireagh. A sept of the Dál gCais who were descendant from Mahon son of Torlough. In 1890 Boland was principally found in Clare, Kildare and Roscommon, and the estimated number of bearers was 2,550. In the United States it is the 4,207th most numerous surname with an estimated 8,250 bearers.

Bolger, ó Bolguidhir
A Gaelic surname meaning descendant of *Bolgodhar* (*bolg-odhar*) perhaps a nickname. A sept of South Leinster who were medics. Also found in Kildare and Wexford. In 1890 Bolger was numerous in Kildare and principally found in Wexford and Wicklow. The estimated number of bearers was 3,136.

Bonar, Bonner, Crampsey, ó Cnáimhsí
In most instances a Gaelic surname, meaning a descendant of *Cnáimhseach*, perhaps meaning 'midwife'. One of the very few matronymic surnames. Also a Scottish surname from the French *bonnaire* meaning 'courteous'. In Limerick it is a Palatine surname. In 1890 Bonar was principally found in Donegal and the estimated number of bearers was 1,700 (including variants). In the United States it is the 855th most numerous surname with an estimated 38,500 bearers.

Boyce, ó Buadhaigh
A Gaelic surname from *Buadhach* meaning 'victorious'. There must have been a sept in Tir Chonaill, the surname is sometimes anglicised Bogue. There was a sept of the Corca Laoighdhe in Cork that bore the surname. There is also an English and Scottish surname of Norman origin *de Bois*, or *del Bois* from "residence by or near a wood". In 1890 Boyce was principally found in Donegal, Down and Derry, and the estimated number of bearers was 1,790. In the United States it is the 1,046th most numerous surname with an estimated 33,000 bearers. Boyes a variant is the 9,863rd most numerous surname with an estimated 2,750 bearers.

Boyd
A Scottish surname of uncertain origin, which according to Black may be derived from the island of Bute. The marquess of Bute was known as *Morair Bhoid*. The Boyds were vassals of De Morevilles in the regality of Largs in Ayrshire. A Manks surname *Mac Giolla Buidhe* was anglicised as Boyd. In 1890 Boyd was numerous in Antrim, it was also to be found in Down and Derry, and the estimated number of bearers was 6,944. In the United States it is the 134th most numerous surname with an estimated 187,000 bearers.

Boylan, ó Baoighealláin
A Gaelic sept of Oriel who were anciently chiefs of Dartraighe (now the barony of Dartry in Monaghan), descendants of *Baoigheall* meaning 'vain pledge' as in the case of O'Boyle below. At one time they were Lords of Oriel but were reduced by the MacMahons. In 1890 Boylan was principally found in Dublin, Monaghan, Cavan and Meath, and the estimated number of bearers was 2,195. In the United States it is the 5,417th most numerous surname with an estimated 5,500 bearers.

O'Boyle, ó Baoighill, ó Baoill
A Gaelic surname meaning descendant of *Baoigheall*, which was a rare early Irish personal name *baoith-gheall*, meaning 'vain pledge. A leading sept of the Cineál Chonaill and were originally Chiefs of the Three Tuath in the north-west of Donegal. When their territory passed into the hands of Mac Suibhne (MacSweeney), they moved to Tír Ainmhireach in west Donegal, now known as the barony of Boylagh (*Críoch Bhaoigheallach* : O'Boyles Country). In 1890 Boyle was the forty-seventh most numerous surname in Ireland, the estimated number of bearers was 13,000, and the surname was principally to be found in Donegal, Antrim, Mayo, Tyrone, Armagh and Louth. In the United States Boyle is the 989th most numerous surname with an estimated 33,000 bearers. It is numerous in the state of Pennsylvania. In England and Wales in 1996 Boyle was the 447th most numerous surname. In Scotland in 1995 Boyle was the 84th most numerous surname.

Bradley, ó Brolcháin, ó Brallaghan
A Gaelic surname meaning descendant of *Brolachán* (diminutive of *Brólach*). A sept of who according to Woulfe were originally seated in the barony of Clogher in Tyrone, but moved north to Derry and Donegal. A branch of the family appears to have settled in Cork. In 1890 Bradley was numerous in Derry, it was also to be found in Antrim, Tyrone, Donegal, Dublin and Cork, and the estimated number of bearers was 6,048. In the United States it is the 181st most numerous surname with an estimated 148,500 bearers. It is numerous in the state of Delaware. In England and Wales in 1996 it was the 124th most numerous surname.

Brady, Mac Brádaigh
A Gaelic surname meaning son of *Brádach*, which personal name meant 'spirited'. A leading sept of East Breffny (Cavan) who were chiefs of Cúl Brigde, the district around Stradone in the barony of Upper Loughtee. Also see O'Grady. In 1890 Brady was the fifty-seventh most numerous name in Ireland and the estimated number of bearers was 11,600. In that year the surname was chiefly found in Cavan, Dublin, Antrim, Meath and Longford. In the United States it is the 448th most numerous surname with an estimated 68,750 bearers. In England and Wales in 1996 it was the 456th most numerous surname.

46

Brannigan, Branagan, ó Branagáin
A Gaelic surname meaning descendant of *Branán*, a diminutive of *Bran* meaning a 'raven'. A sept of the Cineál Eoghain. In 1890 Brannigan was principally found in Armagh and Monaghan and Branagan was principally found in Dublin. The estimated number of bearers including variants was 1,700.

Breen, Bruen, ó Braoin
A Gaelic surname meaning descendant of *Braon*, meaning 'sadness, sorrow'. A sept of Breaghmhaine, now the barony of Brawney in Westmeath, adjoining Athlone and the Shannon. The surname has been translated as O'Brien in this area. A sept of Luighne, now the barony of Lune, in the west of Mayo. A sept of Loch Gealgosa, probably in the barony of Costello in Mayo. A sept of Roscommon, who were erenagh of the church of St. Coman. The surname has been translated as Bruen here. *Mac Braoin* was a sept in Osraighe (Ossory) in the barony of Knocktoper in Kilkenny. In 1890 Breen was principally found in Wexford, Dublin and Kerry, and the estimated number of bearers was 5,000. Bruen was found in Roscommon and the estimated number of bearers was 450. In the United States Breen is the 3,011st most numerous surname with an estimated 11,000 bearers.

Breheny, see **Judge**

Brennan, ó Braonáin, ó Branáin
A Gaelic surname meaning descendant of *Braonán*, which personal name is a diminutive of *Braon* meaning 'sorrow'. A sept of Ossairge (Ossory) who were Chiefs of Uí Dhuach, in the north of the present Kilkenny. A sept of Crevagh in Westmeath. A sept of Síol Anmchadha, of the same stock as the *ó Madáin* (O'Madden), seated in the barony of Longford in south-east Galway. A sept of Dunkerron, who were followers of *ó Súileabháin More* (O'Sullivan More), in Kerry. It is difficult to distinguish the anglicised form of *ó Braonáin* from *ó Branáin* : A Gaelic surname meaning descendant of *Branán*. The personal name *Branán* is a diminutive of *Bran*, which means 'a raven'. An ecclesiastical sept, who were erenaghs of the church of Derry and of Derryvullan in Fermanagh also anglicised Brannan. In 1890 Brennan was the twenty-eight most numerous surname and the estimated number of bearers was 16,000. It was the most numerous surname in Kilkenny and Sligo, and was also principally found Dublin, Mayo, Carlow and Roscommon. In the United States it is the 744th most numerous surname with an estimated 44,000 bearers. It is numerous in the states of New Jersey, New York, and Pennsylvania. In England and Wales in 1996 it was the 340th most numerous surname.

Breslin, ó Breasláin
A Gaelic sept who were a branch of the Cinel Enda and were originally chiefs of Fanad, in the Barony of Kilmacrenan, Donegal. In the thirteenth century they were driven out of this territory to Fermanagh and became brehons (judges) to the Maguires. They were

also erenaghs of the church of Derryvullen in Fermanagh. There was also a sept of the Uí Fiachrach, who were chiefs of Kilanely, in the barony of Tireragh, in Sligo. In 1890 Breslin was principally found in Donegal and the estimated number of bearers was 1,920.

McBride, Mac Giolla Bhríghde
A Gaelic surname meaning son of the servant of St. Brigid. A surname anciently found in many parts of Ireland. A sept of the Cineál Chonaill who were erenaghs in the parish of Raymunterdoney, now in the barony of Kilmacrenan in Donegal. Also a Scottish surname of the same derivation, which established itself in Arran. In 1890 McBride was principally found in Antrim, Donegal and Down, and the estimated number of bearers was 5,280. In the United States it is the 433rd most numerous surname with an estimated 71,500 bearers.

O'Brien, ó Briain,
A Gaelic surname meaning descendant of Brian, the personal name *Brian*, may have meant 'high, noble'. High King Brian Boru, who was victor at the Battle of Clontarf in 1014 was ancestor of the *ó Briain* of Thomond (Thuas Mhumhan). A sept of the Uí Toirdealbhaigh of Dál gCais. They divided into several sub-septs. A sept of Ara in north Tipperary, whose chief was known as Mac Uí Bhriain Ara. A sept of Coonagh in east Limerick. A sept of Pobelbrien in Limerick, whose stronghold was Carrigogonnell. A sept of Aherlow by the Galtees in Tipperary. A sept of Cumaragh near Dungarvan in Waterford. O'Brien was the sixth most numerous name in Ireland in 1890, the estimated number of bearers was 33,400, and the surname was found in every county in Munster and also in Dublin, Cavan and Galway. In the United States it is the 281st most numerous surname with an estimated 107,250 bearers. It is numerous in the states of Connecticut, Massachusetts, and New York. In England and Wales in 1996 it was the 130th most numerous surname.

Broderick, ó Bruadair
A Gaelic surname meaning descendant of *Bruadar* (from the Norse *Broddr*). A sept of Ossory, who were chiefs of Iverk in the south of Kilkenny; A sept of Galway; A sept of Carraic Brachaidhe in Inishowen in Donegal; A sept of Ui Ceinnsealaigh in Wexford; A sept of Corca Laoighdhe in Cork. In 1890 Broderick was principally found in Galway, Cork, Kerry and Dublin, and the estimated number of bearers was 1,750.

Brogan, ó Brógáin
A Gaelic surname derived from *bróg* meaning 'sorrowful'. A sept anciently possessed lands at Breachmaigh and Cnoc Spealain in the Barony of Carra in Mayo. In 1890 Brogan was principally found in Mayo and Donegal, and the estimated number of bearers was 1,480. In the United States it is the 4,273rd most numerous surname with an estimated 8,250 bearers.

Brophy, ó Bróithe
A Gaelic surname. The original territory of the sept was Magh Sedna,
in the barony of Galmoy, Kilkenny. After the Cambro-Norman
Invasion they were driven into Upper Ossory, when their chief settled
at Ballybrophy in Laois. In 1890 Brophy was principally to be found
in Dublin, Kilkenny, Laois and Tipperary, and the estimated number
of bearers was 2,240. In the United States it is the 6,983rd most
numerous surname with an estimated 5,500 bearers.

Brosnan, ó Brosnacháin
A Gaelic surname meaning descendant of *Brosnachán*, meaning a
native of Brosna. A sept of Kerry. In 1890 Brosnan was numerous in
Kerry (55 births), and the estimated number of bearers was 2,956.

Brown, Browne, de Brún
A surname of Irish, English, and Scottish origin. In Scotland *Mac a'
Bhriuthainn* meaning "son of the brehon (judge)", *M'Ille dhuinn* or
M'Mhaoil duinn (Mackduin) meaning "son of the brown lad", *Le
Brun* of Cumberland, also a sept of Clan Macmillian. An English
surname from the nickname : *Brun* Old English meaning "brown of
hair or complexion". Browne has been Gaelicised as *de Brún*. The
most important families were : Browne of Galway, one of the 'Tribes
of Galway'. Browne of the Neale in Mayo. Browne of Mulrankin in
the parish of Kilmore in Wexford, whose lands were forfeited after the
Rising of 1641. Browne of Hariston, Waterford. Browne of Aney,
Limerick. Brown of Kilpatrick, Westmeath. Browne of Dunbrowne,
Kerry. Brownes of Kenmare, Killarney, Kerry, who arrived during the
time of Elizabeth I, the later Earls of Kenmare. Browne was the thirty-
seventh most common name in Ireland in 1890 and the estimated
number of bearers was 14,600. The surname was to be found as
'Brown' in Antrim, Derry, Down and Dublin and as 'Browne' in
Cork, Mayo, Wexford and Dublin. In the United States Brown is the
5th most numerous surname with an estimated 1,707,750 bearers. In
England and Wales in 1996 it was the 5th most numerous surname. In
Scotland in 1995 it was the 2nd most numerous surname.

Bruen, see **Breen**

Bryan
A family of Cambro-Norman origin which settled in Kilkenny. There
are many variants and is sometimes confused with Byrne. In 1890
Bryan was principally found in Dublin, Kilkenny, Wexford, Cork and
Down, and the estimated number of bearers was 2,105. In the United
States it is the 487th most numerous surname with an estimated
66,000 bearers. It is numerous in the states of Connecticut, Delaware,
Maryland, Massachusetts, New Jersey, New York, Pennsylvania. In
England and Wales in 1996 it was the 439th most numerous surname.

Buckley, ó Buachalla
A Gaelic surname meaning descendant of *Buachaill*, a personal name

which meant 'boy', and may have meant a boy left in charge of a cowherd. Anglicised as Buckley, which is an English surname with which these families have no connection. A sept which inhabited the Blackwater valley in north east Cork and who were dispossessed by the Cambro-Normans during the twelfth and thirteenth centuries. To-day Cork and Kerry have the largest concentrations of the surname. A sept of which originated in Tipperary-Offaly and which was numerous during the seventeenth century. Buckley was the ninety-ninth most numerous name in Ireland in 1890 and the estimated number of bearers was 8,200. In that year the surname was chiefly found in Cork, Kerry, Dublin, Kilkenny and Tipperary. In the United States it is the 749th most numerous surname with an estimated 44,000 bearers. In England and Wales in 1996 it was the 234th most numerous surname.

Burke, Bourke, de Búrca
The surname adopted by the descendants of the Cambro-Norman *Richard de Burgh*, who was regranted Connacht by King Henry III of England. Gaelicised as *de Burca*, the anglicisation is either Burke or Bourke. In the fourteenth century the Burkes divided Connacht between themselves. They became completely hibernicized and considered themselves Irish Chiefs of which there were two septs : *MacWilliam Uachtar* (Upper) in Galway; *MacWilliam Iochtar* (Lower) seated in Mayo. Minor branches assumed the surnames of MacDavid, MacPhilpin, MacGibbon, *MacSeoin* (See Jennings), MacRedmond, from their respective ancestors. They were also lords of the barony of Clanwilliam, Limerick. Burke was the twenty-ninth most numerous name in 1890 and the estimated number of bearers was 15,900. The surname was principally to be found in Galway, Cork, Dublin, Mayo, Tipperary and Waterford. In the United States it is the 243rd most numerous surname with an estimated 121,000 bearers. It is numerous in the state of New Jersey. In England and Wales in 1996 it was the 222nd most numerous surname.

Burns
A Scottish surname of local origin: From the town of Burness, Argyllshire; Burneshead, Cumberland, was the seat of a family of Burnes up to the reign of Edward I; and Bernes in the parish of Glenbervie. It would have spread to east Ulster perhaps prior to the Plantation. Burns was the sixty-eight most numerous name in Ireland in 1890, the estimated number of bearers was 9,800. In that year the surname was chiefly found in Antrim, Down and Armagh. In Munster it was to be found in Clare, Cork, Kerry and Tipperary. In the United States it is the 142nd most numerous surname with an estimated 178,750 bearers. In England and Wales in 1996 it was the 182nd most numerous surname. In Scotland in 1995 it was the 60th most numerous surname.

Butler, de Buitléir
A surname of Norman origin. Theobald Walter de Valognes came to Ireland and by 1185 was Chief Butler to the King, he was granted Ur

50

Mhumhan (Ormond) and became Earl of Ormond. In 1890 the name was numerous in Kilkenny and principally found in Dublin, Tipperary and Waterford. The estimated number of bearers was 7,705. In the United States it is the 91st most numerous surname with an estimated 250,250 bearers. In England and Wales in 1996 it was the 92nd most numerous surname.

O'Byrne, ó Broin
A Gaelic surname meaning descendants of *Bran*, which personal name meant 'a raven'. The ancestor of this sept was a son of *Maolmhórdha* King of Leinster who died in 1052. The original territory of the sept was Uí Faoláin in the north of the present Kildare. They were forced into the mountains of Wicklow by the Cambro-Norman invaders. Their country was called Críoch Bhranach, which comprised the barony of Newcastle. A sub-sept inhabited part of Arklow and Ballinacor, known as Gabhal Raghnaill or Ranelagh. In Wicklow many who are described as Brien or O'Brien are actually *ó Broin*. Not to be confused with *ó Birn* also anglicised as Byrne, but more frequently as Beirne. Byrne was the seventh most numerous surname in Ireland in 1890, the estimated number of bearers was 33,300, and it was the most numerous surname in Louth and Wicklow. In that year the surname was also principally found in Dublin and Wexford. It was also found in Carlow, Kildare and Kilkenny; in Cork and Waterford; Donegal; Galway, Mayo and Roscommon. In the United States Byrne is the 1,224th most numerous surname with an estimated 27,500 bearers. In England and Wales in 1996 it was the 192nd most numerous surname.

McCabe, Mac Cába,
A surname of Scottish galloglass origin, descendants of a family of Norse origin, a branch of the Macleods (son of *Leod*, from the Norse name *Ljótr*) of Arran who came over from the Hebrides in the fourteenth century and became a sept of Breifne (Breffny). They were captains to the *ó Ruairc* (O'Rourkes) and *ó Raghallaigh* (O'Reillys) and were known by the titles Constables of Oriel, Constable of Breffny and Constable of the two Breffnys. Distinctive Hebridean personal names, such as Alan (Aleinn), Somhairle (Sumarlidi), were formerly frequent amongst the McCabes. In 1890 McCabe was numerous in Monaghan, and was also found in Cavan and Dublin.The estimated numer of bearers was 6,496. In the United States it is the 1,200th most numerous surname with an estimated 27,500 bearers.

Caffrey
See immediately below. In 1890 Caffrey was principally found in Dublin, Meath and Cavan, and the estimated number of bearers was 1,570.

McCaffrey, MacGafraidh
A Gaelic surname, meaning son of Godfrey. A sept who were a branch of the Maguire's of Fermanagh. In 1890 McCaffery was principally found in Fermanagh and Tyrone, and the estimated number of bearers

51

was 2,730 (including variants). In the United States it is the 3,874th most numerous surname with an estimated 8,250 bearers.

Cahill, ó Cathail
A Gaelic surname meaning descendant of *Cathal* (strong in battle). A sept of Cinel Aodha, in south west Galway, of the same stock as the O'Shaughnessy's. A sept of Crumthann in east Galway. A sept of Corca Thine, now Corkehenny, in the parish of Templemore in Tipperary, who gave their name to Ballycahill. A sept of Loch Lein, who were lords of the Eoghanacht of that district before the O'Donoghues. A sept of Ui Flaithri, near Corofin in Clare. In 1890 Cahill was principally to be found in Cork, Kerry, Dublin, Kilkenny and Tipperary, and the estimated number of bearers was 6,580. In the United States it is the 1,673rd most numerous surname with an estimated 19,250 bearers.

Cain, ó Catháin
A sept of the Ui Fiachrach. Also see Kane. In 1890 Cain was principally found in Mayo, and the estimated number of bearers was 1,390. In the United States it is the 486th most numerous surname with an estimated 66,000 bearers.

Cairns
A Scottish surname of territorial origin from Cairns in the parish of Mid-Calder, Midlothian. There was a family of the name in Galloway. In 1890 the surname was principally found in Antrim, Down and Armagh, and the estimated number of bearers was 1,970.

Caldwell
A Scottish surname of territorial origin from Renfrewshire. Also an English surname of territorial origin from the many places so called meaning 'A cold spring or stream'. An anglicised form of *ó hUarghuis*, or *ó hUairisce* (Horish, Houriskey) in Tyrone, and *Mac Conluain* (Cullivan, Colavin) in Cavan. In 1890 the surname was principally found in Antrim, Derry and Tyrone, and the estimated number of bearers was 1,880. In the United States it is the 272nd most numerous surname with an estimated 107,250 bearers.

O'Callaghan, ó Ceallacháin
A Gaelic surname meaning descendant of *Ceallachán*, which was a diminutive of *Ceallach*. The personal name *Ceallach* meant 'bright-headed'. The name could be male or female, however it was more common as a male name. The principal sept of the name were originally chiefs of Cineál Aodha, now the barony of Kinalea, in south Cork. After the Cambro-Norman Invasion they were driven from there and settled on the banks of the river Blackwater, to the west of Mallow, in an area known as Pobal Uí Cheallacháin, comprising the parishes of Kilshannig and Clonmeen. Also a sept of the Uí Fiachrach, who were lords of Erris in Mayo. In 1890 Callaghan was the forty-third most numerous surname, the estimated number of bearers was

14,000, and the surname was principally to be found in Cork, Kerry and Dublin. O'Callaghan was principally found in Cork and the estimated number of bearers was 2,870. In the United States Callahan is the 621st most numerous surname with an estimated 52,250 bearers, Callaghan was the 4,560th most numerous surname with an estimated 8,250 bearers, and Callihan was the 8,667th most numerous surname with an estimated 2,750 bearers.

Callan, ó Cathaláin
A sept of Oriel, from a diminutive of *Cathal* meaning 'strong in battle'. There are many similar corruptions. In 1890 Callan was principally found in Louth and Monaghan, and the estimated number of bearers was 1,480.

Callanan, Callinan, ó Callanáin
A Gaelic surname. A sept who were hereditary physicians to the MacCarthy's in south Munster. A sept who were co-arbs of Kilcahill in Galway. In 1890 Callanan was found in Galway and Cork, and Callinan was found in Clare. The estimated number of bearers was 1,790 (all variants).

Cameron
A Scottish surname, both Lowland and Highland. The Lowlands surname is of territorial origin from three places so named. The Highland clan name is derived from *cam-shron* meaning 'hook nose'. The Clan Cameron had three main branches. Also see Martin. In 1890 Cameron was principally found in Antrim and Derry, and the estimated number of bearers was 1,340. In the United States it is the 561st most numerous surname with an estimated 57,750 bearers. In England and Wales in 1996 it was the 442nd most numerous surname. In Scotland in 1995 it was the 35th most numerous surname.

Campbell, Caimbeul, Mac Cathmhaoil
A Scottish surname which according to tradition was *ó Duibhne*. Caimbeul was a name applied to an early chief of the Clann Duibhne from Diarmuid of Lochow, said to be of the Siol Diarmid. The Gaelic *cam beal* meant 'wry' or 'crooked mouth'. The Clan Campbell divided into three septs : Clan Dubhgal Craignish, Clan Mac Iver of Asknish, Clan MacArthur of Strachur. Many Campbells came to Ireland with the Ulster plantation. In west Donegal Campbell is usually of Galloglass origin. The Gaelic surname *Mac Cathmhaoil*, meaning 'son of Cathmhaol' has been anglicised as Campbell. *Cathmhaol* was an uncommon early name meaning 'battle chief'. They were a sept of Tír Eoghain whose territory was Cineal Farry now the barony of Clogher. According to Woulfe there was another such sept in Down. In 1890 Campbell was the thirty-first most numerous surname; the estimated number of bearers was 15,600; and the surname was principally to be found in Antrim, Down, Armagh, Tyrone, Derry and Donegal. In the United States it is the 46th most numerous surname with an estimated 409,750 bearers. In England and Wales in 1996 it

was the 83rd most numerous surname. In Scotland in 1995 it was the 6th most numerous surname.

McCann, Mac Cana
A Gaelic surname meaning son of *Cana*, 'wolf-cub', meaning a young warrior. A sept who were lords of Cinel Aonghusa, or Clann Breasain on the south side of Lough Neagh in Armagh. In 1890 McCann was numerous in Armagh, it was also to be found in Antrim, Dublin and Tyrone. The estimated number of bearers was 7,929.

Cannon, ó Canannáin
A sept who were anciently Kings of the Cineál Chonaill in Donegal. Their original territory would seem to have been Tír Aeda (now the barony of Tirhugh). The personal name *Canannán* is a diminutive of *Cano* meaning 'wolf-cub'. After the death of *Niall ó Canannáin* in 1250, the sept declined greatly in power. In 1890 Cannon was principally found in Donegal, Leitrim and Mayo, and the estimated number of bearers was 2,195. In the United States it is the 373rd most numerous surname with an estimated 82,500 bearers.

Carey, ó Ciardha
A Gaelic surname meaning descendant of *Ciardha*, from *Ciar* meaning 'black'. A sept of the southern Uí Néill who were lords of Cairbre, the present barony of Carbury in Kildare. Anglicised as Carey and difficult to distinguish from many other names similarly anglicised. Carey is the anglisication of a variety of Gaelic surnames.
ó Ciardha a sept who were lords of Carbury until the Cambro-Norman invasion. Also a synonym of Kerin, *ó Céirín. Mac Fhiachra*, *Mac Fhiachrach* : A sept of Cineál Eoghain, who were anciently chiefs of Cinel Fearadhaigh, in the barony of Clogher in Tyrone. A sept who were chiefs of Oga Beathra in south-west Galway. A sept of Meath. In 1890 Carey was principally found in Cork, Dublin, Tipperary, Mayo and Kerry, and the estimated number of bearers was 5,280. In the United States it is the 627th most numerous surname with an estimated 52,250 bearers.

Carmody, ó Cearmada
A Gaelic surname meaning descendant of *Cearmaid*. A sept of Thomond. In 1890 Carmody was principally found in Clare, Kerry and Limerick, and the estimated numer of bearers was 1,480.

Carney, see Kearney

Carolan, ó Cearbhalláin, ó Caireálláin
A Gaelic sept of south Ulster. Difficult to distinguish from the *ó Caireálláin* a sept of the Cineál Eoghain who were anciently chiefs of Clandermot, in Derry. In 1890 Carolan was principally found in Mayo and Cavan, and the estimated number of bearers was 2.110.

Carr
An anglicised form of several Gaelic surnames. Also see Kerr. In 1890 was principally found in Donegal, Galway and Dublin, and the estimated number of bearers was 3,800. In the United States it is the 205th most numerous surname with an estimated 140,250 bearers. In England and Wales in 1996 it was the 149th most numerous surname.

O'Carroll, ó Cearbhaill
A Gaelic surname meaning descendant of *Cearbhall*, which personal name meant 'brave in sword fighting, valorous in battle'. A sept who were Lords of Eile, which comprised the baronies of Clonlisk and Ballybritt, in Offaly and Ikerrin and Eliogarty in Tipperary. After the Cambro-Norman Invasion, Ikerrin and Eliogarty became tributory to the Earl of Ormond and only that part of Eile known as Eile ó Cearbhaill remained in the possession of the ó Cearbhaill whose headquarters was at Birr. A sept of who were chiefs of Oriel, who were of the same stock as the MacMathghamhna and the Maguires. A sept who were Chiefs of the Eoghanacht of Loch Léin, the district about Killarney in Kerry. They were dispossessed by the ó Donnchadha (O'Donoghue). A sept who were Chiefs of Ossory (Ossairge). A sept of Tara who were a branch of the southern Uí Néill. A sept of Calry in Sligo and Leitrim. Can be confused with *Mac Cearbhaill* of which there were two septs: one in south Leinster and another in Ulster anglicised as MacCarvill. In 1890 O'Carroll was the twenty-second most numerous surname; the estimated number of bearers was 17,500; and the surname was principally found in Dublin, Kilkenny, Cork, Tipperary and Limerick, but found in all counties of Leinster, Munster and Connaught. In the United States it is the 176th most numerous surname with an estimated 151,250 bearers. In England and Wales in 1996 it was the 283rd most numerous surname.

McCarron, MaCearáin, MacCiaráin
A sept of Donegal derived from *ciar* meaning 'black'. *Mac Carrghamhna* (son of spear-calf), an ancient sept of Westmeath is sometimes so translated. In 1890 McCarron was principally found in Donegal and Derry, and the estimated number of bearers was 1,480.

Carson
A Scottish surname, of Galloway. Carsons were provosts of Drumfries for several generations and were also prominent in local affairs of Kirkcudbrightshire. In 1890 carson was principally found in Antrim, Down and Tyrone, and the estimated number of bearers was 3,450. In the United States it is the 472nd most numerous surname with an estimated 66,000 bearers.

Carter
An English surname perhaps from the occupation of driver of a cart. In 1890 Carter was principally found in Dublin and Galway and the estimated number of bearers was 1,700. In the United States it is the 40th most numerous surname with an estimated 445,500 bearers. In

England and Wales in 1996 it was the 54th most numerous surname.

Carthy, ó Cárthaigh
A Gaelic surname meaning grandson of *Cárthach*, which personal meant "lover, or loving person" (as in the case of MacCarhty below). In 1890 Carthy was principally found in Wicklow, Waterford and Cork, and the estimated number of bearers was 1,120.

MacCarthy, Mac Carthaigh
A Gaelic surname meaning son of *Cárthach*, which personal meant 'lover, or loving person'. It was a common early Irish name in the south of Ireland. These were the chief sept of the Eoghanacht, whose ancestor was Cárthach mac Saírbrethaig. In the period prior to the Cambro-Norman Invasion, the septs were Kings of Desmond (Deas Mhumhan), shortly after the invasion they were driven from Tipperary into the present counties of Cork and Kerry. They divided into sub-septs : Mac Carthaigh More in Kerry; Mac Carthaigh Reagh, lords of Carbery in west Cork; Mac Carthaigh Muscraidhe (of Muskerry). Mac Carthaigh Dúthaigh Ealla (Duhallow). Wolfe states that there were numerous minor branches. In 1890 McCarthy was the thirteenth most numerous surname; the estimated number of bearers was 22,300, and the surname was principally found in Cork, which had 277 births. It was also principally found in Kerry and Limerick. Outside of Munster the surname was only found in appreciable numbers in Dublin and Antrim. In the United States McCarthy is the 409th most numerous surname with an estimated 74,250 bearers, McCarty is the 851st most numerous surname with an estimated 38,500 bearers. It is numerous in the states of Connecticut, Massachusetts, New Jersey, and New York. In England and Wales in 1996 it was the 205th most numerous surname.

McCartney,
A Scottish surname from the Gaelic meaning son of *Artan*, a diminutive of *Art*. The name was to be found in Ayrshire. In 1890 the surname was principally found in Antrim and the estimated number of bearers was 2,370.

McCartan, Mac Artáin
A Gaelic sept meaning son of *Artán* (a diminutive of *Art*, an ancient word for a bear). This sept were lords of Cinel Faghartaigh, now the barony of Kinelarty in Down. In 1890 McCartan was principally found in Down and Armagh, and the estimated number of bearers was 1,570.

Carty, ó Cárthaigh
A Gaelic surname meaning descendant of *Cárthach* meaning 'loving'. There were septs in Tipperary, Clare and Roscommon. In 1890 the surname was principally found in Roscommon, Wexford, Galway and Longford, and the estimated number of bearers was 3,050.

Casey, ó Cathasaigh, Cathasach

A Gaelic surname meaning descendant of *Cathasach*, which personal name meant 'vigilant in war, watchful'. A sept of Meath, who were lords of Saithne, in the north of Dublin. These were dispossessed by Hugh de Lacy soon after the Cambro-Norman Invasion. A sept of the Dál gCais, who occupied the barony of Coshlea in Limerick. A sept in Cork whose territory Coillte Maibineacha was near Mitchelstown. A sept of Tirawley who were erenaghs of Kilarduff, in the parish of Dunfeeny, Mayo. A sept of Fermanagh, who were erenaghs of Devinish. In 1890 Casey was the fifty-ninth most numerous surname, the estimated number of bearers was 11,300 and the surname was chiefly found in Cork, Kerry, Dublin and Limerick. In the United States it is the 479th most numerous surname with an estimated 66,000 bearers. It is numerous in the state of Connecticut.

Cassidy, ó Caiside,

A Gaelic surname meaning descendant of *Caiside*. A sept of Fermanagh who were hereditary physicians to the Mag Uidhir (Maguires). Branches of this family had settled in the midland counties before the end of the sixteenth century according to Woulfe. In 1890 Cassidy was numerous in Fermanagh, and principally found in Donegal, Dublin and Antrim, and the estimated number of bearers was 6,316. In the United States it is the 1,505th most numerous surname with an estimated 22,000 bearers.

McCauley, see McAuley

Caulfield

An English surname of habitation, a Toby Caulfield came to Ulster in 1607. A possible synonym for MacCall, Caffery, and Gaffney. Also a possible anglicisation of *MacConghamhna*, meaning son of *Cú-ghamhna* (calf-hound). A sept who were a branch of the Ui Fiachrach Aidhne from south Galway. In 1890 Caulfield was principally found in Mayo, Antrim and Monaghan, and the estimated number of bearers was 2,640.

Chambers

A surname of Norman origin from the Old French *de la Chambre*, pretaining to an officer charged with the management of the private chambers of sovereign or nobleman. The Scottish form is Chalmers. In 1890 Chambers was principally found in Antrim, Mayo, Down and Armagh, and the estimated number of bearers was 3,090. In the United States it is the 290th most numerous surname with an estimated 101,750 bearers. In England and Wales in 1996 it was the 206th most numerous surname.

Christy, Christie

A Scottish surname, a diminutive of Christian, or Christopher. A surname of Fife. In 1890 the surname was principally found in Antrim, and the estimated number of bearers was 1,480.

Clancy, Clancey, MacFhlannchadha
A Gaelic surname meaning son of *Flannchadh* perhaps meaning 'red warrior, battler'. A sept who were chiefs of Dartry, now the barony of Rosclogher in Leitrim. A sept of Thuas Mhumhan (Thomond), a branch of the MacNamaras who were hereditary judges to the O'Briens and resided at Knockfin and Cahermaclancy in north-west Clare. In 1890 Clancey was numerous in Clare, it was also to be found in Leitrim, Galway and Tipperary. The estimated number of bearers was 4,256. In the United States it is the 3,043rd most numerous surname with an estimated 11,000 bearers.

Clarke
An English or Scottish surname of occupation. The original meaning of the name was 'a man in a religious order, cleric, or clergyman'. All writing and secretarial work in the Middle Ages being done by the Clergy. Later many merchants and tradesmen whose chief business was to draw up deeds etc. were called clerks. It may also have been a nickname for a person who could read and write. In 1863 it was the eighteenth most numerous surname in Scotland and in 1853 was the twenty-seventh most numerous surname in England. Clarke was the thirty-second most numerous surname in Ireland in 1890; the estimated number of bearers was 15,400, and the surname was principally to be found in Antrim, Dublin, Mayo, Cavan and Louth. See also, *ó Cléirigh* below. In the United States Clark is the 21st most numerous surname with an estimated 635,250 bearers, Clarke is the 482nd most numerous surname with an estimated 66,000 bearers. In England and Wales in 1996 Clarke was the 23rd most numerous surname and Clark was the 34th most numerous surname. In Scotland in 1995 Clark was the 14th most numerous surname.

Cleary, Clarke, ó Cléirigh,
A Gaelic surname *ó Cléirigh*, meaning descendant of *Cléireach* meaning a 'clerk'. A sept who anciently ruled Aidhne, co-extensive with the diocese of Kilmacduagh in south Galway, from which they were driven in the thirteenth century and dispersed to different parts of Ireland. A branch settled in Tirawley in Mayo from which they spread to Tir Chonaill and one of whom became a compiler of the Annals of the Four Masters. Branches settled in both Cavan and Kilkenny. In 1890 Cleary was principally found in Dublin, Tipperary, Clare, Limerick and Waterford and the estimated number of bearers was 5,500. In the United States it is the 2,478th most numerous surname with an estimated 13,750 bearers.

MacClelland
A surname of Scottish origin, perhaps derived from the Cleland in the parish of Dalziel, Lanarkshire. In 1890 McClelland was principally found in Antrim, Down, Armagh, Derry and Monaghan, and the estimated number of bearers was 2,960 (including variants).

Clifford, de Clifford, ó Clúmháin
A Gaelic surname meaning descendant of *Clúmhán*, diminutive of *cúmhach*, hairy. A sept of Ui Fiachrach in Sligo who were a bardic family and poets and chroniclers to the O'Haras. According to Woulfe branches of the family settled in south Leinster and west Munster. Also anglicised as Coleman in Kerry, for which see: *ó Colmáin*. Also an English surname from the placename Clifford meaning 'dweller at the ford by the steep bank'. In 1890 Clifford was numerous in Kerry (45 births), and the estimated number of bearers was 3,718. In the United States it is the 1,630th most numerous surname with an estimated 22,000 bearers.

McCloskey, McCluskey, Mac Bhloscaidh,
A Gaelic surname meaning descendant of *Bloscadh*. A sept of Derry who were descendant of *Bloscadh ó Catháin*. They were numerous in the parish of Dungiven at the time of the first ordinance survey. In 1890 McCloskey was numerous in Derry, and McCluskey in Antrim and Dublin. The estimated number of bearers for McCloskey was 2,105, and for McCluskey was 1,075. In the United States it is the 5,948th most numerous surname with an estimated 5,500 bearers.

McClure, Mac Giolla Uidhir
A Scottish surname, meaning son of the pale youth. In 1890 McClure was principally found in Antrim and Down, and the estimated number of bearers was 1,570. In the United States it is the 653rd most numerous surname with an estimated 49,500 bearers.

Coakley, Mac Caochlaoich
A Gaelic surname meaning 'son of the blind hero', it may have been *Mac Caochfhile* meaning 'son of the blind poet'. A sept of west Cork. Also anglicised as Kehilly, Also see Kiely. In 1890 Coakley was principally found in Cork and the estimated number of bearers was 1,390. In the United States it is the 5,553rd most numerous surname with an estimated 5,500 bearers.

Cochrane
A Scottish surname of local origin, from Cochrane, near Paisley, in Renfrewshire. In 1890 the surname was principally found in Antrim, Derry, Down and Tyrone. The estimated number of bearers was 1,880.

Coady, Cody, Mac Oda
In Kilkenny a patronymic surname assumed by the family of Archdeacon. *Oda*, or *Otho* being a Teutonic personal name introduced by the Normans. In 1890 the surname was principally found in Kilkenny, Tipperary, Galway and Cork, and the estimated number of bearers was 1,570.

Cock, see Cox

Coen, ó Comhdhain
A Gaelic surname derived from *Comhghan* meaning 'co-birth', also see Cowen. In 1890 Coen was principally found in Galway and Roscommon, and the estimated number of bearers was 1,210. In the United States it is the 8,587th most numerous surname with an estimated 2,750 bearers.

Coffey, ó Cobhthaigh
A Gaelic surname meaning descendant of *Cobhthach* (victorious), A sept of Corcu Lóighdhe in west Cork of the same stock as the O'Driscoll's. They were seated at Dun Ui Chobhthaigh (Duncowhey) in the barony of Barryroe. Somtimes anglicised Cowhig. A sept of the Uí Mhaine of the same stock as the O'Madden's. They were seated at Tuaim Catraigh (Tomcatry), in the barony of Clonmacnowen, Galway. A sept who were anciently lord of Umhall in Mayo. A sept of Westmeath who were bards. A sept of Derry who were ecclesiastics. In 1890 Coffey was principally found in Kerry, Tipperary, Dublin, Cork and Roscommon, and the estimated number of bearers was 4,390. In the United States it is the 850th most numerous surname with an estimated 38,500 bearers.

Cole
An English surname perhaps derived from the Old English *col* in the sence 'coal-black, swarthy'. There is also a Scottish surname Coles of Galwegian origin, a fom assumed by the MacDowall. In 1890 was principally found in Dublin, Derry, Armagh, Down and Offally, and the estimated number of bearers was 1,660. In the United States it is the 108th most numerous surname with an estimated 22,000 bearers. It is numerous in the states of Connecticut, Delaware, Maryland, Massachusetts, New Jersey, New York, Pennsylvania. In England and Wales in 1996 it was the 122nd most numerous surname.

Coleman, ó Colmáin,
A Gaelic Surname meaning descendant of *Colmán* (diminutive of *Columb*, from Latin *columba*, meaning 'a dove'). A sept of Uí Fiachrach, who were anciently seated in the townland of Grangemore, in the parish of Templeboy in Sligo. There must have been other septs throughout Ireland. Coleman is also an English surname, in many case based upon the personal name introduced into England by Scandinavians to from Ireland. In Sussex it probably means charcoal-burner. Also see Clifford above. In 1890 Coleman was principally found in Cork, Roscommon, Dublin and Waterford, and the estimated number of bearers was 6,180 (including variants). In the United States it is the 82nd most numerous surname with an estimated 261,250 bearers. In England and Wales in 1996 it was the 202nd most numerous surname.

Colgan, Mac Colgan, ó Colgan
A sept of the Oirghilla, who were chiefs of Ui MacCarthainn now the Barony of Tirkeevan in Derry, until dispossessed by the Cineál

Eoghain, and afterwards they were erenaghs of Donaghmore, in Inishowen. A sept of Offaly who were of the same stock as the O'Connors, O'Dempseys, and O'Dunnes. In 1890 Colgan was principally found in Dublin, Offaly and Antrim, and the estimated number of bearers was 1,430.

Coll, Mac Colla
A gallowglass family that settled in Donegal. In 1890 Coll was principally found in Donegal and the estimated number of bearers was 1,250.

Collins, ó Coileáin, ó Cuileáin
A Gaelic surname meaning descendant of *Coilean*, meaning 'whelp'. A sept of the Uí Fidhgheinte in the present Limerick, who are the same stock as *ó Donnabháin* (O'Donovan) and were originally lords of Uí Chonaill Gabhra, now the baronies of Upper and Lower Connello. In 1178 they were expelled from this territory and then settled in west Cork, until the end of the thirteenth Century, when they were dispossessed by the Fitzgeralds. *ó Cuileáin* meaning descendant of *Cuileáin*; a variant of *ó Coileáin* and also anglicised as Collins.
There were according to Woulfe distinct septs of the name in Galway, Tyrone, Tipperary and Cork. A sept of the Uí Mhaine in Galway. Also anglicised Cullane, Cullan, Cullen, Quillan. A sept of the *ó Coiléain* of the Corcu Lóighdhe in Cork. A sept in Tyrone who were erenaghs of Clogher. An *ó Cuileain* sept of Uí Chonaill Gabhra. In 1890 Collins was the thirtieth most numerous name, the estimated number of bearers was 15,700, and the surname was principally to be found in Cork, Limerick, Dublin, Galway and Antrim, many were also found in Kerry and Clare. In the United States it is the 50th most numerous surname with an estimated 368,500 bearers. In England and Wales in 1996 it was the 57th most numerous surname.

Comber, Comer, see **Kerrigan**

Comerford
A surname of Anglo-Norman origin. In 1890 Comerford was principally found in Kilkenny and Dublin, and the estimated number of bearers was 1,340.

Condon, de Caunteton, Condun
A surname of Cambro-Norman origin. Derived from Caunteton or Canton, a parish in Glamorgan. In the late twelfth century this family acquired land in south Leinster and east Cork. In 1890 Condon was principally found in Cork, Tipperary and Kerry, and the estimated number of bearers was 2,870.

Conlan, Conlon, Connellan, ó Conalláin, ó Caoindealbháin,
A Gaelic surname and in the anglicised form of Conlan, Conlon and Connellan, the origins are difficult to distinguish. *ó Conalláin* meaning descendant of *Conallán* (diminutive of *Conall*), A sept of

61

Roscommon, sometimes *ó Coinghiollái*n. *ó Caoindealbháin* meaning descendant of *Caoindealbháin* (gracefully shaped), a sept of Meath who were Chiefs of Cinel Laoghaire, near Trim until the time of the Cambro-Norman Invasion. In 1890 Conlon was principally found in Roscommon, Mayo and Sligo and was generally distributed in Leinster and Ulster. The estimated number of bearers for Conlon was 2,960 and for Conlan was 1,600. In the United States Conlon is the 5,551st most numerous surname with an estimated 5,500 bearers, Conlin is the 7,688th most numerous surname with an estimated 2,750 bearers.

Conneely, Mac Conghaile,
A Gaelic surname meaning son of *Conghal* (fierce as a hound). A sept of west Connacht. In its anglicised form difficult to distinguish from *MacConghaola* (son of *Cú-Ghaola*, the hound of Gaola) a sept of Uí Fiachrach in the south of Galway. Also difficult to distinguish from *ó Conghalaigh*, or *ó Conghaile*, usually anglicised as Connolly (see immediately below). Also see Kenneally. In 1890 Conneely was numerous in Galway. The estimated number of bearers was 4,121 (including variants). In the United States it is the 1,683rd most numerous surname with an estimated 19,250 bearers.

McConnell, MacDhomhnaill,
This means son of *Conall*, however the origin of this anglicisation appears to be MacDomhnaill. In 1890 McConnell was principally found in Antrim, Down and Tyrone, and the estimated number of bearers was 4,520 (including variants). In the United States it is the 722nd most numerous surname with an estimated 44,000 bearers.

O'Connell, ó Chonaill
A Gaelic surname meaning descendant of *Conall*, which personal name meant 'strong as a wolf', it is a very old Celtic name which was borne by the legendary kings and warriors of Ireland. A sept who were anciently Lords of Uí Mhac Charthainn, now the barony of Tirkeeran in Derry, a branch of the Oirghialla. A sept of the Uí Mhaine, who anciently possessed a territory in the south of Galway, between the river Grian and the borders of Thomond (Thuas Mhumhan). A leading septs of Kerry, who were anciently Chiefs of Magh ó gCoinchin in the east of that county, until displaced by *ó Donnchadha* (O'Donoghue) about the middle of the eleventh century. From the time of the Cambro-Norman Invasion down to the seventeenth century, they were followers of MacCarthy More and hereditary castellans of Ballycarbery. In 1890, O'Connell was the twenty fifth most numerous surname, the estimated number of bearers was 16,600, and the surname was principally to be found Cork, Kerry, Limerick, Tipperary and Galway. In the United States O'Connell is the 1,013rd most numerous surname with an estimated 33,000 bearers, Connell is the 1,827th most numerous surname with an estimated 19,250 bearers. It is numerous in the states of Connecticut, and Massachusetts.

Connolly, ó Conghaile,

A Gaelic surname meaning descendant of *Conghalach*, which personal name comes from the name *Congal* meaning 'brave, fierce as a hound'. A sept of the southern Uí Néill in east Meath, who were one of the four tribes of Tara. They were dispossessed soon after the Cambro-Norman Invasion and moved to Monaghan, where they placed themselves under the MacMahons. A sept of the Dál gCais in Thuas Mhumhan (Thomond) who are said to be descended from Mahon brother of Brian Boru. A sept of the Uí Mhaine in Galway related to the O'Madens. A sept whose territory was in Roscommon. *ó Coingheallaigh* or *ó Cionnfhaolaidh* in Munster. In 1890, Connolly was the twenty-third most numerous surname; the estimated number of bearers was 17,000, and the surname was principally to be found in Cork, Monaghan, Galway, Antrim and Dublin. It was to be found as Connelly in Galway. In the United States it is the 1,350th most numerous surname with an estimated 24,750 bearers. It is numerous in the state of Massachusetts. In England and Wales in 1996 it was the 396th most numerous surname.

O'Connor, ó Conchobhair

A Gaelic surname meaning descendant of *Conchobhar*, which personal name may have meant 'patron of warriors', it was and still is a most popular Irish name. The most famous bearer of the name was Conchobhar mac Nessa, the legendery King of ancient Ulster. A sept of Connacht, whose ancestor was *Ruaidrí ó Conchobair* last High King of Ireland who died in 1198. This sept split into three sub-septs : *ó Conchobhair Donn* (the brown O'Connor), *ó Conchobhair Ruadh* (the red O'Connor), and *ó Conchobhair Sligeach*. A sept in Offaly the O'Connor Faly, their chief stronghold was a Daingean, they were dispossessed during the reign of Philip and Mary. A sept known as the O'Connor Kerry. Prior to the Cambro-Norman Invasion they were Lords of an area of Kerry lying between Tralee and the Shannon, because of the encroachment of the Fitzmaurices and others their territory was narrowed down to the barony of Iraghticonor (Oireacht Uí Chonchobhair). Their stronghold was at Carrigafoyle near Ballylongford. During the reign of Elizabeth I, they were dispossessed and their lands were given to Trinity College Dublin. A sept in north Clare the O'Connor of Corcomroe, now a barony. A sept of Keenaght, in Derry. They were Lords of Cianachta until dispossessed by the *ó Cathain* (O'Kane, Keane) shortly before the Cambro-Norman Invasion. A sept of Uí Bhreasaíl, a branch of the Oirghialla. The ninth most numerous name in Ireland in 1890, the estimated number of bearers was 31,200, and the surname was principally found in Kerry, Dublin, Mayo and Cork. It was also found to a large extent in Roscommon and Galway and in Antrim and Derry. In the United States Conner is the 393rd most numerous surname with an estimated 79,750 bearers, O'Connor is the 530th most numerous surname with an estimated 60,500 bearers, Connor is the 1,077th most numerous surname with an estimated 30,250 bearers Connors is the 1,866th most numerous surname with an estimated 19,250 bearers, and Conners is the 4,400th most numerous surname and the estimated number of bearers is 8,250. The surnames are numerous in the states of Connecticut, Delaware, Massachusetts, New Jersey, and New York. In England and Wales in 1996 O'Connor was the 200th most numerous surname, and Connor was the 478th most numerous surname.

Conroy
The anglicisation of a number of Gaelic surname. *Mac Conraoi* meaning son of *Cúraoi* (hound of the plain, or of battle). A sept of Dál Cais who were lords of Dealbna Thíre-da-locha, now the barony of Moycullen in Galway. *ó Conraoi* a sept of the Uí Maine in Galway. *ó Conaire* meaning descendant of Conaire (probably dog-keeper). In 1890 Conroy was numerous in Laois, it was also to be found in Galway and Dublin. The estimated number of bearers was 3,494. It is difficult to distinguish Conroy from Conry. In 1890 Conry was principally to be found in Mayo and Roscommon, and the estimated number of bearers was 2,330. In the United States it is the 2,215th most numerous surname with an estimated 16,500 bearers.

Conway
The anglicisation of a number of Gaelic surnames. *ó Conbhuidhe*, meaning descendant of *Cú-buidhe* meaning 'yellow hound'. A sept of the Ui Fiachrach who anciently occupied Dunneil in the barony of Tireragh, Sligo and later moved to Easky. A sept of Uí Maine in Galway. *ó Connmhacháin*, meaning descendant of Connmhachán, diminutive of Connmhach meaning 'wolf-son, hound-son'. A sept found in Sligo who were followers of the *ó hEaghra* (O'Hara's). *ó Connmhaigh*, meaning descendant of Connmhach meaning 'wolf-son, hound-son'. Otherwise *MacConnmhaigh*, A sept of Dál Cais who were formerly ollaves of music in Thuas Mhumhan (Thomond).
Mac Conmidhe, meaning son of *Cú Midhe* meaning 'hound of Meath'. A sept who were hereditary poets of the *ó Neill*, hence found in Tyrone. In 1890 Conway was principally found in Mayo, Tyrone and Dublin, and generally in Munster, and the estimated number of bearers was 7,571. In the United States it is the 654th most numerous surname with an estimated 49,500 bearers. In England and Wales in 1996 it was the 440th most numerous surname.

Coogan, ó Cuagáin
A Gaelic surname meaning descendent of *Cuagán*. A sept of Uí Maine which before the end of the sixteenth century had spread into Kildare and Kilkenny. In 1890 Coogan was principally found in Dublin, Kilkenny and Monaghan, and the estimated number of bearers was 1,030. In the United States Cogan is the 9,460th most numerous surname with an estimated 2,750 bearers.

Cooke
A surname of English, Scottish and Cambro-Norman origin. The English and Scottish surname derived from the occupation of 'cook'. MacCook were from Kintyre and Arran. In Connacht *Mac Dhabhóc*,

a branch of the Burkes has been anglicised as Cooke. In 1890 Cooke was principally found in Antrim, Dublin, Cork, Limerick, Galway and Sligo, and the estimated number of bearers was 3,990 (including variants). In the United States Cook is the 56th most numerous surname with an estimated 330,000 bearers, and Cooke is the 996th most numerous surname with an estimated 33,000 bearers. In England and Wales in 1996 Cook was the 56th most numerous surname and Cooke was the 176th most numerous surname.

Cooney, ó Cuana
A Gaelic surname meaning descendant of *Cuana* meaning 'handsome, elegant'. A sept who were chiefs of Clann Fergus in Tyrone. They subsequently migrated to north Connacht. In 1890 Cooney was principally found in Mayo and Dublin, and the estimated number of bearers was 3,400. In the United States it is the 2,880th most numerous surname with an estimated 11,000 bearers.

Cooper
An English occupational surname, derived from the Middle English *couper* 'maker or repairer of wooden casks, buckets or tubs'. In 1890 the surname was to be found mostly in Antrim and Dublin, and the estimted number of bearers was 1,610. In the United States it is the 62th most numerous surname with an estimated 310,750 bearers. In England and Wales in 1996 it was the 29th most numerous surname.

Corbett
An English surname, from the Old French *corbet* meaning 'raven', probably a nickname for a person with dark hair or complexion. In 1890 Corbett was principally found in Cork, Tipperary and Galway, and the estimated number of bearers was 2,870 (including variants).

Corcoran, ó Corcráin
A Gaelic surname meaning descendant of *Corcrán* (probably from *corcur* meaning red, crimson, purple). According to Woulfe the name of an ecclesiastical, literary and bardic family in many parts of Ireland. In 1890 Corcoran was principallly found in Mayo, Cork, Tipperary, Dublin and Kerry, and the estimated number of bearers was 5,900 (including variants). In the United States it is the 1,968th most numerous surname with an estimated 16,500 bearers.

Corish, see Bermingham

McCormick, McCormack, MacCormaic,
A Gaelic surname meaning son of *Cormac*. A sept of Longford Fermanagh. In east Ulster a Scottish surname. In 1890 McCormick was numerous in Westmeath, it was also to be found in Antrim, Dublin and Down. McCormack was found in nearly every county, chiefly in Dublin, Mayo, Roscommon and Limerick. The estimated number of bearers for McCormick was 7,347, and for McCormack was 4,972. In

65

the United States McCormick is the 449th most numerous surname with an estimated 68,750 bearers, and McCormack was the 2,412th most numerous surname with an estimated 13,750 bearers.

Corr, Ó Corra

A sept of Ulster, perhaps meaning descendant of *Corra* for 'spear'. In 1890 Corr was principally to be found in Dublin and Tyrone, and the estimated number of bearers was 2,464. In the United States it is the 9,351st most numerous surname with an estimated 2,750 bearers.

Corrigan, Ó Corragáin

A Gaelic sept who were of the same stock as the Maguire's of Fermanagh. Branches of the sept appear to have migrated south, well before the Plantation of Ulster. In 1890 Corrigan was principally found in Dublin, Mayo, Fermanagh Monaghan and Louth, and the estimated number of bearers was 3,315.

Corry

It is difficult to distinguish this from Curry and Currie (see below). A Gaelic surname most likely Irish rather than Scottish. Perhaps it is : *Ó Corra*, or *Ó Corraidh*. In 1890 the surname was principally found in Antrim and Clare, and the estimated number of bearers was 1,970. In the United States Corey is the 2,201st most numerous surname with an estimated 16,500 bearers.

Cosgrave, Cosgrove, Ó Coscraigh

A Gaelic surname meaning descendant of *Coscrach* meaning 'triumphant, victorious'. A sept of Wicklow who were lords of Feara Cualann, comprising the manor of Powerscourt, until dispossessed soon after the Cambro-Norman invasion by the O'Tooles and O'Byrnes. In 1890 Cosgrove was principally found in Mayo, Galway and scattered in Ulster, and the estimated number of bearers was 1,790. In 1890 Cosgrave was principally found in Dublin and Wexford, and the estimated number of bearers was 1,520. In the United States Cosgrove is the 4,098th most numerous surname with an estimated 8,250 bearers.

Costello/e, MacOisdealbhaigh

A surname of Cambro-Norman origin. *Oisdealbh* was the father of Gilbert de Nagle, an example of a Cambro-Norman family using a *Mac* name. Also see Waldron. In 1890 the surname was found as Costello in Mayo, Dublin and Galway and Costelloe, in Limerick, Galway and Clare. The estimated number of bearers was 6,585. In the United States Costello is the 1,297th most numerous surname with an estimated 27,500 bearers.

Cotter, Mac Coitir, Mac Oitir

A Gaelic surname meaning descendant of *Ottar* (a Norse personal name). A sept who were seated at Carrigtwohil, near the city of Cork. In 1890 Cotter was principally to be found in Cork, and the estimated number of bearers was 2,870. In the United States it is the 3,199th most numerous surname with an estimated 11,000 bearers.

Coughlan, Coghlan, ó Cochláin
A Gaelic surname meaning descendant of *Cochlán* (diminutive of *cochal*, a cape or hood), a sept of Barrymore in Cork. *Mac Cochláin* a sept who were lords of Dealbhna Eathra called in later times Delvin MacCoghlane which comprised almost the entire of the present barony of Garrycastle in Offaly. A branch settled in Castlebar in Mayo. In 1890 Coughlan was principally to be found in Cork, and Coghlan in Cork and Dublin, and the estimated number of bearers was 5,600 (including variants).

Coulter, ó Coltaráin, ó Coltair.
A Gaelic sept whose territory was in the parish of Ballycolter in Down. Also a Scottish surname of territorial origin from Lanarkshire, and from Aberdeenshire. In 1890 the surname was principally found in Antrim, Down and Fermanagh, and the estimated number of bearers was 2,020. In the United States it is the 1,586th most numerous surname with an estimated 22,000 bearers.

McCourt, MacCuarta, MacCuairt
According to Woulfe a corruption of *MacMhuircheartaigh*. A Gaelic surname meaning son of *Muirchertach* (skilled in seacraft, mariner).
In 1890 McCourt was numerous in Louth, it was also to be found in Armagh and Antrim. The estimated number of bearers was 1,971. In the United States it is the 7,591st most numerous surname with an estimated 2,750 bearers.

McCoy, Mac Aodha
A variant of the Scottish surname MacKay meaning son of *Aodh*. The came to Ireland as galloglasses by MacDonnell of the Glens of Antrim. A Gaelic sept who were chiefs of Clann Choscraigh, the same stock as the O'Flahertys, in the Barony of Clare in Galway. In 1890 the surname was principally found in Antrim, Armagh and Monaghan, and the estimated number of bearers was 1,840. In the United States it is the 218th most numerous surname with an estimated 132,000 bearers.

Courtney, ó Curnáin
A surname of varied origin. An English surname of Norman origin from Courtenay in Loiret or Gatinais, the surname later spread to Scotland. *ó Curnáin*, a sept of Kerry. In 1890 Courtney was principally to be found in Kerry, Antrim and Dublin, and the estimated number of bearers was 2,640. In the United States it is the 1,273rd most numerous surname with an estimated 27,500 bearers.

Cowan, ó Comhdhain
A Gaelic surname derived from *Comhghan* meaning 'co-birth'. In 1890 Cowan was principally found in Antrim, Down and Armagh, and

the estimated number of bearers was 1,480. In the United States it is the 1.008th most numerous surname with an estimated 33,000 bearers.

Cox, Cock, Mac Quilly, Mac an Choiligh
The Gaelic surname *Mac an Choiligh* (perhaps from *coileach* meaning cock), has been anglicised as Cox. The sept of Roscommon were an erenagh family. The English surname Cox, or Cock has many derivations, and this surname was also to be found in Scotland. In 1890 Cox was principally to be found in Roscommon and Dublin, and the estimated number of bearers was 3,360. In the United States Cox is the 64th most numerous surname with an estimated 302,500 bearers. In England and Wales in 1996 it was the 62nd most numerous surname.

Coyle, Mac Giolla Chomhgaill
A Gaelic sept of Donegal, meaning devotee of Saint Comgall. In 1890 Coyle was principally to be found in Donegal, Cavan, Derry, Dublin, Tyrone and Longford, and the estimated number of bearers was 4,030.

Coyne, ó Cadhain
A sept of the Uí Fiachrach, from *cadhan* perhaps meaning 'a wild goose, a barnacle goose'. Sometimes Kyne in translation. In 1890 Coyne was principally to be found in Galway and Mayo, and the estimated number of bearers was 2,420. In the United States it is the 3,669th most numerous surname with an estimated 8,250 bearers.

Craig
A Scottish surname of local origin, for someone who lived near a steep or precipitous rock, for *creag*. The surname was numerous in Edinburgh in the fifteenth and sixteenth centuries and throughout the Lowlands. In 1890 Craig was principally found in Antrim, Derry and Tyrone, and the estimated number of bearers was 5,370. In the United States it is the 62nd most numerous surname with an estimated 104,500 bearers. In England and Wales in 1996 it was the 492nd most numerous surname. In Scotland in 1995 it was the 55th most numerous surname.

Crawford
A Scottish surname of territorial origin from the old barony of Crawford in the Upper Ward of Lanarkshire. The Earldom of Crawford created in 1398 is the oldest in Scotland still extant. In 1890 Crawford was principally to be found in Antrim, Down, Derry and Tyrone, and the estimated number of bearers was 4,300. In the United States it is the 132nd most numerous surname with an estimated 187,000 bearers. In England and Wales in 1996 it was the 376th most numerous surname. In Scotland in 1995 it was the 75th most numerous surname.

McCready, Mac Conriada, Mac Riada
A Gaelic surname meaning 'son of *Cú-Riada*' (Riada's hound). A
sept of Donegal who were erenagh in Raphoe. In 1890 McCready was
principally found in Down, Antrim and Derry, and the estimated
number of bearers was 1,750. In the United States it is the 7,740th
most numerous surname with an estimated 2,750 bearers.

Cre(e)gan, ó Croidheáin, Mac Riagáin
A Gaelic sept of the Cineál Eoghain who settled in Sligo, derived from
croidhe meaning 'heart'. Perhaps a translation of *Mac Riagáin*, via
Mac Criagáin in other parts. In 1890 Cregan was principally found in
Limerick and Meath, and Creegan was principally found in Leitrim
and Sligo. The estimated number of bearers was 1,480.

MacCreesh, see **MacGuinness**

Cronin, ó Cróinín
A Gaelic surname meaning descendant of *Crónán*, derived fron *Crón*
meaning 'swarthy, yellow'. A sept of the Corcu Loíghdhe who were
chiefs of Tuath ó bhFithcheallaigh, a streatch of territory west of
Clonakilty reaching to the coast between Inchydoney and Galley
Head. The records indicate that they were involved in ecclesiastical
affairs. In 1890 Cronin was numerous in Cork (102 births) and Kerry
(43 births), it was also to be found in Limerick. The estimated number
of bearers was 7,884. In the United States it is the 2,016th most
numerous surname with an estimated 16,500 bearers.

McCrory, Mac Ruaidhrí
A Gaelic sept who were anciently chiefs of *Tellach Ainbhith* and
Muinntear Birn in Tyrone, and who were erenaghs of Ballynascreen in
Derry. Also a surname of Scottish origin of the same stock as the
MacDonnells, who came to Ireland as gallowglasses in the fourteenth
century. In 1890 McCrory was principally found in Tyrone and
Antrim, and the estimated number of bearers was 1,520.

Crowe, Mac Enchroe, Mac Conchradha
A Gaelic sept of Thomond. Also an English and a Scottish surname.
In 1890 Crowe was principally to be found in Antrim, Tipperary and
Clare, and the estimated number of bearers was 3,046.

Crowley, ó Cruadhlaoic
A Gaelic surname meaning descendant of *Cruadhlaoch*, meaning the
'hard warrior'. A sept who were related to the *MacDiarmada*
(MacDermotts) in Roscommon. MacFirbis gives their pedigree as
descent from *Diarmaid an cruadhlaoch*, who was fourth in descent
from *Diarmaid* the eponymous ancestor of the *MacDiarmada*. It
appears that in the thirteenth century this family moved south and
subsequently established itself in Carbery in west Cork. In 1890
Crowley was numerous in Cork (116 births). The estimated number of
bearers was 7,212 (including variants). In the United States it is the

1,057th most numerous surname with an estimated 30,250 bearers.

Cullen, Collins, ó Cuilinn
A Gaelic surname meaning descendant of *Cuileann*, which personal name meant 'holly'. A sept of the Uí Mhaine in Galway. A sept of the Corcu Loíghdhe in Cork. *ó Cuileamhain* meaning descendent of Cuileannán, who were a sept of south Leinster. In 1890 Cullen was the eighty-fourth most numerous surname and the estimated number of bearers was 9,000. In that year the surname was chiefly found in Dublin and Wexford. In the United States Cullen is the 1,859th most numerous surname with an estimated 19,250 bearers. In England and Wales in 1996 Collins was the 57th most numerous surname.

McCullough, McCullagh, Mac Cú Uladh, Mac Con Uladh
A Gaelic surname meaning 'son of the hound of Ulster', a sept of east Ulster. *MacCulloch* is a Scottish surname of which Black states: 'much obscurity enshrouds the origin of this old Galwegian name, and no satisfactory pedigree of the family exists.'. There can be no doubt that many bearers of the surname in east Ulster are of Scots origin. In 1890 McCullough was principally found in Antrim, Tyrone and Down. The estimated number of bearers for McCullough, which is particular to Antrim and Down was 3,090, and the estimated number of bearers for McCullagh was 1,790. The total estimated number of bearers including variants was 5,800. In the United States McCullough is the 739th most numerous surname with an estimated 44,000 bearers.

Cummins
It is difficult to ascertain which Gaelic surname Cummins is a translation of. The following may be considered. An *ó Coimín* sept were erenaghs of the church of St. Cuimín Fada. There is a parish of Kilcummin in the barony of Tirawley in Mayo. An *ó Comáin* sept found throughout Munster. There is a parish of Kilcummin in the barony of Magunihy in Kerry. In 1890 Cummins was principally to be found in Dublin, Cork and Tipperary, and the estimated number of bearers was 3,450.

Cunningham
A Scottish surname derived from a place name Cunningham in Ayrshire. These lands were granted to a Norman whose descendant Richard de Cunningham was using the name of the land as a surname by 1210. The name came to Ulster in particular Donegal at the time of the Ulster Plantation. Also the anglicisation of a number of Gaelic surnames : *ó Connacháin; Mac Connagháin; Mac Coinneagáin; ó Cuinneagáin; ó Cuinneacháin;* and *Mac Cuinneagáin.* In each case based on a diminutive of *Conn.* In 1890 Cunningham was the seventy-fourth most numerous surname, the estimated bearers was 9,600 and principally found in Down, Antrim, Dublin, Galway, Roscommon, and Cork. In the United States it is the 180th most numerous surname with an estimated 148,500 bearers. In England

and Wales in 1996 it was the 254th most numerous surname. In Scotland in 1995 it was the 78th most numerous surname.

Curley, Mac Thoirdealbhaigh
A Gaelic surname meaning son of *Toirdealbhach* (from the Scandinavian *Thor*). There is a Ballymacurley and Curley's Island in Roscommon. In 1890 Curley was principally found in Roscommon, Galway and Dublin, and the estimated number of bearers was 1,610.

Curran, Currane, Ó Corráin
A Gaelic surname meaning descendant of *Corrán* (diminutive of *Corradh*, according to Woulfe). A surname adopted by several distinct septs, none of whom it is possible to clearly identify. In 1890 Curran was principally to be found in Donegal, Dublin, Waterford and Galway and, the estimated number of bearers was 7,570. Currane was found exclusively in Kerry and the estimated number of bearers was 850. In the United States Curran is the 1,435th most numerous surname with an estimated 24,750 bearers.

Curry, Currie, Ó Comhraidhe
Both an Irish and a Scottish surname. *Ó Comhraidhe*; a sept who were chiefs of Mac Uais, now the Barony of Moygoish in Westmeath; a sept of the Corca Loíghdhe, in south-west Cork; a sept of the Dál gCais in Thomond. In Scotland Corrie, of which Currie is a varint is of local origin, from the parish of Hutton-Corrie, Drumfriesshire. It is also the anglicisation of a branch of the Clan McDonald. Also see Corry above. In 1890 the surname was principally found in Antrim, and the estimated number of bearers was 3,360. In the United States Curry is the 313rd most numerous surname with an estimated 96,250 bearers, and Currie is the 1,791st most numerous surname with an estimated 19,250 bearers.

(Mac) Curtin, Mac Cuirtín
A Gaelic sept of Thomond, whose territory was near Ennistymon in the barony of Corcomroe in Clare. In 1890 Curtin was principally to be found in Cork, Limerick, Clare and Kerry, and the estimated number of bearers was 3,090.

Cusack,
A surname of Norman origin from *Cussac* in France. At the time of the Cambro-Norman invasion they were granted lands in Meath and other parts of Leinster. In 1890 the surname was principally found in Limerick, Cavan and Clare, and the estimated number of bearers was 2,060. In the United States Cusack is the 9,719th most numerous surname with an estimated 2,750 bearers, and Cusick was the 6,233rd most numerous surname with an estimated 5,500 bearers.

MacCutcheon, see **Hutchinson**

McDaid, McDevitt, MacDaibhéid

A Gaelic surname meaning son of David; a branch of the O'Dohertys of Inishowen. In 1890 the surname was principally found in Donegal, Derry and Tyrone. The estimated number of bearers for McDaid was 2,150 and the estimated number of bearers for McDevitt was 670. In the United States McDade is the 4,489th most numerous surname with an estimated 8,250 bearers, McDevitt was the 5,397th most numerous surname with an estimated 5,500 bearers.

Dalton, D'Alton, de Dalatún

An Anglo Norman surname from the place name Dalton in the north of England. Daltons were lords of Rathconrath in Westmeath, but lost their estates in the seventeenth century. A surname of Norman extraction from *de Autun* in Normandy, a family of which settled in Kilkenny. In 1890 Dalton was numerous in Westmeath, it was also to be found in Dublin, Waterford Limerick and Kilkenny. The estimated number of bearers was 3,360. In the United States it is the 608th most numerous surname with an estimated 52,250 bearers.

Daly, ó Dálaigh

A Gaelic surname meaning descendant of *Dálach*, which personal name meant 'one given to frequenting assemblies'. A sept of the Uí Mhaine who were originally Chiefs of Corcu Adain, or Corcu Adhaimh in the present Westmeath. They were a famous bardic family. Raghnall ó Dálaigh, who settled in Deas Mhumhan (Desmond) about the middle of the twelfth century, became chief poet to *Mac Carthaigh* (MacCarthy), he was ancestor of the sept of Muintir Bhairre in O'Keeffe's country. A sub-sept settled at Finavarra, in the Burren, Clare about the middle of the thirteenth century, where they became poets to the *ó Loghlens*. A branch of these settled in Uí Mhaine in Galway. Another branch settled in Cavan and became poets to the *ó Raghallaigh* (O'Reilly); while other branches were poets to the *O'Neill* of Ulster and *ó Conchobhair* (O'Connor) of Connacht. In 1890 Daly was the twenty-fourth most numerous name, the estimated number of bearers was 17,000, and was principally to be found in Cork, Dublin, Kerry, Galway and Offaly. In the United States Daly is the 1,349th most numerous surname with an estimated 24,750 bearers, Daley is the 1,511th most numerous surname with an estimated 22,000 bearers and Daily is the 3,250th most numerous surname with an estimated 11,000 bearers. It is numerous in the states of Connecticut, and New Jersey. In England and Wales in 1996 Daly was the 443rd most numerous surname.

Darcy, Dorcey, ó Dorchaidhe

A surname of Norman origin, *de Arcy* from *Arci* in Normandy. John D'Arcy was chief justiciar of Ireland in the fourteenth century, he received grants of land in Meath and it is from him that most Dary's in Leinster are descended. It is also the anglicised form of many Gaelic surnames. A Gaelic surname meaning descendant of *Dorchaidhe* meaning 'dark'. A sept of Mayo. A sept who were one of

72

the 'Tribes of Galway'. In 1890 Darcy was principally found in Dublin and Tipperary, and the estimated number of bearers was 3,850.

Davidson
A Scottish surname of which there appears to three clans. Two Kings of Scotland were called David. The personal name is from the Hebrew meaning 'beloved one'. In Roxburg a small clann seems to have been formed in the sixteenth and seventeenth centuries. In 1863 Davidson was the thirty-fourth most numerous surname in Scotland and the estimated number of bearers was 12,600. In Ireland in 1890 Davidson was principally to be found in Antrim and Down, and the estimated number of bearers was 2,600. In the United States it is the 262nd most numerous surname with an estimated 112,750 bearers. In England and Wales in 1996 it was the most numerous surname. In Scotland in 1995 it was the 24th most numerous surname.

Davis, Dav(e)y
A Welsh surname, from *Dafydd* through Davys meaning son of Davy, from David a Hebrew name meaning 'beloved'. In 1890 Davis was principally found Dublin and Antrim and the estimated number of bearers was 4,660 (including variants). Davey/Davy was principally found in Sligo and Antrim and the estimated number of bearers was 1,390. In the United States Davis is the 6th most numerous surname with an estimated 1,320,000 bearers. In England and Wales in 1996 Davis was the 45th most numerous surname.

Davison,
Both an English and a Scottish surname, see Davidson above. In 1890 the surname was principally found in Antrim and the estimated number of bearers was 2,020. In England and Wales in 1996 it was the 328th most numerous surname.

Dawson
Both an English and Scottish surname. The English surname meaning 'son of Dawe' i.e. David. In 1890 Dawson was principally to be found in Antrim, and the estimated number of bearers was 2,465. In the United States it is the 307th most numerous surname with an estimated 96,250 bearers. In England and Wales in 1996 it was the 127th most numerous surname.

O'Dea, ó Deaghaidh
A Gaelic surname meaning descendant of *Deaghadh*. A sept of the Dál gCais, who were chiefs of Ui Fearmaic, which comprised the greater part of the barony of Inchquin in Clare. They had their principal strongholds at Tullyodea and Dyserttola. A sept of Tipperary who were anciently chiefs of Sliabh Ardacha, now Slewardagh. In 1890 O'Dea was principally found in Clare and Limerick, and the estimated number of bearers was 2,020.

73

Deane, Deeney
One of the 'Tribes of Galway'; said to be descendant of William Allen, or Den who came from Bristol, England in the reign of Henry VI. In Donegal *Mac an Deagháin*, meaning son of the Dean. According to Woulfe the families so named seem to have been originally O'Donnells and O'Gallaghers. *ó Deaghain* meaning descendant of the Dean was to be found in Donegal and parts of the South. In 1890 Deane was principally found in Mayo, Cork and Donegal, and the estimated number of bearers was 2,020; Deeney and Deeny were principally found in Donegal and Derry and the estimated number of bearers was 670. In the United States Denney is the 2,924th most numerous surname with an estimated 11,000 bearers.

Deasy, Déiseach, Mac an Déisigh
A Gaelic surname meaning a native of Decies in Waterford. Woulfe suggests a sept of Sligo. In 1890 Deasy was principally found in Cork (1,075 bearers) and Mayo. The estimated number of bearers was 1,570.

Deegan, ó Duibhginn
A Gaelic surname meaning descendant of *Dubhceann* 'black head'. A sept of Wexford. A sept of Laois-Offaly. Sometimes confused with Duggan (see below), which is to be found in Wexford. In 1890 the surname was principally found in Dublin, Laois and Offaly, and the estimated number of bearers was 1,250. In the United States it is the 9,348th most numerous surname with an estimated 2,750 bearers.

Delaney, Delany, ó Dubhshláine, ó Dúláinne
A Gaelic surname meaning descendant of *Dubhsláine* (black, of the river Slaney). A sept of Laois who were chiefs of Coill Uachtarach in Ossairge (Ossory), now the barony of Upper Woods at the foot of Slieve Bloom. In its anglicised form it is difficult to distinguish from *ó Dubhláin* (black defiance, challenge) In 1890 Delaney was the second most numerous surname in Laois, it was also to be found in Dublin, Tipperary and Kilkenny. The estimated number of bearers for Delaney was 4,166, and for Delany was 2,912. In the United States Delaney is the 929th most numerous surname with an estimated 35,750 bearers.

Dempsey, ó Díomasaigh
A Gaelic surname meaning descendant of *Diomasach* meaning 'proud, arrogant'. A sept whose territory was Clann Mhaoilughra a district on both sides of the river barrow comprising the baronies of Portnahinch in Laois and Upper Philipstown in Offaly. One of the few who defeated Strongbow in battle they were dispossessed after the defeat of James II. In 1890 Dempsey was numerous in Offaly, and principally found in Dublin, Antrim, Cork, and Wexford. The estimated number of bearers was 5,241. In the United States it is the 1,253rd most numerous surname with an estimated 27,500 bearers. It is numerous in the state of Delaware.

74

Dennehy, ó Duineachdha
A Gaelic surname meaning descendant of *Duineachaidh* meaning 'humane'. In 1890 Dennehy was principally found in Cork and Kerry, and the estimated number of bearers was 1,610.

Denning, see Dinneen

Desmond, ó Deasmumhnaigh
A Gaelic surname meaning a native of Desmond (south Munster). In 1890 Desmond was principally found in Cork and the estimated number of bearers was 1,520. In the United States it is the 5,129th most numerous surname with an estimated 5,500 bearers.

MacDermot(t), Mac Diarmada
A Gaelic surname meaning son of *Diarmaid*, the meaning of which personal name is unclear. A sept of Moylurgh, who were a branch of the Síl Muireadaigh. There were of the same stock as *ó Conchobhair*, their clan name was Clann Mhaoilruanaidh, from *Maolruanaidh* a son of *Tadgh ó Conchobhair*, King of Connacht in the eleventh century. They took their name from *Diarmaid* who died in 1159 a grandson of *Maolruanaidh*. In the fourteenth century they divided into three distinct septs. MacDermott of Moylurgh who was overlord and had his fortress at the Rock of Lough Key, near Boyle in Roscommon. *Mac Diarmada Ruadh*, who was chief of Tír Tuathail, comprising the parish of Kilronan and had his residence at Alderford, in the barony of Boyle, Roscommon. *Mac Diarmada Gall*, the anglicised MacDermott, who was chief of Artagh, comprising the parish of Tibohine, in the barony of Frenchpark, Roscommon. The anglicised form of *ó Duibh Dhíorma* a sept of the Cineál Chonaill, who were lords of An Bhréadach (Bredagh) in Inishowen, Donegal. In 1890 McDermott was the ninety-sixth most numerous surname, the estimated number of bearers was 8,400, the surname was the second most common in Roscommon and also to be found in Dublin, Donegal, Galway and Tyrone. In the United States it is the 1,212nd most numerous surname with an estimated 27,500 bearers.

Devany, Devaney, Devenny,
Much confusion arises between these surnames: *ó Duibheamhna*; a sept who were anciently chiefs of Ui Breasail near Armagh; *ó Duibheannaigh* a sept of Down and a sept of Donegal; *ó Duibhín* a scattered surname. In 1890 the surname was principally found in Mayo, Galway and Leitrim. In the United States Devaney is the 8,580 most numerous surname with an estimated 2,750 bearers.

Devine, Divine, ó Daimhín, ó Duibhín
A Gaelic surname but it is not clear which surname the anglicisation Devine refers too. *ó Daimhín* descendant of *Daimhín* diminutive of *damh* meaning 'bard, poet'. They were a sept of Oriel a branch of the Maguires who were chiefs of Tirkennedy in Fermanagh, and who may have spread to the midland counties. In 1890 Devine was principally

75

to be found in Tyrone, Dublin and Roscommon, and the estimated number of bearers was 3,630. In the United States Devine is the 1,522nd most numerous surname with an estimated 22,000 bearers.

Devlin, ó Doibhilin, ó Dobhailein
A Gaelic surname. A sept of the Cineál Eoghain, who were chiefs of Muintar Devlin on the west side of Lough Neagh. They were heriditory sword-bearers to ó Neill and part of his cavalry. It is a most numerous surname in Tyrone. ó Dobhailein. A sept who were chiefs of Corca Firthri in Sligo, sometimes anglicised Dolan. In 1890 Devlin was principally found in Antrim, Tyrone, Dublin, Armagh and Derry, and the estimated number of bearers was 5,010. In the United States it is the 3,284th most numerous surname with an estimated 11,000 bearers.

McDevitt, see McDaid

Dillon, Diolún
A surname of Norman origin formed from an old Teutonic personal name *Dill*, according to Woulfe. The Dillons came to Ireland at the time of the Cambro-Norman invasion, and were granted land in Westmeath and Annaly by King John, known in later times as Dillon's Country, they became barons of Kilkenny West. A branch of the family settled in Mayo. In 1890 Dillon was principally found in Dublin, Limerick, Antrim and Galway, and the estimated number of bearers was 5,240. In the United States it is the 825th most numerous surname with an estimated 41,250 bearers.

Dinneen, Dineen, ó Duinnín
A Gaelic surname meaning descendant of *Duinnín* (diminutive of *donn* meaning 'brown'). A sept of the Corca Loíghdhe in south-west Cork, who were hereditary historians to MacCarthy More. A sept of the midlands, where it is anglicised as Dunning and as Denning. In 1890 the surname was principally found in Cork and the estimated number of bearers was 1,880. In the United States Dineen is the 9,849th most numerous surname with an estimated 2,750 bearers.

Diver, ó Duibhidhir
A Gaelic surname, a variant of ó Dubhuidhir. See O'Dwyer. In 1890 Diver was principally found in Donegal and the estimated number of bearers was 1,300.

Dixon, Dickson
An English surname meaning Dick's son, the Scottish Dickson sometimes takes this form. In 1890 Dixon was principally found in Dublin and Mayo and the estimated number of bearers was 2,280. Dickson was principally found in Down and Antrim and the estimated number of bearers was 2,200. In the United States Dixon is the 139th most numerous surname with an estimated 181,500 bearers. In England and Wales in 1996 Dixon was the 99th most numerous

surname, and Dickinson was the 285th most numeroussurname. In Scotland in 1995 Dickson was the 72nd most numerous surname.

Dodds, Dodd
Both an English and a Scottish surname. In Scotland perhaps of local origin, there were lands of Doddis in the barony of Bowne, in Berwickshire. In England from the Old English a nickname perhaps 'something rounded' (a reference to a stupid person), 'deceiver, rascal', or 'the hairless, close-cropped one'. In 1890 the surname was principally found in Down and Armagh, and the estimated number of bearers was 1,390. In England and Wales in 1996 Dodd was the 365th most numerous surname.

O'Doherty, ó Dochartaigh
A Gaelic surname meaning descendant of *Dochartach*, which personal name meant 'hurtful'. A leading sept of the Cineál Chonaill, and of the same stock as the *ó Domhnaill* (O'Donnell), were originally Chiefs of Cineál Enna and Ard Midhir, now Ardmire, in the barony of Raphoe. At the beginning of the fifteenth century they moved north and became lords of the Inishowen peninsula. Cahir ó Dochartaigh rose against the English in 1608 and following his defeat Inishowen was given to Sir Arthur Chichester. A very numerous surname in the Inishowen peninsula of Donegal and in the city of Derry. This surname has also been anglicised as Dogherty. In 1890, Doherty was the fifteenth most numerous surname in Ireland; the estimated number of bearers was 20,800, and it was the most numerous surname in Derry. So numerous is Doherty in Inishowen, that bearers are distinguished by nicknames, amongst those attributed to my ancestors were: 'Ownes"; "the Moon' and 'the Big Hill". As well as Donegal the surname was also to be found in Mayo. In the United States Doherty is the 1,467th most numerous surname with an estimated 22,000 bearers. It is numerous in the state of Massachusetts. In England and Wales in 1996 it was the 395th most numerous surname.

Dolan, ó Dúbhláin, ó Dobhailen, ó Dúláin
A Gaelic surname, a sept of the Uí Mhaine who were chiefs in the baronies of Clonmacnowen in Galway, and Athlone in Roscommon.
In 1890 Dolan was numerous in Fermanagh, Cavan and Leitrim, it was also to be found in Roscommon, Galway and Dublin. The estimated number of bearers was 6,361. In the United States it is the 1,510th most numerous surname with an estimated 22,000 bearers.

MacDonagh, MacDonnchadha, MacDonncha
A Gaelic surname meaning son of *Donnchadh* meaning 'brown warrior'. A sept who were chiefs of Tirerrill and Corran in Sligo, a branch of the *MacDiarmada* (MacDermotts) of Moylurg. The Book of Ballymote was compiled under their patronage. Also a sept who were a branch of the *MacCarthaigh* (MacCarthys) who were chiefs of Duhallow in Cork. In 1890 McDonagh was numerous in Galway and Roscommon, it was also to be found in Mayo. The estimated number

of bearers was 7,795 (including variants). In the United States McDonough is the 1,604th most numerous surname with an estimated 22,000 bearers.

Donaghy
A variant of *MacDonnchadha* (see MacDonagh above) in Tyrone and Derry according to MacLysaght. Donaghty is also to be found in Donegal. In 1890 the surname was principally found in Antrim, Derry and Tyrone, and the estimated number of bearers was 2,200.

Donaldson
An anglicisation of the Scottish surname MacDonald. In 1890 Donaldson was principally found in Antrim and Armagh, and the estimated number of bearers was 1,480. In the United States it is the 786th most numerous surname with an estimated 181,500 bearers. In Scotland in 1995 it was the 90th most numerous surname.

Donegan, ó Donnagáin
A Gaelic surname meaning descendant of *Donnagán* (diminutive of *donn* for 'brown'). A surname adopted by several septs. A sept who were chiefs of Ara, now the Barony of Ara (or Duhara) in Tipperary, and of Ui Cuanach, now the Barony of Coonagh in Limerick. A sept who were anciently chiefs of Muscraighe-tri-maighe, or Muskerry of the Three Plains, now the Barony of Rathluirc in Cork. In addition there were a number of septs in Ulster. In 1890 the estimated number of bearers was 1,390. In the United States it is the 9,580th most numerous surname with an estimated 2,750 bearers.

Donnellan, Donelan, Donlon, Donlan, ó Domhnalláin
A surname adopted by several septs, from the personal name *Domhnall* meaning 'world mighty'. A sept of Uí Mhaine who were chiefs of Clann Bhreasail, a district between Ballinasloe and Loughrea centered upon Ballydonnellan in Galway. A sept of the Oirghialla who were anciently lords of Ui Tuirtre, comprising the baronies of Upper and Lower Toome in Antrim. A sept in Offally who were brehons (judges). A sept who were chiefs of Teallach Ainbhith in Tyrone. In 1890 Donnellan was principally to be found in Clare and Mayo, Donelan and Donlan was to be found in Galway, and Donlon in Longford, and the estimated number of bearers for all variants was 3,400.

Donnelly, ó Donnghaile
A Gaelic surname meaning descendant of *Donnghaile*, which personal name meant 'brown-valour'. A sept of Cineál Eoghain who derive their descent from *Donnghal* the fourth in descent from *Domhnall*, King of Aileach. The sept originally occupied Druim Lighean, anglicised. Drumleene, north of Lifford in Donegal. They were expelled by the Cineál Chonaill and settled at Ballydonnelly, now Castlecaulfield, to the west of Dungannon in Tyrone. The sept were hereditary marshal to ó Neill. A sept of the Uí Fiachrach, who

78

occupied an area at Dun Uí Chobhthaigh, anglicised Doonycoy, in the parish of Templeboy, Sligo. A sept of the Corcu Loíghdhe, whose territory was near Dunmanway in Cork. In 1890, Donnelly was the sixty-fifth most numerous name in Ireland and the estimated number of bearers was 10,700. In that year the surname was chiefly found in Antrim, Tyrone, Armagh and Dublin. In the United States it is the 1,312th most numerous surname with an estimated 24,750 bearers. In England and Wales in 1996 it was the 468th most numerous surname.

Donohoe, O'Donoghue, ó Donnchadha, ó Donnchú

A Gaelic surname meaning descendent of *Donnchadh* meaning 'brown warrior, strong warrior'. A sept who derive their name and descent from Donnchadh, son of Ceallachan, King of Cashel, they were seated at Magh Feimhin now the barony of Iffa and Offa in Tipperary. A sept of Desmond, a branch of the Uí Eathach Mumhan and of the same stock as the O'Mahonys. Their original territory was in west Cork, but around the begining of the thirteenth century they were driven out by the MacCarthys and O'Mahonys and settled in Kerry. They became lords of the country about Killarney, which was named Eoghanacht Ui Dhonnchadha. In 1890 Donohoe was numerous in Cavan, and principally found in Dublin, Longford, and Galway. The estimated number of bearers was 7,257 (including variants). In 1890 O'Donoghue was principally found in Kerry and Cork, and the estimated number of bearers was 1,750. In the United States Donahue is the 3,024th most numerous surname with an estimated 11,000 bearers, Donohoe is the 8.946th most numerous surname with an estimated 2,750 bearers.

O'Donovan, ó Donnabháin

A Gaelic surname meaning descendant of *Donndubhán*, which personal name meant 'brown black'. A sept of Munster who were chiefs of Uí Chairpri Aebhdha, an area lying along the river Maigue in Limerick. Their stronghold was at Bruree, but around the year 1178 they were forced into south-west Cork and settled in O'Driscoll's (ó hEidersceoil) country of Corcu Loíghdhe, to which they gave their clan name of Uí Chairpri. They retained possession until the Jacobite Wars. Branches of the sept settled in both Wexford and Tipperary.
ó Donnamháin, a sept of the Corcu Loíghdhe. The name means descendant of *Donndamhán, Donn* meaning 'brown', and *Damh* meaning 'poet'. This sept were seated in Tuath O Feehily, in O'Driscolls (*ó hEidersceoil*) country. In 1890 Donovan was the sixty-seventh most numerous surname and the estimated number of bearers was 9,900. In that year the surname was chiefly found in Cork (175 births). In the United States Donovan is the 897th most numerous surname with an estimated 35,750 bearers. It is numerous in the states of Connecticut, Delaware, and Massachusetts.

MacDonnell, MacDonald, Mac Domhnaill

A Gaelic, both Irish and Scottish surname meaning descendant of *Domhnall*, which personal name meant 'world-mighty'. A leading sept of the Highland Clans of Scotland, the MacDonnells, or MacDonalds. They derive their descent from *Domhnall*, grandson of Somhairle thane of Argyle about the middle of the twelfth century. In the fourteenth and fifteenth century they came to Ireland as Galloglass. They settled in Laois and in Wicklow. In 1520 they established themselves in Antrim. A sept of Clann Cellacháin (Kelly) in Fermanagh. A sept of Thomond (Thuas Mhumhan), who were descended from Domhnall, who was son of Murtagh Mor O'Brien, High King of Ireland. In 1863 McDonald was the second most numerous surname in Scotland and the estimated number of bearers was 36,600. In 1890 MacDonald was the ninty-fifth most numerous surname in Ireland and was principally to be found in Dublin, Antrim, Cavan, Wexford and Carlow, and the estimated number of bearers was 8,560. In 1890 MacDonnell was the sixty-third most numerous surname and the estimated number of bearers was 11,000. In that year the surname was generally distributed throughout the country, but was chiefly found in Dublin, Mayo, Antrim, Galway and Cork. In the United States McDonald is the 117th most numerous surname with an estimated 206,250 bearers, and McDonnell is the 3,058th most numerous surname with an estimated 11,000 bearers. In England and Wales in 1996 McDonald was the 194th most numerous surname. In Scotland in 1995 McDonald was the 26th most numerous surname.

O'Donnell, ó Domhnaill
A Gaelic surname meaning descendant of *Domhnall*, which personal name meant 'world-mighty' it was a very common Irish name. The leading sept of the Cineál Chonaill in Donegal (Tír Chonaill), the original territory of the sept was Cineál Luighdheach, a mountainous district between the Swilly and the Dobhar. In the later part of the twelfth century they established themselves as Lords of Tír Chonaill. A sept who were Lords of Corcubaskin, in west Clare. They were dispossessed by the MacMahons early in the fourteenth century. A sept of the Uí Mhaine, who were chief of Clann Flaitheamhail in the present Galway. A sept who were Lords of Uí Dhróna, now the barony of Idrone in Carlow. A sept of the Oirghialla, who were Chiefs of Uí Eathach in the present Armagh. In 1890, O'Donnell was the forty-fourth most numerous surname, the estimated number of bearers was 13,900, and the surname was principally to be found in Donegal, Mayo and Galway. It was distributed generally in Munster. In the United States O'Donnell is the 875th most numerous surname with an estimated 38,500 bearers, and Donnell was the 3,974th most numerous surname with an estimated 8,250 bearers. It is numerous in the states of Connecticut, Massachusetts, and Pennsylvania. In England and Wales in 1996 it was the 491st most numerous surname.

Doolan, Doolin, ó Dubhláin, ó Dubhlainn
It is unclear which Gaelic sept this anglicised form relates to. *ó Dubhláin*, a scattered surname; or *ó Dubhlainn*, a sept of the Uí Mhaine. In 1890 it was principally found in Dublin, Louth, Cork and Tipperary. The estimated number of bearers was 2,960 (all variants).

Dooley, ó Dubhlaoich
A Gaelic surname meaning descendant of *Dubhlaoch* meaning 'black hero'. A sept who, before the Cambro-Norman Invasion were lords of Feara Tulach, now the barony of Fertullagh, in the south-east of Westmeath. A sept of Clann Mhaonaigh. They were banished from Meath in the eleventh century, and settled on the western side of the Slieve Bloom mountains in Ely O'Caroll. Their chief had the privilege of inaugurating O'Carroll as king of Ely. A sept of Siol Anmchadha who were originally located in the south-east of Galway. In 1890 Dooley was principally found in Dublin and Offaly, and the estimated number of bearers was 2,690. In the United States it is the 1,236th most numerous surname with an estimated 27,500 bearers.

Doran, Dorran, ó Deoráin
A Gaelic surname meaning descendant of *Deóradhán* diminutive of Deóradh meaning 'an exile, stranger'. One of the seven septs of Laois and a brehon family. In 1890 Doran was principally found in Dublin, Wexford, Down and Armagh and the estimated number of bearers was 4,350. In the United States it is the 1,961st most numerous surname with an estimated 16,500 bearers.

Douglas
A Scottish surname of local origin. Originally the name of a stream and lands in upper Lanarkshire, from *dubh glais* meaning 'black water'. The principal branches of this family were: The Black Douglases of Lanarkshire; The Douglas Earls of Morton in Drumfriesshire; The Red Douglas Earls of Angus; and The Drumlanrig-Queensberry Douglases.In 1890 Douglas was principally found in Antrim and Derry, and the estimated number of bearers was 2,420. In the United States it is the 257th most numerous surname with an estimated 112,750 bearers. In England and Wales in 1996 it was the 284th most numerous surname. In Scotland in 1995 it was the 89th most numerous surname.

O'Dowd, ó Dubhda
A Gaelic surname from *dubh* meaning 'dark, black'. This sept were head family of the northern Ui Fiachrach. Before the English conquest of Connacht in 1237, they ruled Lower Connacht, including the greater part of Mayo and Sligo. In the fourteenth century they drove the English out of their territory, but never regained their previous power. After the Cromwellian and Jacobite wars their lands were confiscated. A branch of this sept settled in Munster before the end of the sixteenth century, where the surname is anglicised Doody. There was also a sept of the Cineál Eoghain who bore this surname. In 1890 Dowd was principally found in Roscommon, Dublin, Kerry and Galway, and the estimated number of bearers was 3,760. In the United States Dowd is the 2,660th most numerous surname with an estimated 13,750 bearers.

McDowell, MacDougal, Mac Dubhghaill

A Scottish surname from *dubh* for 'black' and *gall* for 'foreigner' (a reference to the Norse or Danes). A sept of Galloway, they came to Ireland as galloglasses, and settled in Roscommon. In 1890 McDowell was principally found in Antrim and Down, and the estimated number of bearers was 4,080. In the United States it is the 626th most numerous surname with an estimated 52,250 bearers.

Dowling, ó Dunlaing, ó Dúlllaing

A Gaelic surname meaning descendant of *Dunlaing*, an ancient personal name of Leinster and Munster. One of the seven septs of Laois, whose territory lay along the river Barrow. A branch may have settled in Corcu Loíghdhe. In its anglicised form difficult to distinguish from *ó Dubhlainn* (black Flann), a sept of the Uí Maine. It is also difficult to distinguish from *ó Dubhláin*, descendant of *Dubhshlán*, meaning black defiance, challenge. In 1890 Dowling was numerous in Kilkenny and also to be found in Dublin and Laois. The estimated number of bearers was 4,883. In the United States it is the 2,305th most numerous surname with an estimated 13,750 bearers.

Downey, ó Dúnadhaigh

A Gaelic surname derived from *Dúnadhach* meaning 'one who leads on campaigns'. A sept of Siol Anmchadha in Galway, who are of the same stock as the O'Maddens; A sept of Corcu Loíghdhe in south-west Cork, who are of the same stock as the O'Driscolls. A sept of Luachair a districk on the borders of Cork, Kerry and Limerick. In Limerick the surname has been anglicised as Downing. In 1890 Downey was principally found in Cork, Kerry, Antrim and Limerick, and the estimated number of bearers was 4,080. In the United States it is the 1,235th most numerous surname with an estimated 27,500 bearers.

Doyle, ó Dubhghaill, ó Dúill

A surname meaning descendant of *Dubhghall*, which personal name meant 'black foreigner', it was one of the Irish name for the Vikings. A surname adopted by several septs of Danish origin. It is to be found in the neighbourhood of the old Danish settlements. Doyle was the twelfth most numerous name in Ireland in 1890, the estimated number of bearers was 23,000, and the surname was to be found in every county in Ireland. It was principally found in Dublin, Wexford, Wicklow, Carlow, Kerry and Cork. In the United States it is the 419th most numerous surname with an estimated 74,250 bearers. It is numerous in the state of Connecticut. In England and Wales in 1996 it was the 216th most numerous surname.

O'Driscoll, ó hEidersceoil, ó Drisceoil,

A Gaelic surname derived from *Eidirsceól* meaning 'interpreter'. A sept who were chiefs of Corcu Loíghdhe, which included the baronies of Carbery, Beare and Bantry. After the Cambro-Norman invasion this territory was encroached upon by the O'Donovans, O'Mahonys and

O'Sullivans, and narrowed down to a strip of territory around the Bay of Baltimore. However the O'Driscolls possessed considerable power and had several strong castles until the end of the Elizabethan period. After the defeat of Kinsale, their property was confiscated and given to Lord Castlehaven. In 1890 Driscoll was most numerous in Cork (110 births), and the estimated number of bearers was 5,420. In the United States Driscoll is the 1,569th most numerous surname with an estimated 22,000 bearers. It is numerous in the state of Massachusetts.

Duff
Clearly from the Gaelic *dubh* meaning 'dark, black'. It may be an abbreviated form of Duffy (see immediately below); or of the Scottish surname MacDuff. In 1890 the surname was principally found in Antrim, Dublin and Louth, and the estimated number of bearers was 2,020.

Duffy, ó Dubhthaigh, ó Dufaigh
A Gaelic surname meaning descendant of *Dubhthach*, which personal name comes from *Dubh* meaning 'dark, black' which was either a male or female name in early Ireland. A sept in Roscommon who had strong ecclesiastical connections. A sept in Donegal, who also had ecclesiastical connections. A sept in Monaghan. In 1890, Duffy was the forty-fifth most numerous surname; the estimated number of bearers was 13,600, and it was the most common surname in Monaghan. The surname was principally to be found in Mayo, Monaghan, Donegal, Dublin, Louth and Roscommon. In the United States Duffy is the 889th most numerous surname with an estimated 35,750 bearers, and Duffey is the 7097th most numerous surname with an estimated 5,500 bearers. It is numerous in the states of Connecticut, Delaware, Maryland, Massachusetts, New Jersey, New York, Pennsylvania. In England and Wales in 1996 it was the 352nd most numerous surname.

Duggan, Dugan, Doogan, Dougan, ó Dubhagáin
The anglicised forms of several Gaelic septs, meaning descendant of *Dubhagán* (diminutive of *dubh*, 'dark, black', perhaps 'little dark lad'). A sept of Fermoy who before the Cambro-Norman Invasion were lord of the northern half of Feara Maighe, which comprised the baronies of Fermoy, Condons, and Clangibbon. A sept of Uí Mhaine, a literary family who were heritary historians to the O'Kenllys and compilers of the Book of Uí Mhaine, and had their residence at Ballydugan, near Loughrea in Galway. A sept of Tirawley who were anciently seated in the parish of Kilmore-Moy, to the north-west of Ballina in Mayo. A sept of the Corca Laoighdhe in Cork. A sept of Aidhne in south-west Galway. In 1890: Duggan was principaly found in Cork, Dublin, Tipperary and Waterford, and the estimated number was 3,990; Dugan was principally found in Antrim, Down and Derry and the estimated number of bearers was 900; Doogan was principally found in Donegal, Dougan in Antrim and Armagh, and the estimated number of bearers was 2,375 (including variants). In the United States

Dugan is the 1,705th most numerous surname with an estimated 19,250 bearers, and Duggan is the 2,799th most numerous surname with an estimated 11,000 bearers.

Duncan
A Scottish surname derived from the Gaelic *Donnchad* meaning 'brown warrior'. In 1890 Duncan was principally found in Antrim and Tyrone, and the estimated number of bearers was 1,840. In the United States it is the 177th most numerous surname with an estimated 151,250 bearers. In England and Wales in 1996 it was the 407th most numerous surname. In Scotland in 1995 it was the 36th most numerous surname.

Dunleavy, Mac Dhuinnshléibhe, ó Duinnshléibhe
A Gaelic surname derived from *Donnshléibhe* (brown of the mountain). A sept of Ulidia, who lost their territory to John de Courcy in 1177, they then moved to Tirconnell and other parts. Also see Leavy. In 1890 Dunleavy was principally found in Mayo and Sligo, and the estimated number of bearers was 1,790. In the United States it is the 8,576th most numerous surname with an estimated 2,750 bearers.

Dunlop
A Scottish surname derived from the lands of Dunlop in the district of Cunningham in Ayrshire. In 1890 Dunlop was principally found in Antrim, and the estimated number of bearers was 1,570. In the United States Dunlap is the 846th most numerous surname with an estimated 38,500 bearers.

Dunne, Dunn, ó Duinn
A Gaelic surname meaning descendant of *Donn*, which personal name means either 'brown' or metaphorically 'king,' or 'lord'. A midland sept who were Lords of Uí Riagáin, a branch of the Uí Fáilghe. Uí Riagáin anglicised Iregan, which was co-extensive with the present barony of Innahinch in Laois. A sept of Tara, which was dispossessed soon after the Cambro-Norman Invasion. The surname is also spelt as Dunn in Ulster being found in Antrim, Down, Derry and Tyrone. It may be the English surname Dunn, from the Old English *dunn* meaning 'dull, brown' or 'dark, swarthy'. The twenty-seventh most numerous name in Ireland in 1890; the estimated number of bearers was 16,300, and it was the most numerous surname in Laois. It was also to be found in Dublin, Kildare, Offaly, Kilkenny, Cork and Tipperary. In the United States Dunn is the 160th most numerous surname with an estimated 159,500 bearers, and Dunne is the 4,053rd most numerous surname with an estimated 8,250 bearers. In England and Wales in 1996 Dunn was the 154th most numerous surname.

Dunning, see Dinneen

Dunphy, Ó Donnchadha
A Gaelic sept of Ossory of the same stock as the Fitzpatricks, and were anciently one of the ruling families of Ossory. Also see O'Donoghue. In 1890 Dunphy was principally found in Waterford and Dublin, and the estimated number of bearers was 1,520.

Durkan, Mac Dhurcáin MacDhuarcáin
A Gaelic surname meaning son of *Duarcán* (perhaps from *Duairc*, sad melancholy). A sept of north Connacht who were lords of Cúl Neiridh in Sligo and were probably a branch of the O'Haras. In 1890 Durkan was numerous in Mayo and Sligo. The estimated number of bearers was 2,777 (including variants).

O'Dwyer, Ó Du(i)bhir
A Gaelic surname meaning descendant of *Dubhodhar*, which personal name meant 'black'. A sept in Tipperary of Leinster origin who were chiefs of Coill na Manach, now the barony of Kilnamanagh. A sept of Donegal. The hundredth most numerous name in Ireland in 1890 and the estimated number of bearers was 8,100. In that year the surname was chiefly found in Tipperary, Cork, Dublin, Limerick, Kerry and Kilkenny. In the United States Dwyer is the 1,368th most numerous surname with an estimated 24,750 bearers. It is numerous in the states of Massachusetts.

Eames
A surname which may be English or Irish. The Gaelic surname is particular to Leitrim (where I have been told it is pronounced "Aimes"), which would indicate a sept of Breffney. The Book of Arms compiled by James Terry, Athlone Herald in 1690 lists Mac Iames as an Irish sept. The English surname perhaps from the Middle English *eme* meaning 'uncle'.

Early, Ó Maolmhochóir, Ó Mochóir
A Gaelic surname meaning descendant of *Maolmhocheirghe*, meaning chief of early rising or fond of early rising. An ecclesiastical sept in the diocese of Kilmore, the head of which was coarb of Drumreilly in Leitrim and of Drumlane in Cavan. In 1890 Early was principally found in Leitrim and the estimated number of bearers was 1,880. In the United States it is the 3,283rd most numerous surname with an estimated 11,000 bearers.

Edwards
Both an English and a Scottish surname. In 1890 Edwards was principally found in Dublin, Wexford and Antrim, and the estimated number of bearers was 1,610. In the United States it is the 49th most numerous surname with an estimated 376,750 bearers. In England and Wales in 1996 it was the 17th most numerous surname.

(Mac)Egan, MacAodhagáin
A Gaelic surname meaning son of *Aodhagán*, a diminutive of *Aodh*

meaning fire. A sept who originated in Uí Maine; but in the fourteenth and fifteenth centuries branches of the sept settled in Ur Mhumhan (Ormond). They were a distinguished brehon (judicial) family. Also see Keegan. In 1890 Egan was numerous in Offaly and principally found in Galway, Dublin, Offally, Mayo and Roscommon. The estimated number of bearers for Egan was 7,660. In the United States it is the 1,621st most numerous surname with an estimated 22,000 bearers.

Elliott
An English surname. A diminutive of *Elias* from the Old French *élie* and *-ot*. A Scottish surname. A border name from the Old English *Aelfweald* meaning 'elf-ruler'. In 1890 Elliott was numerous in Fermanagh and principally found in Antrim, Donegal and Dublin. The estimated number of bearers was 3,404. In the United States it is the 193rd most numerous surname with an estimated 143,000 bearers. In England and Wales in 1996 it was the 111th most numerous surname.

Ellis
An English surname, from the Middle English *Elis, Elias*, the Greek form of the Hebrew *Elijah*. In 1890 Ellis was principally found in Dublin and Antrim, and the estimated number of bearers was 1,700. In the United States it is the 114th most numerous surname with an estimated 211,750 bearers. In England and Wales in 1996 it was the 68th most numerous surname.

English
Clearly a reference to the origin of the bearer, in Limerick since the thirteenth century and completely hibernicized. In 1890 English was principally found in Tipperary, Antrim and Dublin, and the estimated number of bearers was 2,375. In the United States it is the 649th most numerous surname with an estimated 49,5000 bearers.

Ennis, ó hAonghuis
A Gaelic surname meaning son of *Aonghus* perhaps meaning 'unique choice'. The origin of the surname are unclear. It has been anglicised as Ennis. See also *ó hAonghusa* below. In 1890 Ennis was principally found in Dublin and Kildare, and the estimated number of bearers was 1,970.

(Mac)Enright, Mac Ionnrachtaigh
A Gaelic surname from the personal name *Ionnrachtach* perhaps meaning 'attacker'. A sept of the Dál gCais. In 1890 Enright was principally found in Limerick, Kerry, Cork and Clare, and the estimated number of bearers was 2,200.

MacEoin, see MacKeown

Evans
A Welsh surname (son of Evan), *Evan* is the Welsh form of John. In 1890 it was principally found in Dublin, Derry and Antrim, and the estimated number of bearers was 2,460. In 1853 Evans was the eight most numerous surname in England and Wales. In the United States it is the 48th most numerous surname with an estimated 387,750 bearers. In England and Wales in 1996 it was the 7th most numerous surname.

MacEvoy, Mac Fhíodhbhuidhe, Mac Fhíodhbhadhaigh
A Gaelic surname derived from *Fhíodhbhadhach* meaning 'of the wood. the woodman'. One of the seven septs of Laois who were anciently chiefs of Tuath-Fiodhbhuidhe, which appears to have been situated in the Barony of Stradbally. In 1890 McEvoy was principally found in Dublin, Louth, Armagh and Laois, and the estimated number of bearers was 4,440 (including variants). In the United States it is the 5,364th most numerous surname with an estimated 5,500 bearers.

MacFadden, MacPháidín
A Gaelic surname meaning son of *Paidin* a variant of Patrick. The name is particular to west Donegal and may be of Galloglass origin. A Scottish surname of the same Gaelic derivation. In 1890 the estimated number of bearers was 3,500 and it was principally found in Donegal, Antrim and Derry. In the United States it is the 949th most numerous surname with an estimated 35,750 bearers.

Fagan
A surname of Norman origin. In 1890 the surname was principally found in Dublin, and the estimated number of bearers was 2,150.

Fahy, Fahey, ó Fathaigh, ó Fathhaidh
A Gaelic surname meaning descendant of *Fathadh* meaning 'foundation'. A sept of Uí Mhaine who were chiefs of Poblewinterfahy now in the barony of Loughrea in Galway. They remained in possession of a considerable portion of their property down to the Cromwellian confiscations. According to O'Donovan was sometimes anglicised as Green from its resemblance to *Faithche*, a green, a field. In 1890 Fahy was numerous in Galway, it was also to be found in Tipperary and Mayo. The estimated number of bearers for Fahy was 3,225, and for Fahey was 2,105. In the United States Fahey is the 3,902nd most numerous surname with an estimated 8,250 bearers.

MacFall, see **Lavelle**

Fallon, ó Fallamhain
A Gaelic surname derived from *Fallamhan* meaning 'ruler'. A sept of Leinster who were lords of Crioch na gCeadach which comprised the present parish of Castlejordan in Offaly. A sept of Connacht who were lords of Clann Uadach, which comprised the parishes of Camma

87

and Dysart in the Barony of Athlone. In 1890 Fallon was principally found in Roscommon and Galway, and the estimated number of bearers was 3,140. In the United States it is the 3,613rd most numerous surname with an estimated 8,250 bearers.

Fanning, Fannin
A surname of Canbro-Norman origin, branches of which family settled in south Leinster and Limerick. In 1890 the surname was principally found in Wexford, Tipperary and Waterford, and the estimated number of bearers was 2,200. In the United States Fanning is the 3,062nd most numerous surname with an estimated 11,000 bearers.

McFarland, see **MacParland**

O'Farrell, Ó Fearghail
A Gaelic surname meaning descendant of *Fearghal*, which personal name meant 'manly valour', it was a popular name in early Ireland. The leading sept of Anghaile (Annaly), the town of Longford was formerly called Longphort Uí Fhearghail (the fortress of Ó Fearghail). The sept divided into two sub-septs : *Ó Fearghail Buidhe* (yellow) of Upper Annaly in the south and west of Longford and part of Westmeath. *Ó Fearghail Ban* (white/fair) of Lower Annaly in the north and east of Longford. Both branches of Ó Fearghail managed to hold on to land in Longford well into the seventeenth century. The thirty-fifth most numerous name in Ireland in 1890, the estimated number of bearers was 14,700, and the surname was to be found in every county, but chiefly in Dublin, Longford (second most numerous), Louth, Meath, Westmeath, and Roscommon. In the United States Farrell is the 658th most numerous surname with an estimated 49,500 bearers, and Ferrell is the 859th most numerous surname with an estimated 38,500. It is numerous in the states of Connecticut, New Jersey, and New York. In England and Wales in 1996 it was the 361st most numerous surname.

Farrelly, Ó Faircheallaigh, Ó Fearghaile
A Gaelic surname meaning descendant of *Faircheallach*. An ecclesiastical sept who were erenaghs of Drumlane in Cavan. In 1890 Farrelly was numerous in Cavan and Meath, it was also to be found in Dublin. The estimated number of bearers was 3,091.

Faulkner
An English surname of occupation, from the Old French *fau(l)connier* 'one who hunts with falcons'. There are other possible meanings. In 1890 was Faulkner principally found in Antrim and the estimated number of bearers was 1,570.

Feely, Ó Fithcheallaigh
A Gaelic surname derived from *Fithcheallach* meaning 'chess-player'. There was clearly a sept in the North-West. A sept of the

Corca Laoighdhe, who were chiefs of Tuath O Fithcheallaigh, an extensive district in the neighbourhood of Baltimore in Cork. In Cork the surname has been anglicised as Field. In 1890 Feely was principally found in Donegal and Roscommon, and the estimated number of bearers was 1,840. Field was principally found in Dublin and Cork and the estimated number of bearers was 1,300. In the United States Feeley is the 8,299th most numerous surname with an estimated 2,750 bearers.

Feeney, Ó Fiannaidhe, Ó Fidhne
A Gaelic surname meaning descendant of *Fiannaidhe* meaning 'soldier'. A sept of the Uí Fiachrach who were chiefs of Finghid now Finned, in the parish of Easkey in Sligo. In its anglicised form difficult to distinguish from *Ó Fídhne*, a sept of Galway, there is a Ballyfeeny in Roscommon. In 1890 Feeney was numerous in Sligo, it was also to be found in Mayo and Galway, and Feeny was found in Galway and Roscommon. The estimated number of bearers for Feeney was 2,060, and for Feeny was 1,164. In the United States it is the 4,027th most numerous surname with an estimated 8,250 bearers.

Fennell, Ó Fionnghail
An English surname from *atte Fenegle* meaning a 'Grower of fennel', a plant cultivated for its use in sauces, or from *fenel* used metonymically. May be an anglicisation of *Ó Fionnghail*, from *Fionnghal* (meaning 'fair-valour'). See immediately below. In 1890 it was principaly found in Clare and Dublin, and the estimated number of bearers was 1,300.

Fennelly, Ó Fionnghalaigh
A Gaelic surname meaning descendant of *Fionnghalach*, derivative of *Fionnghal* meaning 'fair-valour'. A sept of Ormond who were descendent of *Fionnghalach* son of Donnchuan an ally of Brian Boru at Clontarf. To be distinguished from the English surname Fennell (see immediately above). Also see Finlay. In 1890 Fennelly was principally found in Kilkenny, Laois and Offaly, and the estimated number of bearers was 670.

Ferguson, MacFergus
A Scottish surname meaning son of Fergus. According to Black they were one of the septs of Mar and Atholl in Perthshire. There were also families in Aberdeenshire and Ayrshire. In Scotland in 1853 Ferguson was the thirty-first most numerous surname, and the estimated number of bearers was 13,200. In Ireland in 1890 Ferguson was principally found in Antrim, Down and Derry, and the estimated number of bearers was 5,950. In the United States it is the 156th most numerous surname with an estimated 162,250 bearers. In England and Wales in 1996 it was the 281st most numerous surname. In Scotland in 1995 it was the 34th most numerous surname.

89

Ferris, Fergus, ó Fearghuis, ó Fearghusa
A Gaelic surname meaning descendant of *Fearghus* meaning 'super-choice'. A sept of west Connacht who were hereditary physicians to the O'Malleys. A sept of of Leitrim who were co-arbs of St Mogue, or erenaghs of Rossinver. Also a Scottish surname, in Aberdeenshire it is a contraction of Ferguson (see immediately above). In 1890 Ferris was principally found in Antrim and the estimated number of bearers was 1,480. In the United States it is the 1,405th most numerous surname with an estimated 24,750 bearers.

Ferry, ó Fearadhaigh
A Gaelic surname meaning descendant of *Fearadhach* (manly). In 1890 Ferry was principally found in Donegal and the estimated number of bearers was 1,210. In the United States it is the 3,839th most numerous surname with an estimated 8,250 bearers.

Field, see Feely

Finlay
A Scottish surname, same meaning as above, sometimes anglicised MacKinley. Most likely the Gaelic *ó Fionnghalaigh* above. Finlay used as a synonym of Fennelly in Laois Offaly. In 1890 Finlay was principally found in Antrim and Down, and the estimated number of bearers was 3,400. In the United States Finley is the 734th most numerous surname with an estimated 44,000 bearers.

Finegan, Finnegan, ó Fionnagáin,
A Gaelic surname meaning descendant of *Fionnagán* diminutive of *Fionn*, 'fair', for fair-headed. A sept of Uí Fiachrach in Mayo. There are two places called Ballyfinnegan, one in the barony of Ballymoe and the second in the barony of Castlereagh, on the borders of Galway and Roscommon. A sept of Breifne (Breffney), bearers of the surname are now found in Cavan. In 1890 Finegan was principally found in Monaghan, Galway and Louth, and Finnegan was principally found in Armagh and Cavan, and the estimated number of bearers was 5,150. In the United States Finnegan is the 4,158th most numerous surname with an estimated 8,250 bearers.

Finn, ó Finn
A Gaelic surname meaning descendant of *Fionn* meaning 'fair'. A sept of Breifney who were chiefs of Calraighe of Lough Gill, now the parish of Calry in Sligo. A sept who were lords of Feara Rois near Carrickmacross in Monaghan. A sept who were erenaghs of Kilcolgan in Galway. In 1890 the estimated number of persons bearing the name was 5,000 and it was principally to be found in Cork, Mayo, Dublin and Roscommon. In the United States it is the 1,626th most numerous surname with an estimated 22,000 bearers.

Fisher
An English surname of occupation, from Old English *fiscere* meaning

'fisherman', or alternatively derived from a place: 'dweller by an enclosure for catching fish'. In 1890 Fisher was principally found in Antrim and Wicklow, and the estimated number of bearers was 1,300.

Fitzgerald, Mac Gearailt
A surname of Cambro-Norman origin. Fitz from the Latin *filius* meaning son hence son of Gerald. The personal name Gerald is from the Old German *Gairovald*, a compound of *ger* 'a spear' and *vald* 'rule'. They derive their descent from Gerald, Constable of Pembroke. His son Maurice came to Ireland with Strongbow. Gaelicised as *Mac Gearailt*. They divided into two branches : Desmond (Deas Mhumhan) and Kildare. In 1890 Fitzgerald was the thirty-sixth most numerous name in Ireland, the estimated number of bearers was 14,700, and the surname was principally to be found in Munster, but most numerous in Cork, Limerick and Kerry. It was also to be found in Dublin. In the United States it is the 417th most numerous surname with an estimated 74,250 bearers. It is numerous in the states of Connecticut, and Massachusetts. In England and Wales in 1996 it was the 412th most numerous surname.

Fitzgibbons, Gibbons, Mac Giobúin
A sept who were a branch of the Burkes of Connacht, who were seated to the west of Croagh Patrick in Mayo. A family descendant from Gilbert de Clare who, at the begining of the fourteenth century, possessed the manor of Mahoonagh and other estates in Limerick. In 1890 Gibbons was numerous in Mayo, it was also to be found in Galway. The estimated number of bearers was 3,494.

Fitzhenry, see **Henry**

Fitzpatrick, Mac Giolla Padraigh
A Gaelic surname meaning 'son of the servant of Patrick'. It became anglicised as FitzPatrick, the only Fitz name of Gaelic origin. A sept of Ossairge (Ossory) who took their name from Giolla Padraigh lord of Ossairge in the tenth century. In early times they ruled over Kilkenny and part of Laois. After the Cambro-Norman invasion they were forced by the Butlers into the Barony of Upper Ossory. In 1890, Fitzpatrick was the sixty-first most numerous surname and the estimated number of bearers was 11,100. In that year the surname was to be found throughout Ireland, but chiefly found in Dublin, Laois, Cork, Tipperary, Cavan, Antrim, Down, Mayo and Galway. In the United States it is the 890th most numerous surname with an estimated 35,750 bearers. It is numerous in the state of New Jersey.

Fitzsimons
An English surname, Fitz from the Latin *filius* for 'son', son of Simon, came to Leinster from England in 1323. The Gaelic name *Mac an Ridire* 'son of the knight' was assumed by the family in Westmeath. In 1890 Fitzsimons was principally found in Dublin, Down and Cavan, and the estimated number of bearers was 3,580. In

the United States it is the 3,901st most numerous surname with an estimated 8,250 bearers.

Fitzwilliam, Mac Liam
A surname of Norman origin, Fitz from the Latin *filius* for 'son' hence 'son of William'. William was a very popular first name in England and the most common until the thirteenth century. The most famous bearer of the name was William, Duke of Normandy. The surname was most likely introduced into south east Leinster from England. It has been Gaelicised as *Mac Liam*.

O'Flanagan, ó Flannagáin
A Gaelic surname meaning descendant of *Flannagán*, which personal name meant 'red or ruddy'. A sept of the Oirghialla, who were chiefs of Tuath rátha anglicised Toorah an extensive area in the barony of Magheraboy in the north-west of Fermanagh. A sept of the Síl Muireadaigh, who were hereditary stewards to the *ó Conchobhair* (O'Connor), Kings of Connacht. They were chiefs of Clann Cathail, a district which embraced several parishes near Elphin in Roscommon. A sept who were lords of Comar and sometimes of all Teffia in Westmeath. A sept of Ely O'Carroll, who were chiefs of Cenél Arga, a district co-extensive with the barony of Ballybritt in Offaly. A sept who were chiefs of Uachtar tíre, now the barony of Upperthird in the north-west of Waterford. These were dispossessed by the Powers soon after the Cambro-Norman invasion. In 1890 Flanagan was the sixty-ninth most numerous name in Ireland and the estimated number of bearers was 9,800. In that year the surname was chiefly found in Roscommon, Mayo, Dublin, Clare and Galway. In Ulster it was to be found in Fermanagh, Cavan and Monaghan. In the United States Flanagan is the 1,102nd most numerous surname with an estimated 30,250 bearers, and Flanigan is the 4,670th most numerous surname with an estimated 8,250 bearers.

O'Flaherty, ó Flaithbheartaigh, ó Flaitheartaigh
A Gaelic surname meaning descendant of *Flaithbheartach* meaning 'bright ruler'. A sept of Connacht who were originally chiefs of Muinntear Mhurchadha (Muntermorroghœ), a district on the east side of Lough Corrin in the barony of Clare in Galway. They were expelled by the English in the thirteenth century from their original territory and settled on the other side of Lough Corrib, in the barony of Moycullen and were styled lords of Iar-Connacht. There is a similarly named sept in Thuas Mhumhan (Thomond). In its anglicised form difficult to distinguish from *ó Fathartaigh*, a sept of Galway, who were formerly chiefs of Dealbhna Cuile Fabhair, on the east side of Lough Corrib. In 1890 Flaherty was numerous in Galway, it was also to be found in Kerry. The estimated number of bearers was 3,942. In the United States Flaherty is the 2,115th most numerous surname with an estimated 16,500 bearers.

Flannery, Ó Flannabhra
A Gaelic surname meaning descendant of *Flannabhra* meaning 'red-eyebrows'. A sept of the Ui Fidhgheinte, in the present Limerick. A sept of Ui Fiachrach who were formally based around Killala, but who subsequently dispersed throughout Connacht. In 1890 Flannery was principally found in Mayo, Tipperary, Galway and Clare, and the estimated number of bearers was 2,870. In the United States it is the 3,392nd most numerous surname with an estimated 11,000 bearers.

Fleming, Pléimeann
A surname of Norman origin from Old French *Flamanc* meaning 'a native of Flanders'. They came to Ireland from Wales with the Cambro-Normans. It is Gaelicised as *Pléimeann*. In 1890 Fleming was principally found in Antrim, Dublin, Galway, Derry, Cork and Mayo, and the estimated number of bearers was 7,030. In the United States it is the 258th most numerous surname with an estimated 112,750 bearers.

Flood
An English surname from the Old English *flod* meaning 'dweller by the stream or channel, gutter'. The Gaelic surname *Mac an Tuile*, a corruption of *Mac Mhaoltuile*, a sept of Roscommon who were hereditary physicians to the O'Connors, has been so translated. Also the English pronunciation of the Welsh surname Lloyd. Also see Tully. In 1890 Flood was principally found in Dublin and the estimated number of bearers was 2,870. In the United States it is the 1,997th most numerous surname with an estimated 16,500 bearers.

O'Flynn, Ó Floinn
A Gaelic surname meaning descendant of *Flann* meaning 'ruddy'. A sept who were chiefs of Siol Maolruain now in the parishes of Kiltulagh and Kilkeevin in the west of Roscommon. A sept who were erenaghs of the church of St. Dachonna at Eas Ui Fhloinn, to the west of Boyle in Roscommon. A sept of Tirawley who were seated at Magh hEleog now in the parish of Crossmolina a branch of this family were hereditary erenaghs of the church and monastery of St. Tighearnan at Errew on Lough Conn. A sept of the Corcu Loíghdhe who were anciently chiefs of Ui Baghamhna, now the barony of Ibawn in south Cork. A sept who were lords of Muscrige Ui Fhloinn in the barony of Muskerry in Cork, who were displaced by the MacCarthaigh (MacCarthy) of Blarney. In 1890 Flynn was the forty-first most numerous surname, the estimated number of bearers was 14,300, and was principally found in Cork, Dublin, Waterford, Roscommon and Leitrim. In Ulster it was to be found in Cavan. In the United States it is the 520th most numerous surname with an estimated 60,500 bearers. It is numerous in the states of Massachusetts, and New Jersey. In England and Wales in 1996 it was the 367th most numerous surname.

Fogarty, Fogarthy, Ó Fogartaigh
A Gaelic surname meaning descendant of *Fogartach* perhaps

93

meaning 'one who inflames'. A sept of Dal Cais who were chiefs of Eile Ui Fhogartaigh, now the barony of Elyogarty in Tipperary. In 1890 Fogarty was principally found in Tipperary and Dublin, and the estimated number of bearers was 2,730.

Foley, ó Foghladha
A Gaelic surname meaning descendant of *Foghladha*, which personal name meant 'plunderer'. A sept of Waterford, which later spread throughout Munster and South Leinster. Also see MacSharry. In 1890 Foley was the sixtieth most numerous name in Ireland and the estimated number of bearers was 11,200. In that year the surname was chiefly found in Kerry, Cork, Waterford and Dublin. In the United States it is the 692nd most numerous surname with an estimated 46,750 bearers. It is numerous in the states of Connecticut, and Massachusetts.

Forde, Ford
A surname of English origin from the Old English *ford* meaning 'dweller by the ford'. May be the anglicised form of a number of Gaelic surnames. *ó Fuarráin* meaning descendant of *Fuarrán* or Fuarthán (diminutive of fuar, cold). A sept of Munster. *Mac Giolla na Naomh*, meaning son of the servant of the saints a sept of west Connacht. Corrupted to Mac Giollanáth and erroneously translated from the resemblance of the final syllable to *áth*, a ford. *Mac Conshnámha* meaning son of *Cú-shnámha* (swimming hound). A sept of Leitrim who were chiefs of Muinter Kenny in the present barony of Dromahaire. It was popularly supposed to be *Mac an átha*, son of the ford and translated accordingly. In 1890 Forde was numerous in Galway, it was also to be found in Cork, Mayo and Dublin. The estimated number of bearers for Forde was 5,107, and for Ford was 1,747. In the United States Ford is the 102nd most numerous surname with an estimated 225,500 bearers, and Forde is the 5,451st most numerous surname with an estimated 5,500. In England and Wales in 1996 Ford was the 116th most numerous surname.

Forsythe
A Scottish surname of local origin, or from the Gaelic *Fearsithe* meaning 'man of peace'. In 1890 Forsythe was principally found in Antrim and Down, and the estimated number of bearers was 1,480.

Foster
An English surname from the Middle English *foster* meaning 'foster-parent, nurse' or from *Forseter* meaning a 'shearer'. The Scottish Foster is a contracted form of Forrester, families were to be found in Edinburgh and Stirlingshire. In 1890 Foster was principally found in Antrim and Dublin, and the estimated number of bearers was 2,555. In the United States it is the 93rd most numerous surname with an estimated 250,250 bearers. In England and Wales in 1996 it was the 73rd most numerous surname.

Fox, Sionnach
An English surname that derived from a nickname. A family settled in Limerick, hence Mountfox near Kilmallock. May be the anglicised form of a number of Gaelic surnames. *Mac an tSionnaigh* meaning son of the fox. *ó Sionnaigh*, a sept of Corca Laoighdhe in south west Cork. *Mac Seancha* meaning son of the historian, a sept of Sligo, now found in Leitrim, erroneously translated as Fox. *ó Sionacháin*, a sept found in Westmeath or Cavan. *ó Catharnaigh* meaning descendant of Catharnach (warlike). A sept of Meath, who were chiefs of Teffia, but whose territory was narrowed down to Muinntear Tadhgain, now the barony of Kilcoursey in Offaly. They were also known by the surname *Sionnach*, hence Fox. In 1890 the surname was to be found in every county in Ireland, but principally in Dublin, Longford, Tyrone and Leitrim, and the estimated number of bearers was 5,500. In the United States it is the 186th most numerous surname with an estimated 145,750 bearers. In England and Wales in 1996 it was the 115th most numerous surname.

Foy
An anglicisation of a number of Gaelic surnames : *ó Fiach*, meaning descendant of *Fiach* meaning a 'raven', a bardic sept of Ulster, usually anglicised as Fee. *ó Fathaigh* or *ó Faith*, a sept of Uí Mhaine in Galway, usually anglicised as Fah(e)y. In 1890 Foy was principally found in Mayo, Cavan and Dublin, and the estimated number of bearers was 1,700.

Frazer, Fraser
A Scottish surname, which was originally *de Frisselle*. In 1863 it was the twenty-first most numerous surname in Scotland and the estimated number of bearers was 17,500. In Ireland in 1890 the surname was principally found in Dublin, Antrim and Down, and the estimated number of bearers was 1,840.

Friel, ó Firghil
A Gaelic surname meaning descendant of *Fearghal* meaning 'valorous'. A sept of the Cineál Chonaill who were hereditary erenaghs of Kilmacrenan in Donegal. They were responsible for the inauguration of the *ó Domhnaill* and the *Mac Suibhne Fánad*. In 1890 Friel was principally found in Donegal, Tyrone, and Derry, and the estimated number of bearers was 1,930. In the United States it is the 7,409th most numerous surname with an estimated 5,500 bearers.

Fulton
A Scottish surname of local origin. It may also be an English surname from Foulden in Norfolk. In 1890 Fulton was principally found in Antrim, and the estimated number of bearers was 1,430. In the United States it is the 861st most numerous surname with an estimated 38,500 bearers.

Furlong
An English surname perhaps having some relationship to the furlong length. May have come to Ireland at the time of the Norman invasion and by the fourteenth century the name was established in Wexford. In 1890 Furlong was principally found in Wexford, and the estimated number of bearers was 1,610. In the United States it is the 4,780th most numerous surname with an estimated 5,500 bearers.

Gaffney
An anglicised form of a number of Gaelic surnames: *ó Gamhna, ó Caibheanaigh, Mac Conghamhna, Mac Carrghamhna,* or *Mag Fhachtna*. Also see Caulfield. In 1890 Gaffney was found in Cavan and Dublin and principally in Roscommon, and the estimated number of bearers was 3,050. In the United States it is the 2,759th most numerous surname with an estimated 11,000 bearers.

Gallagher, ó Gallchobhair, ó Gallchóir
A Gaelic surname meaning descendants of *Gallchobhar*, which personal name may have meant 'lover of foreigners. A leading sept of the Cineál Chonaill, they were Marshalls to the *ó Domhnaill* (O'Donnell). In 1890, Gallagher was the fourteenth most numerous surname, the estimated number of bearers was 21,800, and it was the most numerous surname in Donegal. In that year the surname was also principally found in Mayo, Tyrone, Sligo, Derry and Dublin. In the United States it is the 547th most numerous surname with an estimated 57,750 bearers. It is numerous in the states of Delaware, New Jersey, New York, and Pennsylvania. In England and Wales in 1996 it was the 266th most numerous surname.

Galligan, ó Gealagáin
A Gaelic surname meaning descendant of *Gealagán*, diminutive of *geal*, meaning 'bright, white'. A sept of Sligo. It is also anglicised as White in Cavan. In 1890 Galligan was numerous in Cavan, and the estimated number of bearers was 1,164. In the United States it is the 9,336th most numerous surname with an estimated 2,750 bearers.

Gallivan, ó Gealbháin
A Gaelic surname meaning descendant of *Gealbhán* (bright-white). A sept of the Dál gCais. In 1890 Gallivan was principally found in Kerry and the estimated number of bearers was 1,430.

Galvin, ó Gealbháin
A Gaelic surname meaning descendant of *Gealbhán* meaning 'bright-white'. A sept of the Dál gCais. In the 1659 census they were numerous in Barony of Athlone, in Roscommon. In 1890 Galvin was principally found in Cork, Clare, Kerry, and Roscommon, and the estimated number of bearers was 2,777. In the United States it is the 3,666th most numerous surname with an estimated 8,250 bearers.

Gamble,
A surname of English origin from the Scandanavian *Gamall*, or *Gamal* meaning 'old'. In 1890 the surname was principally found in Antrim, Down and Derry, and the estimated number of bearers was 1,790. In the United States it is the 799th most numerous surname with an estimated 41,250 bearers.

Gannon, Mag Fhionnáin
A Gaelic surname derived from *fionn* meaning 'fair'. A sept of Mayo, who were based in Erris. In 1890 Gannon was principally found in Mayo, Dublin and Leitrim, and the estimated number of bearers was 3,270.

MacGarry, Mag Fheardhaigh
A Gaelic surname meaning son of *Fearadhach* meaning 'manly'. In 1890 McGarry was principally found in Antrim, Dublin, Roscommon and Leitrim, and the estimated number of bearers was 3,540 (including variants). In the United States McGarry is the 6,068th most numerous surname with an estimated 5,500 bearers, and McGary is the 7,590th most numerous surname with an estimated 2,750 bearers.

Garvey, ó Gairbheith
A Gaelic surname descendant of *Gairbhith* meaning 'rough peace'. A sept who were chiefs of Ui Eathach Cobha, the present Barony of Iveagh in Down, who were of the same stock as the MacGuinnesses. A sept of Oriel who were anciently chiefs of Ui Breasain in the present Barony of Oneilland East in Armagh, who were dispossessed by the MacCanns. A sept of the Ui Ceinnsealaigh who were anciently chiefs of Ui Feilmeadha Thuaidh in the present Barony of Rathvilly in Carlow. In 1890 Garvey was principally found in Kerry, Mayo, Galway and Louth, and the estimated number of bearers was 2,870.

McGarvey, Mac Gairbheith
A Gaelic surname meaning son of *Garbhith* (*garbh* meaning 'rough'). A sept of Ulster. In 1890 McGarvey was principally found in Donegal and Derry, and the estimated number of bearers was 1,340.

Gavin, Gavan, ó Gábháin
A Gaelic surname descendant of *Gábhadhán*. A sept of Connacht. A sept of the Corca Laoighdhe, in south west Cork. In 1890 was principally found in Mayo and Galway, and the estimated number of bearers was 2,960 (including variants). In the United States Gavin is the 2,659th most numerous surname with an estimated 13,750 bearers.

Geoghegan. Mag Eochagáin
A Gaelic surname meaning son of *Eochagán*, a diminutive of *Eochaidh*, meaning perhaps 'horse-rider, fighter on horseback'. A sept known as the Cinel Fhiachach, of the southern Ui Neill. Their territory comprised the barony of Moycashel, Westmeath, they were dispossessed by the Cromwellian confiscations. A branch was

transplanted to Galway. In 1890 Geoghegan was principally found in Dublin and Galway, and the estimated number of bearers was 1,700 (including variants).

Geraghty, Mac Oireachtaigh
A Gaelic surname meaning son of *Oireachtach*, a reference to 'a member of a court or an assembly'. A sept who were a branch of the O'Connors, who were chiefs of Muinntear Roduibh in Roscommon. In 1890 the surname was principally found in Galway, Mayo and Dublin, and the estimated number of bearers was 3,230.

Gibbons, see Fitsgibbon

Gibson, Mac Giolla Brighde
A Scottish surname derived from Gib a pet form of Gilbert, a personal name introduced by the Normans. The surname was to be found in Caithness, Orkney, Durie, and in Glendarul in Cowal. It is also an anglicised form of *Mac Giolla Brighde*, a sept that was a branch of the Clan Buchanan. In 1890 Gibson was principally found in Down and Antrim, and the estimated number of bearers was 4,300.

Gill, MacGill, Mac Giolla
An English, Scottish and Irish surname. The English surname is derived from the Irish for 'servant'. The Scottish derivation is similar and there was a Barony of Gillesland in Cumberland. In Ireland, a shortened form of surnames commencing *Mac Giolla*. Also can be confused with *Mac an Ghaill* or *Mac an Ghoill* meaning 'son of the foreigner' a surname given to the decendants of the early Anglo-Norman settlers. In 1890 Gill was principally found in Dublin, Galway, Mayo and Longford, and the estimated number of bearers was 2,777. In the United States Gill is the 424th most numerous surname with an estimated 74,250 bearers, and McGill is the 1,247th most numerous surname with an estimated 27,500 bearers.

Gillan, Gillen, ó Gilín, ó Giolláin
At least two Gaelic surnames: One meaning descendant of *Gilín* (diminutive of *geal* for 'bright, white'). There were two septs in Connacht, one in Tirawley and one in Partry. The other meaning descendant of *Giollán* (diminutive of *Giolla* meaning 'servant, youth'). A sept of the Cineál Eoghain. *ó Giollagáin* (see Gilligan below) is a variant. In 1890 Gillan was principally found in Antrim and Sligo, while Gillen was principally found in Antrim, Donegal and Tyrone. The estimated number of bearers was 1,790 (both variants). In the United States Gillen is the 3,603rd most numerous surname with an estimated 8,250 bearers.

Gillespie, Mac Giolla Easpaig
A Gaelic surname, meaning 'son of the servant of the Bishop', This sept originated in east Ulster. A branch had moved to Donegal by the thirteenth century. They were *archinnigh* in the parishes of Killybegs

and Kilcar. In the census of 1659 the surname was to be found in the Barony of Boylagh and Banagh. Also a Scottish surname of similar derivation. In 1890 Gillespie was principally found in Antrim, Donegal, Armagh and Tyrone, and the estimated number of bearers was 3,850. In the United States it is the 790th most numerous surname with an estimated 41,250 bearers.

Gilligan, ó Giollagáin
A Gaelic surname meaning descendant of *Giollán* (diminutive of *Giolla* meaning 'servant, youth'). *Mac Giollagáin* was a sept of Ulster. See Gillen above. In 1890 Gilligan was principally found in Dublin and the estimated number of bearers was 1,430.

Gillmartin, see Martin

Gilmore, Gilmour, Mac Giolla Mhuire
Both an Irish and a Scottish surname of similar derivation, meaning 'son of the servant of Mary'. It has also been anglicised in Scotland as Morrison (son of *Muire*). From Scotland the surname spread to England. The Gaelic sept were chiefs of Ui Derca Cein in the Barony of Castlereagh in Down. In 1890 Gilmore was principally found in Antrim, and the estimated number of bearers was 3,540 (including variants). In the United States Gilmore is the 538th most numerous surname with an estimated 60,500 bearers.

Gilroy, see MacIllroy

Gilssenan, see de Nugent

MacGinley, Mag Fhionnghaile, Mag Fhionnbharra
A Gaelic surname meaning son of *Fionnghal* meaning 'fair valour'. A sept of Donegal. In 1890 McGinley was numerous in Donegal. The estimated number of bearers was 2,105. In the United States it is the 5,947th most numerous surname with an estimated 5,500 bearers.

Gleeson, ó Glasáin, ó Gliasáin
A Gaelic surname meaning descendant of *Glasán*, diminutive of *glas*, meaning 'grey'. A sept of Ur Mhumhan (Ormond). In 1890 Gleeson was numerous in Tipperary, it was also to be found in Limerick, Dublin, Kilkenny and Cork. The estimated number of bearers was 3,673. In the United States Gleason is the 1,482nd most numerous surname with an estimated 22,000 bearers.

(Mac) Glynn, Mag Fhloinn
A Gaelic surname meaning son of *Flann* meaning 'bright red, blood red'. A sept of Connacht. In 1890 Glynn was principally found in Galway, Mayo, Dublin and Clare, and the estimated number of bearers was 3,225. The estimated number of bearers for McGlynn was 1,750. In the United States Glynn is the 3,591st most numerous surname with an estimated 8,250 bearers, and McGlynn is the 7,193rd most

numerous surname with an estimated 5,500 bearers.

Goggin, de Cogan
A surname of Cambro-Norman origin, from Cogan a parish in Glamorganshire in Wales. *Milo de Cogan* was the first constable of Dublin, and arrived in Ireland with Strongbow in 1170. Other members of this family were granted and later acquired additional lands in Cork. In 1890 Goggin was principally found in Cork and Kerry, and the estimated number of bearers was 1,520.

McGoldrick, Mag Ualghairg
A Gaelic surname meaning son of *Ualgharg* meaning 'proud-fierce'. A sept of Leitrim who were a branch of the O'Rourkes. In 1890 the surname was principally found in Tyrone, Fermanagh and Sligo, and the estimated number of bearers was 1,840.

McGonigle, Mac Conghail
A Gaelic surname meaning son of *Conghal* (for 'brave, fierce as a hound'). A sept of the Cineál Chonaill. In 1890 McGonigle was principally found in Donegal and Derry, and the estimated number of bearers was 1,700.

Gordon
A Scottish surname which is also found in England. May have derived from the place name Gordon in Berwickshire. The name was also to be found in Hampshire in England. In Scotland in 1863 Gordon was the fiftieth most numerous surname in Scotland and the estimated number of bearers was 9,500. In Ireland in 1890 Gordon was principally found in Antrim, Down and Dublin, and the estimated number of bearers was 5,460. In the United States it is the 143rd most numerous surname with an estimated 178,750 bearers. In England and Wales in 1996 it was the 215th most numerous surname. In Scotland in 1995 it was the 50th most numerous surname.

O'Gorman, McGorman, ó Gormáin, MacGormáin
A Gaelic surname either descendant or son of *Gormán* diminutive of *gorm*, meaning 'blue'. A sept of Leinster who were formerly lords of Ui Bairche, in the barony of Slievemargy, in Laois, After the Cambro-Norman invasion they were dispersed to Monaghan and the barony of Ibrickan in Clare. Also a sept who were erenaghs of Callowhill in Fermanagh. In 1890 Gorman was principally found in Antrim, Dublin and Tipperary, and the estimated number of bearers was 6,270. O'Gorman was principally found in Clare and the estimated number of bearers was 1,075. In the United States Gorman is the 1,175th most numerous surname with an estimated 27,500 bearers.

Gormley, ó Goirmleaghaigh
A Gaelic surname derived from *Goirmfhleaghach* meaning 'blue-spearman'. A sept who were chiefs of Cinel Moen and originally seated in Magh Itha, now in the Barony of Raphoe in Donegal. In the

100

thirteenth century they were expelled by the Cineál Chonaill, and settled on the other side of the river Foyle in Ardstraw in Tyrone. In 1890 Gormley was principally found in Antrim and Tyrone, and the estimated number of bearers was 1,970.

Grace
A surname of Cambro-Norman origin. Raymond *le Gros* (the fat) accompanied Strongbow to Ireland. The head of the family had the title Baron of Courtstown. In 1890 Grace was principally found Dublin and Kilkenny, and the estimated number of bearers was 1,610. In the United States it is the 1,167th most numerous surname with an estimated 30,250 bearers.

McGovern, Mag Shamhradháin, Mag Shamhráin,
A Gaelic surname meaning son of *Samhradhán* from *samhra*, meaning 'summer'. A sept of Breifne (Breffny) who were chiefs of Telllach áchach, now the barony of Tullyhaw, in north west Cavan. In 1890 McGovern was numerous in Fermanagh, Cavan and Leitrim. The estimated number of bearers was 4,569 (including variants). In the United States it is the 2,848th most numerous surname with an estimated 11,000 bearers.

MacGowan, see Smith

O'Grady, ó Gráda
A Gaelic surname derived from *Gráda* meaning 'noble, illustrious'. A sept of the Dál gCais who were originally seated in the parish of Killonasoolagh, near the river Fergus in Clare. They subsequently moved to Tomgraney, in the Barony of Tulla Upper in Clare. In some unaccountable way according to Woulfe the surname got anglicised as Brady. The Connacht surname *Mag Riada* or *ó Griada*, usually anglicised as Gready has also been anglicised'a Grady. In 1890 Grady was principally found in Mayo, Clare, Kerry and Roscommon, and the estimated number of bearers was 3,050. O'Grady was principally found in Clare, Limerick, Dublin and Roscommon, and the estimated number of bearers was 2,110. In the United States Grady is the 1,147th most numerous surname with an estimated 30,250 bearers, and O'Grady is the 5,733rd most numerous surname and the estimated bearers is 5,500.

Graham
A Scottish surname of Anglo-Norman origin which settled in Abercorn and Dalkeith (Lothian) in the twelfth century. The name is derived from the Old English *graegham* meaning 'grey home', from the manor of that name. The family were granted lands in Lothian in the twelfth century by King David I of Scotland. The name was introduced to Ulster from Scotland. In 1890 Graham was the eighty-second most numerous surname and the estimated number of bearers was 9,100. In that year the surname was chiefly found in Antrim, Down, Dublin, Tyrone, Armagh and Monaghan. In 1863 it was the

fortieth most common name in Scotland, with an estimated 11,200 bearers. In the United States it is the 104th most numerous surname with an estimated 225,500 bearers. In England and Wales in 1996 it was the 101st most numerous surname. In Scotland in 1995 it was the 30th most numerous surname.

Granny, Mag Ráighne
The Gaelic surname Mag Raighne derived from *Raigne*, a pet form of *Raghnall* (or Reginald), in its anglicised form Granny, has been confused with Grant. This is certaingly the case in Donegal. See Grant immediatly below.

Grant
A Scottish surname of Norman origin, from the Old French *grand, grant* meaning 'great. In 1890 Grant was principally found in Antrim and Donegal, and the estimated number of bearers was 3,460. In the United States it is the 154th most numerous surname with an estimated 165,000 bearers. In England and Wales in 1996 it was the 136th most numerous surname. In Scotland in 1995 it was the 40th most numerous surname.

MacGrath, Magrath, Mac Craith,
A Gaelic surname meaning son of *Craith*, which personal name meant 'son of grace'. A sept of Donegal whose chief was co-arb of St. Daveog, or erenagh of Termon Daveog, now Termon Magrath, at Lough Derg, and who resided at the castle of Termon Magrath north of Lough Erne, near Pettigo. A sept of Thuas Mhumhan (Thomond) who were hereditary poets and chroniclers to *ó Briain* (O'Brien).
A sept of Waterford of which little is known. A sept of Kintail in Scotland, who are to be found in Ulster. In 1890 McGrath was the fifty-fifth most numerous surname, the estimated number of bearers was 11,900 and the surname was to be found in every county in Ireland, but was chiefly found in Tipperary, Cork, Waterford, Antrim and Tyrone. In the United States McGrath is the 1,120th most numerous surname with an estimated 30,250 bearers.

Gray, Grey, de Gray
An English or Scottish surname. From the Old English probably meaning grey-haired. With respect to Scotland of Norman origin, Black suggest that it is perhaps from *Gray*, a town in the department of Haute-Saone in Normandy. Macglashans, that is *M'Ghille ghlais* (son of the grey lad) who settled in the Lowlands anglicised their name as Gray. With respect to Ireland Woulfe suggests that Gray may be a corruption of *Mac Cúilriabhaigh*, a midland sept, and also that a sept of Thuas Mhumhan (Thomond), *Mac Giolla Riabhaigh* was likewise translated. In Scotland in 1853 Gray was the thirty-third most numerous surname and the estimated number of bearers was 12,700. In Ireland in Gray 1890 was principally found in Antrim, Down Derry, and Dublin, and the estimated number of bearers was 5,240. In the United States Gray is the 69th most numerous surname with an

102

estimated 291,500 bearers. In England and Wales in 1996 it was the 78th most numerous surname. In Scotland in 1995 it was the 25th most numerous surname.

Gready, see O'Grady

Greany, ó Gráinne
A Gaelic surname meaning a descendant of *Gráinne* (a female personal name), one of few Irish metronymics. In 1890 Greany was principally found in Kerry and Galway, and the estimated number of bearers was 1,340.

Green, Greene, ó hUaine
An English surname derived from a place, the Old English *grene* 'green' usually from residence near the village green. In 1890 the surname was principally found in Dublin, Antrim, Galway, Tipperary and Clare, and the estimated number of bearers for Green was 4,700, and for Greene was 2,100. In the United States Green is the 35th most numerous surname with an estimated 503,250 bearers, and Greene is the 191st most numerous surname with an estimated 145,750 bearers. In England and Wales in 1996 Green was the 19th most numerous surname.

Greer
A Scottish surname considered to be a shortened form of MacGregor. In 1890 Greer was principally found in Antrim, Armagh and Down, and the estimated number of bearers was 2,820. In the U.S.it is the 426th most numerous surname with an estimated 71,500 bearers.

Griffin, ó Gríobhtha, ó Gríofa, ó Gríobhtháin
A Gaelic surname meaning descendant of *Gríobhtha*, which personal name meant 'griffen-like' or 'fierce warrior'. A sept of Dál gCais, who were chiefs of Cenél Cuallachta, in the south east of the barony of Inchiquin. They had a castle at ballygriffy. *ó Gríobhtháin*, descendent of *Gríobhthán*, diminutive of *Gríobhtha*. A sept of Connacht, found in Galway and Mayo. In 1890 Griffin was the seventy-fifth most numerous surname, the estimated number of bearers was 9,600 and was principally found in Kerry, Clare, Cork, Limerick, Galway, Mayo and Dublin. In the United States it is the 98th most numerous surname with an estimated 231,000 bearers. In England and Wales in 1996 it was the 208th most numerous surname.

Grimes, ó Gréacháin, ó Coinleisc
The anglicisation of at least two Gaelic surnames : *ó Gréacháin*, perhaps a variant of *ó Créachán*, a sept of the Ui Fiachrach who were formerly seated in Tirawley in Mayo. *ó Coinleisc* a literary family in Connacht. In 1890 Grimes was principally found in Tyrone and Mayo, and the estimated number of bearers was 1,750. In the United States it is the 562nd most numerous surname with an estimated 57,750 bearers.

Grogan, Ó Gruagáin, Ó Grúgáin
A Gaelic surname derived from either *gruag* for 'hair', or *grúg* meaning 'fierceness, anger'. A sept of Roscommon who were erenaghs of Elphin. In 1890 Grogan was principally found in Dublin, Tipperary, Mayo and Clare, and the estimated number of bearers was 1,970. In the United States it is the 2,820th most numerous surname with an estimated 11,000 bearers.

McGuigan, Mag Uiginn
This may be *Mag Uiginn* a sept of Tir Eoghain. However it could be a corruption of many different Gaelic surnames. In 1890 McGuigan was principally found in Antrim and Tyrone, and the estimated number of bearers was 1,930. In the United States it is the 8,907th most numerous surname with an estimated 2,750 bearers.

McGuinness, Mag Aonghusa, Mag Aonghuis
A Gaelic surname meaning son of *Aonghus* (meaning 'one choice'). A sept who were chief of all Ui Eathach, now the baronies of Upper and Lower Iveagh in Down. *Mac Raois* a branch of the sept in Orghialla (Oriel), anglicised as McCreesh. In 1890 McGuinness was principally found in Dublin, Monaghan and Louth, and the estimated number of bearers was 5,730 (including variants, of which there were 16 varieties). In the United States it is the 6,745th most numerous surname with an estimated 5,500 bearers.

McGurk, MacGuirk, Mag Oirc
A Gaelic surname, a sept of Tir Eoghain. Their territory appears to have been around Ballygurk (*Baile Mhic Oirc*), in the Barony of Loughshilon in the present County Derry. In 1890 McGurk was principally found in Tyrone and Antrim, McGuirk in Dublin, and the estimated number of bearers was 2,285 (including variants).

(O')Hagan, Ó hAgáin
A Gaelic surname meaning descendant of *Ogán* (diminutive of *óg* meaning 'young'); a northern variant of *Ó hOgáin* (see Hogan). A sept of the Cineál Eoghain who were chiefs of Cineal Fearghusa who were seated at Tullaghoge in Tyrone. It was their privilege to inaugurate *Ó Neill*. A sept of the Cineál Eoghain who were chiefs of Cinel Tighearnaigh. *Ó hAodhagáin* a sept of Orghialla (Oriel) is sometimes so anglicised. In 1890 Hagan was principally found in Antrim, Tyrone and Armagh, and the estimated number of bearers was 2,820. In the same year O'Hagan was principally found in Armagh, Louth and Down, and the estimated number of bearers was 1,480. In the United States Hagan is the 1,651st most numerous surname with an estimated 22,000 bearers.

McHale, Mac hEil, Mac Céile
A surname of Welsh origin meaning son of *Howel*, a family who settled in Tirawley (now in Mayo) in the twelfth and thirteenth century. In its anglicised form difficult to distinguish from *Mac Céile*,

meaning son of *Céile* (companion). A sept of Mayo who were erenaghs of Killala and co-arbs of St. Caillin at Fenaghin in Leitrim. In 1890 McHale was numerous in Mayo. The estimated number of bearers was 2,284. In the United States Hale is the 296th most numerous surname with an estimated 101,750 bearers, and McHale is the 5,774th most numerous surname with an estimated 5,500 bearers.

Hall
An English and Scottish surname. The English surname meaning 'worker in the hall' from the Old English *heall*. The Scottish surname of local origin. In 1853 Hall was the sixteenth most numerous surname in England and Wales, and the estimated number of bearers was 60,400. In Ireland in 1890 Hall was principally found in Antrim, Dublin and Armagh, and the estimated number of bearers was 5,370. In the United States it is the 26th most numerous surname with an estimated 550,000 bearers. In England and Wales in 1996 it was the 20th most numerous surname.

O'Halloran, ó hAllmhuráin
A Gaelic surname meaning descendant of *Allmhurán*, meaning 'stranger from beyond the seas'. A sept who were chiefs of Clann Fearghaile, an extensive district in the neighbourhood of the present city of Galway. A sept of Thuas Mhumhan (Thomand) who were seated in the parish of Ogonnelloe in east Clare. In 1890 Halloran was numerous in Clare, it was also to be found in Galway and Cork, and the estimated number of bearers was 3,000. In the United States Halloran is the 6,917th most numerous surname with an estimated 5,500 bearers.

Halpin, ó hAilpín
A Gaelic surname meaning descendant of *Alpín*, diminutive of *Alp* meaning 'a lump, a stout person'. It appears to have originated in the Clare-Limerick area. It is anglicised as Halpin and should not be confused with the Scottish MacAlpin. In 1890 the name was principally found in Dublin and Clare, and the estimated number of bearers was 1480.

Hamill, ó hAdhmaill
A sept of the Cineál Eoghain descendant of *Adhmall*, meaning 'quick, ready, active'. A Scottish surname of Norman territorial origin, a Hugh Hammill of Roughwood in Ayrshire came to Ireland with Montgomery of Ards. In addition there is an English surname (also spelt Hammel) derived from the Old English *hamel* meaning 'scared, mutilated'. In 1890 Hamill was principally found in Antrim, Armagh and Louth, and the estimated number of bearers was 3,450 (including variants). In the United States it is the 5,273rd most numerous surname with an estimated 5,500 bearers.

Hamilton
A Scottish surname derived from the English place name Hambledon.
Robert de Bruce rewarded Walter de Hamildone with Comyn lands in
Lanarkshire. In 1863 Hamilton was the thirty-sixth most numerous
surname in Scotland and the estimated number of bearers was 12,000.
In Ireland in 1890 Hamilton was principally found in Antrim, Down,
Tyrone and Derry. The estimated number of bearers was 7,481. In the
United States it is the 103rd most numerous surname with an
estimated 225,500 bearers. In England and Wales in 1996 it was the
191st most numerous surname. In Scotland in 1995 it was the 29th
most numerous surname.

Hand, see Lavin

O'Hanlon, ó hAnluain,
A Gaelic surname meaning descendant of *Anluan* meaning 'great
hero, or champion'. A sept of Orghialla (Oriel), who were chiefs of Ui
Niallain (now the barony of Oneilland in Armagh) and formerly of
Oirthear (now the barony of Orier in Armagh). In 1890 O'Hanlon
was principally to be found in Dublin and Armagh. Hanlon was
principally to be found in Dublin, Kerry, Louth and Wexford. The
estimated number of bearers was 4,260. In the United States it is the
3,559th most numerous surname with an estimated 8,250 bearers.

Hanly, Hanley, ó hAinle
A Gaelic surname meaning descendant of *Ainle* meaning 'a hero, a
champion, a warrior'. A sept of Connacht who were chiefs of Cinel
Dobhtha (in later times called Tuaohanly and Doohy Hanly) a district
in Roscommon, extending along the Shannon and comprising the
parishes of Kilglass, Termonbarry, Cloontuskert, and the eastern part
of Lisonuffy. In 1890 Hanly was principally found in Roscommon,
Galway and Limerick and Tipperary, and Hanley was principally
found in Cork. The estimated number of bearers was 4,260. In the
United States Hanley is the 1,850th most numerous surname with an
estimated 19,250 bearers.

Hanna, Hannay, Ahanney
A Scottish surname. In 1890 Hanna was principally found in Antrim,
Down and Armagh, and the estimated number of bearers was 3,850.

Hannigan, ó hAnnagáin
A Gaelic surname meaning descendant of *Annagán* a diminutive of
Annadh meaning 'delay'. According to Woulfe of Limerick origin.
Matheson found the name in Waterford and Tyrone an indication of
two distinct septs. In Wicklow it is more likely to be of the Waterford
connection. In 1890 Hannigan was principally found in Dublin,
Waterford and Tyrone, and the estimated number of bearers was
1,340. In the United States it is the 9,127th most numerous surname
with an estimated 2,750 bearers.

Hannon, Hannan, ó hAnnáin
A Gaelic surname meaning descendant of *Ainchín* (perhaps for *Ainghein*: 'unborn'). A sept of the Siol Anmchadha, in south-east Galway. Difficult to distinguish from *ó hAinnín*, more usually anglicised Hanneen. In 1890 the surname was principally found in Galway, Roscommon, Limerick, Cork and Sligo, and the estimated number of bearers was 4,260. In the United States Hannon is the 2,792nd most numerous surname with an estimated 11,000 bearers.

Hanrahan, Handrahan, ó hAnracháin
A corruption of *ó hAnradháin* (also anglicised Hourihan) according to Woulfe. Such Gaelic surname meaning descendant of *Anradhán* (diminutive of *anradh*, meaning 'warrior, champion'. A sept of the Dál gCais in Thomond. A sept who were anciently erenaghs of Ross in west Cork. A sept who were anciently chiefs of Ui Creamhthainn, a district lying around the rock of Dunamasc in Laois. A sept who were formerly chiefs of Corca Raoidhe, now the Baronyof Corcaree in Westmeath. In 1890 the surname was principally found in Clare and Limerick, and the estimated number of bearers was 2,420. In the United States Hanrahan is the 6,436th most numerous surname with an estimated 5,500 bearers.

Hanratty, ó hAnrachtaigh
A Gaelic surname meaning descendant of *Anrachtach* meaning 'unrighteous, unlawful'. A sept of Orghialla (Oriel) who were chiefs of Ui Méith Macha now the barony of Monaghan in County Monaghan. In 1890 Hanratty was numerous in Louth, it was also to be found in Armagh, Monaghan and Dublin, and the estimated number of bearers was 1,344.

O'Hara, ó hEaghra
A Gaelic surname meaning descendant of *Eaghra*. This sept derive their name and descent from *Eaghra*, Lord of Luighne who died in the year 926, they were for many centuries lords of Luighne, now the barony of Leyney in Sligo. In the fourteenth century they divided in two : *ó hEaghra Buidhe* (yellow) and the *ó hEaghra Riabhach* (speckled or brindled), a branch also settled in the Route, Antrim. In 1890 O'Hara was numerous in Sligo, and was principally found in Dublin and Antrim, and the estimated number of bearers was 4,704. Hara was to be found in Galway only (estimated bearers 225). In the United States O'Hara is the 1,623rd most numerous surname with an estimated 22,000 bearers.

Haran, Haren, ó Eaghráin
A Gaelic surname of uncertain origin. In 1890 Haran was principally found in Mayo, and Haren was principally found in Clare, and the estimated number of bearers was 1,660.

O'Hare, Hare, Haire, ó hír
A Gaelic surname meaning descendant of *ír* meaning 'long, lasting', a

sept of Orghialla (Oriel) who were chiefs of Oirtheara, now the baronies of Orier in the east of Armagh. In its anglicised form difficult to distinguish from *Mag Fhearadhaigh*, meaning son of *Fearadhach* (manly), which is corrupted to *ó Giorraidge*, and erroneously translated O'Hare as if from *Girrfhiadh*, meaning 'a hare'. In 1890 O'Hare was numerous in Armagh, it was also to be found in Louth and Down, and the estimated number of bearers was 2,643. Hare was principally found in Antrim, and the estimated number of bearers for all variants was 985. In the United States Hare is the 1,885th most numerous surname with an estimated 19,250 bearers, and O'Hare was the 7,008th most numerous surname with an estimated 5,500 bearers.

Harkin ó hEarcáin
A sept of the Cineál Eoghain, whose original homeland was in Bredagh in Inishowen. It is most likely that they were descendants of *Ercán*, a diminutive of *Erc* meaning 'speckled, dark-red or a salmon'. They were one of many erenagh (airchinnigh) in the parish of Clonca. In the census of 1659 there were twenty-one families of the surname. There is also a Scottish surname from Aberdeen, probably from Harry (Henry). In 1890 Harkin was principally found in Donegal and Derry, and the estimated number of bearers was 2,510. In the United States it is the 2,695th most numerous surname with an estimated 13,750 bearers.

Harper, Harpur, MacChruiter
In east Ulster Harper is a Scottish surname derived from the office of 'harper', which position was of high standing under the Brehon Law. In Stewarty the surname would be a translation of *MacChruiter*, which means 'son of the harper'. In south Leinster Harpur is a surname of Norman origin from *le Harpur* meaning 'the harper'. The surname was to be found in Leinster from the thirteenth century. There is a Harperstown in the Parish of Taghmon, Barony of Bargy in Wexford. In 1890 Harper was principally found in Antrim, Harpur in Wexford, and the estimated number of bearers was 2,285 (all variants). In the United States Harper is the 185th most numerous surname with an estimated 148,500 bearers. In England and Wales in 1996 Harper was the 201st most numerous surname.

Harrington, ó hIongardail, ó Húrdail
A Gaelic surname meaning descendant of *Indardgal*. A sept who settled in west Cork. In its anglicised form difficult to distinguish from *ó hArrachtáin*, meaning descendant of *Arrachtán* (diminutive of *Arrachta* meaning 'tall, mighty, brave, heroic'). A sept of Uí Mhaine in Galway. In 1890 Harrington was numerous in Cork (82 births), it was also to be found in Kerry and Mayo. The estimated number of bearers was 5,331. In the United States it is the 478th most numerous surname with an estimated 66,000 bearers.

Harris,
Both an English and a Scottish surname, meaning son of Harry, a form of Henry. In Scotland there was a Harris sept of Clan Campbell. In England in 1853 Harris was the twenty-sixth most numerous surname and the estimated number of bearers was 51,900. In Ireland in 1890 the surname was principally found in Dublin, Cork and Antrim, and the estimated number of bearers was 2,640. In the United States it is the 15th most numerous surname with an estimated 756,250 bearers. In England and Wales in 1996 it was the 22nd most numerous surname.

Harrison,
Both an English and a Scottish surname, though more English than Scots. Meaning son of Harry (from Henry through the intermediate form Hanry). In England in 1853 Harrison was the twenty-ninth most numerous surname, and the estimated number of bearers was 47,200. In Ireland in 1890 the surname was principally found in Antrim, Dublin and Down, and the estimated number of bearers was 2,150. In the United States it is the 115th most numerous surname with an estimated 209,000 bearers. In England and Wales in 1996 it was the 38th most numerous surname.

Hart, Harte, ó hAirt
A Gaelic surname meaning descendant of *Art*, meaning 'a bear, a champion'. A sept of Meath who were originally seated in the neighbourhood of Tara, but dispossessed soon after the Cambro-Norman invasion, when they settled in the barony of Carury in Sligo. Also an English surname derived from a nickname. The Middle English *hert*, 'stag', used for someone bearing some fancied resemblence to the animal. In 1890 Harte was numerous in Sligo, Leitrim and Roscommon, Hart was found in Antrim, Dublin and Cork. The estimated number of bearers for Hart was 2,867, and for Harte was 2,598. In the United States Hart is the 179th most numerous surname with an estimated 148,500 bearers.

Harvey
An English surname introduced by Bretons at the time of the Conquest. From the Old Breton *Aeruiu, Haerviu*, meaning 'battleworthy'. It subsequently spread to Scotland. It also takes the form Hervey, Hervie and Harvie. In 1890 Harvey was principally found in Antrim, Dublin, Down and Donegal, and the estimated number of bearers was 2,420. In the United States it is the 225th most numerous surname with an estimated 129,250 bearers. In England and Wales in 1996 it was the 100th most numerous surname.

Hasson, ó hOsáin
A Gaelic surname meaning descendant of *Osán*, diminutive of *Os* meaning 'a deer'. A sept of Derry and Tyrone. In the United States it is the 7,024th most numerous surname with an estimated 5,500 bearers.

Hayden, ó hEideáin
An English surname derived from a place name. From Haydon (Dorset, Somerset, Wiltshire), Haydon Bridge (Northumberland), or Heydon (Cambridgeshire, Norfolk). Also a Gaelic sept of Carlow *ó hEideáin*, sometimes anglicised as Headon. In 1890 Hayden was principally found in Dublin, Carlow and Tipperary, and the estimated number of bearers was 2,020. In the United States it is the 847th most numerous surname with an estimated 38,500 bearers.

Hayes, Hughes, ó hAodha
A Gaelic surname meaning descendant of *Aodh*, which personal name meant 'fire'. A sept who were Chiefs of Uí Dheaghaidh (an ancient subdivision of Uí Cheinnselaigh), a district nearly co-extensive with the barony of Gorey in Wexford. A sept who were Lords of Uí Fiachrach of Ardstraw in Tyrone. A sept of the Cineál Chonaill, who were Chiefs of Eas Ruadh, near Ballyshannon in Donegal. A sept of Oriel (Orghialla), who were Chiefs of Fearnmhaighe, now the barony of Farney in Monaghan. A sept who were Lords of Odhbha, near Navan in Meath. A sept who were Chiefs of east Tír Theathbha in Meath. A sept who were Lords of Muscraighe-Luachra in the north-west of Cork. A sept who were sub-chiefs of Tuath ó Donnghaile in the south-west of Cork, who anglicise the name as O'Hea. A sept of the Dál gCais in Thomond (Thuas Mhumhan). A sept of the Uí Mhaine in Galway. A sept of the Uí Fiachrach, formerly seated at Ard ó hAodha in the parish of Templemurray in Mayo. A sept of the Uí Fiachrach; parish of Ballintober, Mayo. A sept of the Uí Fiachrach, seated at Tonrego in the parish of Dromard in Sligo. Also a surname of Norman extraction *La Heise* or *de la Haye* which originated in La Haye-du-Puits in Manche in Normandy. This Norman family settled in the Barony of Forth in Wexford were known initially as Hay, spread throughout Wexford and Wicklow and became known as Hayes like the Gaelic septs above mentioned. In 1890 Hughes was the thirty-fourth most numerous surname; the estimated number of bearers was 14,900; and it was principally to be found in Armagh, Antrim, Dublin, Tyrone, Monaghan, Galway and Mayo. In 1890 Hayes was the fifty second most numerous surname; the estimated number of bearers was 12,300 and it was chiefly found in Cork, Limerick, Tipperary, Dublin and Wexford, it was also to be found in Antrim and Galway. In the United States Hughes is the 88th most numerous surname with an estimated 253,000 bearers, and Hayes is the 100th most numerous surname with an estimated 228,250 bearers. In England and Wales in 1996 Hughes was the 18th most numerous surname, and Hayes the 141st most numerous surname. In Scotland in 1995 Hughes was the 65th most numerous surname.

O'Hea, see immediately above

Healy, ó hEalaighthe, ó hEalaithe, ó hEilidhe
A Gaelic surname meaning descendant of *Ealadhach* meaning 'artistic, scientific'. The anglicisation is sometimes Healihy. A sept of

110

Donoughmore, in the barony of Muskerry in Cork. Also an anglicised form of *ó hEilidhe*. Also meaning descendant of *Ealadhach*, a sept from Sligo, whose territory consisted of the Curlews, Ballinafad, and the district lying around the western shore of Lough Arrow and had their chief residence at Baile Uí Eilidhe (Ballyhely). Healy was the forty-eight most numerous name in Ireland in 1890; the estimated number of bearers was 13,000, and the surname was principally to be found in Cork, Kerry, Dublin, Galway, Roscommon and Mayo. In the United States Healy is the 1,735th most numerous surname with an estimated 19,250 bearers, and Healey is the 3,466th most numerous surname with an estimated 11,000 bearers.

Heaney ó hEíghnigh
A Gaelic suname: descendants of *Eigneach* perhaps from *écen* 'force'. A sept of Oriel (Oirgialla) who were Lords of Fermanagh in the eleventh and twelfth centuries. A sept of who were chiefs of Clann Chearnaigh in east Armagh. A sept who were chiefs of Clann Laoghaire in Tirawley in Mayo. A sept who were erenaghs (airchinnigh) of Banagher in Derry. In 1890 Heaney was principally found in Antrim, Armagh and Louth, and the estimated number of bearers was 2,510. In the United States Heaney is the 9,021st most numerous surname with an estimated 2,750 bearers.

Heffernan, ó Ifearnáin
A Gaelic surname meaning descendant of *Ifearnán*. A sept who were chiefs of Uaithne-Cliach, now the barony of Owneybeg in east Limerick. They were dispossessed by the O'Mulryans in the fourteenth century. In 1890 Heffernan was principally found in Tipperary, and the estimated number of bearers was 2,370. In the United States Heffernan is the 5,820th most numerous surname with an estimated 5,500 bearers.

O'Hegarty, ó hEigceartaigh
A Gaelic surname meaning descendant from *éigceartach* meaning 'unjust'. A sept of the Cineál Eoghain. A sept of the Eóganacht in Carbery in Cork. In 1890 Hegarty was principally found in Cork, Donegal, Clare, Derry and Mayo and the estimated number of bearers was 4,480 (including variants). In the United States Hegarty is the 9,960th most numerous surname with an estimated 2,750 bearers.

Henderson
A Scotish surname meaning son of Henry, their being many septs and families bearing the surname. A small sept held lands in Upper Liddesdale in the Borders. The chief lowland family of the surname were of Fordell in Fifeshire. A branch of the Clan Gunn bears the surname, they are believed to be descendant of Henry, the younger son of George Gunn, a chief of the clan in the fifteenth century. The MacEanruig (anglicised Henderson) of Glencoe are probably descended from Dughall who lived in the early part of the fourteenth century. In 1890 Henderson was principally found in Antrim and

Tyrone, and the estimated number of bearers was 3,225. In the United States it is the 81st most numerous surname with an estimated 261,250 bearers. In England and Wales in 1996 it was the 177th most numerous surname. In Scotland in 1995 it was the 27th most numerous surname.

Henehan, Heneghan, ó hEineacháin
A Gaelic surname meaning descendant of *Eidhneachán*. A sept of the Ui Fiachrach, who were formerly seated in the parishes of Manulla and Balla in Mayo. *ó hEanacháin* is a variant. Somtimes anglicised Bird, being erroneously supposed to be derived from *ean* meaning a 'bird'. In 1890 the surname was principally found in Mayo and the estimated number of bearers was 2,200.

Hennessy, ó hAonghusa
A Gaelic surname meaning descendant of *Aonghus*, *Aonghus* a variant of *óengus* was the young god of Irish tradition. A sept who were lords of Clann Cholgan, a district co-extensive with the barony of Lower Philipstown in Offaly. A sept who were lords of Ui Mac Uais in the barony of Moyfenrath in Meath. A sept who were chiefs of Gailenga Beaga, in Meath/North Dublin. A sept of Dál Cais in Thuas Mhumhan (Thomand). A sept of Moyfenrath (Meath Westmeath). Anglicised as O'Hennessy and sometimes Ennis. In 1890 Hennessey was principally found in Cork, Limerick, Tipperary and Dublin, and the estimated number of bearers was 4,300. In the United States Hennessey is the 4,497th most numerous surname with an estimated 8,250 bearers, Hennessy was the 5,161st most numerous surname with an estimated 5,500 bearers.

Henry, Fitzhenry, ó hInneirghe, Mac hAonraoi
A Gaelic surname meaning descendant of *Inneirghe* meaning 'early riser'. A sept of the Cineál Eoghain who were chiefs of Cuileanntrach in Tyrone. In its anglicised form difficult to distinguish from *Mac hAnraoi*, meaning son of Henry. Henry was a numerous personal name amongst the Norman settlers in Ireland, accordingly there is a Fitzhenry family in Wexford. Meiler and Robert who landed at Bannow in 1169 were grandsons of King Henry I. The Fitzhenry's were made barons of Kilcavan, near Ballymitty in Wexford. Also a surname found in both England and Scotland. The personal name was introduced by the Normans, amongst whom it was very popular. Derived from the Old German *Haimirich*, compound of *haimi* 'house', 'home' and *ric* 'ruler'. Henry was numerous surname in the districts of Ayr and Fife in Scotland. In 1890 Henry was numerous in Sligo, it was also to be found in Antrim and Tyrone. The estimated number of bearers was 5,913 (including variants). In the United States Henry is the 133rd most numerous surname with an estimated 187,000 bearers. In England and Wales in 1996 Henry was the 374th most numerous surname.

112

(O')Herlihy, ó hIarlaithe
A Gaelic surname meaning descendant of *Iarlaithe* (which is anglicised Jarlath). An ecclesiastical sept who were hereditary erenaghs of St. Gobnait's church at Ballyvourney, in Cork. In 1890 the surname was principally found in Cork and Kerry, and the estimated number of bearers was 1,880.

Her(r)on, ó hEaráin
A Gaelic surname meaning descendant of *Earadhán* (diminutive of *earadh* meaning 'fear, dread'. A sept of Oriel who were lords of Ui Breasail Macha, in the Barony of Oneilland in Armagh. Also a Scottish surname such a family had lands in Kirkcudbrightshire (barony of Heron), *Mac Giolla Chearáin* has been so anglicised. The English surname Heron is derived from the Old English and was a nickname for a thin man with long legs. In 1890 the surname was principally found in Antrim, Donegal and Down, and the estimated number of bearers was 2,020.

Hewitt
An English surname: derived from a diminutive of Hugh; occassionally local in origin from residence in a clearing, from Old English *hiewett* meaning a 'cutting' where trees had been cut down. Also a Scottish surname from the former derivation. In 1890 the surname was principally found in Antrim, and Armagh, and the estimated number of bearers was 1,790. In England and Wales in 1996 it was the 236th most numerous surname.

Hickey, ó hIcídhe
A Gaelic surname meaning descendant of *Iceadh* meaning 'healer'. A sept of Dál Cais who were hereditary physicians to the O'Briens of Thuas Mhumhan (Thomond). They were seated at Ballyhickey in the parish of Clooney, Clare. In 1890 Hikey was principally found in Cork, Tipperary, Dublin, Limerick and Clare, and the estimated number of bearers was 5,900. In the United States it is the 1,173rd most numerous surname with an estimated 27,500 bearers.

Higgins, ó hUiginn
A Gaelic surname meaning descendant of *Uige*, meaning 'knowledge, skill, ingenuity'. A sept of the southern Uí Neill, in the present Westmeath, and one of the most distinguished literary families in Ireland. A branch settled in Sligo, where they acquired large estates in the parishes of Achonry and Kilmacteige which they retained down to the Cromwellian confiscations. In 1890 Higgins was the eighty-third most numerous surname and the estimated number of bearers was 9,100. In that year the surname was chiefly found in Mayo, Galway, Dublin, Roscommon, Cork, and Antrim. In the United States it is the 370th most numerous surname with an estimated 82,500 bearers. It is numerous in the states of Connecticut, Delaware, Maryland, Massachusetts, New Jersey, New York, Pennsylvania. In England and Wales in 1996 it was the 227th most numerous surname.

Hill, An Chnoic

An English surname derived from Old English *hyll*. 'Dweller on a hill'. In 1659 according to Petty, Hill was the principal surname of Antrim. In 1853 Hill was the twenty-fifth most numerous surname in England and Wales, and the estimated number of bearers was 52,200. In 1890 Hill was principally found in Antrim, Dublin and Down, and the estimated number of bearers was 5,280. In the United States it is the 33rd most numerous surname with an estimated 514,250 bearers. In England and Wales in 1996 it was the 30th most numerous surname. In Scotland in 1995 it was the 81st most numerous surname.

Hoare, le Hore, ó hUidhir

A surname of Cambro-Norman origin who settled in South Leinster as well as Cork and Kerry, *le Hore* meaning 'the hoary, greyish-white'. To be distinguished from *ó hUidhir*, from *Odhar* meaning 'dark-grey', a rare Cork sept. In 1890 Hoare was principally found in Kerry, Cork and Dublin, and the estimated number of bearers was 1,340.

Hoey, ó hEochaidh

A sept in Ulster who were subdued by the Mac Dunleavys. A sept of Meath. In 1890 Hoey was principally found in Louth and Dublin, and the estimated number of bearers was 1,480.

Hogan, ó hOgáin

A Gaelic surname meaning descendant of *ógán*, diminutive of *óg* meaning 'young'. A sept of the Dál gCais who derived their descent from *Cosrach*, uncle of Brian Boru. They were seated at Ardcrony, about four miles to the north of Nenagh in Tipperary. A sept of the Corcu Loíghdhe in south-west Cork. In 1890 it was the ninety-first most numerous surname, the estimated number of bearers was 8,600 and was chiefly found in Cork (40 births) and Kerry (21 births). In the United States it is the 489th most numerous surname with an estimated 66,000 bearers.

Holland

An English surname of local origin. From Holland in Essex, Lancashire and Lincoln. In 1890 Holland was principally found in Cork, Galway and Dublin, and the estimated number of bearers was 2,330. In the United States it is the 256th most numerous surname with an estimated 115,500 bearers. In England and Wales in 1996 it was the 160th most numerous surname.

Holmes

An English surname of local origin from Holme in Dorset and Yorkshire (West Riding). From the Old Norse *holmr* meaning 'residence near a piece of flat land in a fen' or 'by a piece of land partly surrounded by streams'. A Scottish surname of local origin, from Holmes near Dundonald in Kyle Stewart and in the Barony of Inchestuir. In 1890 Holmes was principally found in Antrim and Dublin, and the estimated number of bearers was 3,765. In the United

States it is the 145th most numerous surname with an estimated 178,750 bearers. In England and Wales in 1996 it was the 87th most numerous surname.

Hopkins, Hobkin(s), Mac Oibicín
An English surname *hobbe-kin*, a diminutive of Hobb (Robert). Woulfe lists *Mac Oibicín*, with a similar derivation, often pronounced *ó Coibicín* as a Mayo surname. In 1890 the surname was principally found in Mayo and Dublin, and the estimated number of bearers was 1,970. In the United States it is the 263rd most numerous surname with an estimated 112,750 bearers. In England and Wales in 1996 it was the 199th most numerous surname.

Horan, ó hOdhráin
A sept of north Connacht, from descendant of *Odhrán* diminutive of *odhar* perhaps meaning 'dark, sallow, grey-brown'. In 1890 Horan was principally found in Mayo, Kerry, Tipperary and Roscommon, and the estimated number of bearers was 2,820. In the United States it is the 4,072nd most numerous surname with an estimated 8,250 bearers. In the United States it is the 4,072nd most numerous surname with an estimated 8,250 bearers.

Horgan, ó hArgáin
A sept of Cork. There are many similar surnames. In 1890 Horgan was principally found in Cork and Kerry, and the estimated number of bearers was 2,960. In the United States it is the 9,120th most numerous surname with an estimated 2,750 bearers.

Houlihan, Holohan, ó hUallacháin
A Gaelic surname meaning descendant of *Uallachán* diminutive of *uallach* meaning 'proud, arrogant'. There were several septs in Thomand, Cork and Offaly. In 1890 Houlihan was principally found in Kerry, Limerick, Cork and Clare, Holohan in Kilkenny, and the estimated number of bearers was 3,180 (all variants). In the United States it is the 8,190th most numerous surname with an estimated 2,750 bearers.

Houston, Huston, MacGiollatSeachlainn
A Scottish surname of territorial origin from the barony of the name in Lanarkshire. May also mean son of hutchin, a diminutive of Hugh, probably a branch of the MacDonnells. In the Stranorlar area of Donegal sometimes a synonym of *MacGiollatSeachlainn*, or *Mac an Teachlainn*, MacTaghlin. Also see Hutchinson. In 1890 the estimated number of bearers was 3,400 and was principally found in Antrim, Derry, Armagh and Down.

Howard, ó hIomhair
An English surname from the Norman personal name *Huard*, *Heward*, perhaps meaning 'hardy, brave, strong', also from the Anglo-Scandinavian personal name *Haward* perhaps meaning 'high

guardian'. The surname borne by the Dukes of Norfolk. A Gaelic sept of Thomond meaning descendant of *Iomhar* (from the Norse personal name *Ivarr*). In 1890 Howard was principally found in Dublin, Cork, Clare and Limerick, and the estimated number of bearers was 2,730. In the United States it is the 65th most numerous surname with an estimated 302,500 bearers. In England and Wales in 1996 it was the 108th most numerous surname.

McHugh, MacAodha
A Gaelic surname meaning son of *Aodh* meaning 'fire'. A sept who were a branch of the *ó Flaithbheartaigh* (O'Flaherty) and who were chiefs of Clann Choscraigh in the barony of Clare in Galway. According to MacLysaght there was also a sept near Tuam in Galway. In 1890 McHugh was numerous in Mayo, Fermanagh and Leitrim, it was also to be found in Donegal and Galway. The estimated number of bearers was 7,884. In the United States it is the 2,244th most numerous surname with an estimated 16,500 bearers.

Hughes, see Hayes

Hunt
An English surname from the Old English *hunta* meaning 'hunter, huntsman'. MacLysaght suggests that in Connacht that Hunt is used by pseudo-translation for several Irish surnames: Feighney, Feighry and Fey. In 1890 Hunt was principally found in Mayo, Roscommon, Dublin and Waterford, and the estimated number of bearers was 3,400. In the United States it is the 148th most numerous surname with an estimated 173,250 bearers. In England and Wales in 1996 it was the 81st most numerous surname.

Hunter
An English, Irish and Scottish surname. The English surname derived from *hunta* meaning 'to hunt, huntsman'. The Scottish surname of similar derivation. The oldest family of the surname was to be found in Hunterston in Ayrshire. Mac Giolla-Domhnaigh states that in Ulster the surname is the anglicised form of *Mac Fhiachra*, a sept of the Cineál Eoghain, who were anciently chiefs of Cinel Fearadhaigh, in the Barony of Clogher in Tyrone (such surname more usually anglicised as MacKeighry, or MacKeefrey, or MacKeary). In 1890 Hunter was principally found in Antrim, Derry and Down, and the estimated number of bearers was 4,255. In the United States it is the 130th most numerous surname with an estimated 189,750 bearers. In England and Wales in 1996 it was the 147th most numerous surname. In Scotland in 1995 it was the 37th most numerous surname.

Hurley, ó Murthuile, ó Muirthil
A Gaelic surname meaning descendant of *Murthuile*, meaning 'sea tide'. A sept of west Cork. Also an *ó Muirrthaile* sept among the Fir Sceinde of Connacht. In its anglicised form difficult to distinguish from *ó hUrthuile* of Knocklong in Limerick. In 1890 Hurley was

116

numerous in Cork (86 births), it was also to be found in Waterford, Dublin and Galway. The estimated number of bearers was 6,003. In the United States it is the 807th most numerous surname with an estimated 41,250 bearers. It is numerous in the states of Delaware, and Massachusetts.

Hutchinson, Hutchison
A Scottish surname derived from Hutcheon, a diminutive of Hugh. The name can be consfused with both Houston (see above) and MacCutcheon (A branch of the Scottish Clan MacDonald). In 1890 Hutchinson was principally found in Derry, Antrim, Down and Dublin, and the estimated number of bearers was 2,870 (all variants). In the United States Hutchinson is the 602nd most numerous surname with an estimated 55,000 bearers. In England and Wales in 1996 Hutchinson was the 220th most numerous surname.

Hyland, ó hAoláin
A Gaelic surname ; descendant of *Faolán*, diminutive of *Faol* meaning 'wolf'. A variation of *ó Faoláin* (See Phelan and Whelan below). In this anglicisation it was common in Laois Offaly, from whence it spread to other parts. In Connacht it is sometimes corrupted to Holland. In 1890 Hyland was principally found in Mayo, Dublin and Laois, and the estimated number of bearers was 2,465. In the United States it is the 4,445th most numerous surname with an estimated 8,250 bearers.

Hynes, ó hEidhin
A Gaelic surname meaning descendant of *Eidhean* meaning 'ivy'. A sept who were chiefs of Uí Fiachrach Aidhne and lords of Aidhne, a district co-extensive with the diocese of Kilmacduagh in Galway. There was also a sept in the neighbourhood of Caherconlish in Limerick. There is an English surname (sometimes Hines) derived from the Middle English *hine* meaning 'hind, servant'. In 1890 Hynes was principally found in Galway, Clare, Mayo and Dublin, and the estimated number of bearers was 3,720.

McIlroy, McElroy, Gilroy, Mac Giolla Ruaidh
A Gaelic surname meaning son of *Giolla ruadh* meaning 'red (haired) youth'. A sept of Fermanagh whose chief resided at Ballymackilroy, in the parish of Aghalurchur near Lough Erne. Also a Scottish surname of similar derivation from the parish of Ballantrae in Ayrshire. It is also anglicised Gilroy which surname was principally found in Leitrim and Mayo in 1890 (estimated bearers 720). In 1890 McIlroy was principally found in Antrim, Down, Fermanagh and Derry, and the estimated number of bearers was 3,540 (all variants). In the United States Gilroy is the 8,390th most numerous surname with an estimated 2,750 bearers.

McInerney, Mac an Airchinnigh
A Gaelic surname meaning 'son of the erenagh'. A sept of

Roscommon, a branch of the *ó Branáin* who were erenagh of St. Patrick's church at Elphin. A sept of Thuas Mhumhan (Thomand) who were based in the parish of Ballysally. In 1890 McInerney was numerous in Clare, it was also to be found in Limerick, and the estimated number of bearers was 2,867 (including variants). In the United States it is the 8,906th most numerous surname with an estimated 2,750 bearers.

McIntyre, MacAteer, Mac an tSaoir
A Gaelic surname both Irish and Scots, meaning son of the craftsman (from *saor* meaning 'mason, carpenter'). There may have been several Ulster septs, there is a Ballymacateer in Armagh. The Scottish sept was from Glenoe, near Bunawee, Nether Lorn, Argyllshire. In 1890 McIntyre was principally found in Derry, Antrim and Sligo, and the estimated number of bearers was 2,600. In the United States McIntire is the 3,160th most numerous surname with an estimated 11,000 bearers. In Scotland in 1995 McIntyre was the 94th most numerous surname.

Irvine
A Scottish surname of territorial origin. From Irving the name of an old parish in Dumfriesshire and from Irvine in Ayrshire. In 1890 Irvine was numerous in Fermanagh, it was also to be found in Antrim. The estimated number of bearers was 3,046.

Irwin, Erwin
An English surname from the Old English *Eoforwine* meaning 'boar-friend'. This surname is often confused with Irvine. In 1890 Irwin was principally found in Armagh, Antrim, Tyrone and Derry, and the estimated number of bearers was 5,280. In the United States Irwin is the 939th most numerous surname with an estimated 5,500 bearers.

Jackson
An English surname meaning 'son of James' James being *Jacubus* in Latin and *Jacques* in French. It was the twenty-fourth most numerous surname in England and Wales in 1853. In 1890 Jackson was scattered but chiefly found in Antrim, Armagh and Dublin and also in Cork and Mayo. The estimated number of bearers was 4,520. In the United States it is the 13th most numerous surname with an estimated 852,250 bearers. In England and Wales in 1996 Jackson was the 25th most numerous surname.

Jamison, Jameson, Jamieson, Mac Shéamuis
A Scottish surname meaning son of James. A sept of Clan Gunn. A sept of Clan Stuart of Bute. In 1890 Jamison and Jamieson were principally found in Antrim and Down, and Jameson in Dublin, the estimated number of bearers was 2,330 for all variants. In Scotland in 1995 Jamieson was the 96th most numerous surname.

118

Jennings, Mac Sheóinín

A surname of Norman origin meaning son of *Jonin*, a diminutive of John. The surname was adopted by a branch of the Burkes in Connacht. There is also an English surname of similar derivation. In 1890 Jennings was principally found in Mayo, Galway, Cork and Armagh, and the estimated number of bearers was 2,820.

Johnson

Both an English and a Scottish surnsame meaning son of John. See also below. In 1853 it was the tenth most numerous surname in England and Wales and the estimated number of bearers was 69,500. In Ireland in 1890 Johnson was a scattered surname which was principally found in Cork, Dublin, and Antrim, and the estimated number of bearers was 2,600. In the United States Johnson is the 2nd most numerous surname with an estimated 2,227,500 bearers. In England and Wales in 1996 it was the 10th most numerous surname.

Johnston, Johnstone

A Scottish surname derived from a place name Johnstone in Dumfries. An English surname derived from a place name Johnson Hall in Staffordshire or meaning 'son of John'. In 1890 Johnston was the thirty-third most numerous surname, the estimated number of bearers was 15,200 and was principally found in Antrim, Down, Fermanagh, Armagh and Dublin and Johnstone was principally found in Cavan and Derry. In the United States Johnston is the 214th most numerous surname with an estimated 134,750 bearers. In England and Wales in 1996 it was the 214th most numerous surname. In Scotland in 1995 Johnston was the 28th most numerous surname, and Johnstone was the 64th most numerous surname.

Jones

An English and Welsh surname from the Latin *Johannes*, John, which by the fourteenth century rivalled William as the most numerous personal name. In 1853 it was the second most numerous surname in England and Wales. In 1890 Jones was principally found in Dublin, Cork, Antrim and Armagh, and the estimated number of bearers was 6,800. In the United States it is the 4th most numerous surname with an estimated 1,707,750 bearers. In England and Wales in 1996 it was the 2nd most numerous surname. In Scotland in 1995 it was the 59th most numerous surname.

Jordan, MacShiúrtáin

A surname of Norman origin meaning son of Jordan, assumed by the descendants of Jordan D'Exeter who settled in Mayo. In 1890 Jordan was principally found in Dublin, Mayo, Antrim and Galway, and the estimated number of bearers was 4,070. In the United States it is the 110th most numerous surname with an estimated 214,500 bearers. In England and Wales in 1996 it was the 219th most numerous surname.

Joyce, Seóigh
A surname of Welsh origin meaning 'son of joy'. The family became completly hibernicized and acquired territory in the mountainous district of Iar-Connacht called Duthaigh Seoghach (Joyce Country) now the barony of Ross in Galway. They also became one of the 'Tribes of Galway'. In 1890 Joyce was numerous in Galway and Mayo. The estimated number of bearers was 7,347. In the United States it is the 748th most numerous surname with an estimated 44,000 bearers. In England and Wales in 1996 it was the 397th most numerous surname.

Judge, Breheny, Mac an Breitheamhnaigh
A Gaelic surname meaning son of the judge. A surname found in Connacht and West Ulster, whose bearers would have been descendants of the brehon families. It is also anglicised as Breheny, which in 1890 was principally found in Roscommon and Sligo, and the estimated number of bearers being 720. In 1890 Judge was principally found in Mayo, Dublin and Tyrone, and the estimated number of bearers was 1,340.

O'Kane, Ó Catháin
A Gaelic surname meaning descendant of *Cathán*, which personal name is derived from *cath* 'a battle' perhaps meaning 'battler'. A sept of the Cineál Eoghain, who were the leading sept of Keenaght in Derry. They were dispossessed during the Plantation of Ulster. A sept of the Uí Fiachrach in Galway. In 1890 Kane was the seventy-second most numerous surname, the estimated number of bearers was 9,700 and the surname was chiefly found in Antrim, Derry and Dublin. In the United States Kane is the 746th most numerous surname with an estimated 44,000 bearers. It is numerous in the states of Delaware, New Jersey, New York, and Pennsylvania.

Kangley, see **Tighe**

Kavanagh, Caomhánach
A Gaelic surname whose bearers derive their descent from *Domhnall Caomhánach*, the son of *Diarmuid Mac Murchadha*. It is one of the few Gaelic surname without the 'Ó'. The chief of the sept was known as *Mac Murchadha Caomhánach*. The personal name *Murchadh* meant 'sea-warrior' and *Caomhánach*, meant 'comely, mild'. The leading sept of Leinster. Kavanagh was the fifty-third most numerous name in Ireland in 1890 and the estimated number of bearers was 12,200. In that year the surname was chiefly found in Dublin, Wexford and Wicklow. In the United States Kavanagh is the 7,087th most numerous surname with an estimated 5,500 bearers, and Kavanaugh is the 7,325th most numerous surname with an estimated 5,500 bearers.

McKay, MacAoidh
A Scottish surname derived from the Gaelic meaning son of *Aodh*

120

(Hugh). There appears to be two families of the name from : Moray in the north, and from Invernessshire (*Mac Ai*). Also see: McCoy, McHugh, and Keys. In 1890 the surname was principally found in Antrim, and the estimated number of bearers was 2,870. In the United States it is the 849th most numerous surname with an estimated 38,500 bearers. In Scotland in 1995 Mackay was the 42nd most numerous surname, and McKay was the 83rd most numerous surname.

McKee,
A Scottish surname a variant of McKay (see immediately above). In 1890 the surname was principally found in Antrim, Down and Armagh, and the estimated number of bearers was 4,300. In the United States it is the 699th most numerous surname with an estimated 46,750 bearers.

Keane, Mac Cahan(e), ó Céin
Keane is an anglicisation of two Gaelic surnames. *ó Céin* meaning descendant of *Cian*, which personal name meant 'ancient, enduring'. A sept who were chiefs of a district bordering the river mahon in Waterford. A sept in Derry, difficult to distinguish from *ó Catháin*. *Mac Catháin* meaning son of *Cathán*, which means 'battler'. A sept of Clare who were co-arbs of St. Senan at Inis Cathaigh. In 1890 Keane was the eighty-fifth most numerous surname, the estimated number of bearers was 9,000, and the surname was chiefly found in Galway, Clare, Kerry and Mayo. In the United States Kean is the 7,017th most numerous surname with an estimated 5,500 bearers.

Keany, ó Caoinnigh
A Gaelic surname meaning descendant of *Caoinneach* (a variant of *Coinneach*). In 1890 Keany was numerous in Leitrim, it was also to be found in Galway and Donegal. The estimated number of bearers was 1,478 (including variants).

Kearney, Carney, ó Cearnaigh
A Gaelic surname meaning descendant of *Cearnach* meaning 'victorious'. A sept of Uí Fiachrach, who formerly held extensive possessions in the parishes of Moynulla and Balla in Mayo. A sept of the Dál Cais who migrated to Cashel. A sept who were erenaghs (airchinnigh) of Derry. In its anglicised form difficult to distinguish from *ó Ceithearnaigh*. In 1890 Kearney was principally found in Dublin, Cork and Antrim, and the estimated number of bearers was 6,585 (including variants); with respect to Carney there were twenty-one births in Mayo, eight in Ulster and seven in Leinster. The estimated number of bearers was 2,195. In the United States Kearney is the 1,750th most numerous surname with an estimated 19,250 bearers.

Kearns, Kiernan, ó Ciaráin
A Gaelic surname meaning descendant of *Ciarán* diminutive of *ciar*

meaning 'black'. A sept who were lords of Fearmhaigh, Tir Connell, Donegal. A sept who were originally seated in the barony of Imokilly in Cork. See also *ó Céirín*. In 1890 Kearns was principally found in Dublin and Mayo, and the estimated number of bearers was 3,900. In the United States Kerns is the 1,771st most numerous surname with an estimated 19,250 bearers.

Keating
A surname of Cambro-Norman origin whose original settlement was in South Leinster. In 1890 Keating was principally found in Cork, Kerry, Tipperary and Dublin, and the estimated number of bearers was 5,820 (including variants). In the United States it is the 2,420th most numerous surname with an estimated 13,750 bearers.

Keaveny, Mac Géibheannaigh, ó Géibheannaigh
Mac Géibheannaigh, from *Géibheannach* meaning 'fettered, prisoner' originally a sept of Fermanagh. *ó Géibheannaigh* from the same, a sept of the Uí Mhaine in Galway. In 1890 Keaveny was principally found in Galway and Sligo, and the estimated number of bearers was 1,480.

O'Keeffe, ó Caoimh
A Gaelic surname meaning descendant of *Caomh*, which personal name meant 'gentle'. A sept of Munster, who derive their descent from *Art Caomh* who was son of *Fionghuine*, King of Munster in the tenth century. They are of the same stock as the *Mac Carthaigh* and the *ó Ceallacháin*. *Donnchadh* the first to bear the surname lived in the reign of *Ceallachán* of Cashel. They were originally seated at Glanworth and possessed the district now called Roches' Country, in the barony of Fermoy. They were driven from their territory by the Cambro-Norman invaders and settled in a district in the north-west of the barony of Duhallow, to which they gave the name Pobul Uí Chaoimh. In 1890 O'Keeffe was the ninety-second most numerous surname, the estimated number of bearers was 8,600, and in that year the surname was chiefly found in Cork, Waterford, Kerry and Kilkenny. In the United States O'Kefe is the 2,499th most numerous surname with an estimated 13,750 bearers, and numerous in the state of Massachusetts.

Keegan, MacAodhagáin
A Gaelic sept meaning son of *Aodhagán*, diminutive of *Aodh*. A sept of Uí Maine who were brehons. In the fourteenth and fifteenth centuries they settled in Ormond and Desmond. Also see Egan. In 1890 Keegan was principally found in Dublin, Roscommon, Wicklow and Leitrim, and the estimated number of bearers was 4,250. In the United States it is the 3,631st most numerous surname with an estimated 8,250 bearers.

Keenan, ó Cianáin
A Gaelic surname meaning descendant of *Cianáin* diminutive of

Cian meaning 'ancient, enduring'. A sept of Ulster who were hereditary historians to the Maguires. In 1890 Keenan was principally found in Antrim, Monaghan, Dublin and Down, and the estimated number of bearers was 4,610.

McKeever, Mac Íomhair

An Irish and a Scottish surname, derived from *Ivarr* (a Scandinavian personal name). MacLysaght suggests *Mac éimhir* a sept of Oriel who were a branch of the Mac Mahons. In 1890 McKeever was principally found in Derry and Antrim, and the estimated number of bearers was 1,520. In the United States Keever is the 9,550th most numerous surname with an estimated 2,750 bearers.

Kehoe, see Keogh

Kelleher. Kelliher, ó Céileachair

A Gaelic surname meaning descendant of *Céileachar* (companion-dear, spouse-loving). A sept of Dál Cais (being descendant of Donnchuan, brother of Brian Boru). In 1890 Kelleher was numerous in Cork (92 births), it was also to be found in Kerry. The estimated number of bearers for Kelleher was 4,121, and for Kelliher was 1,075.

O'Kelly, ó Ceallaigh

A Gaelic surname meaning descendant of *Ceallach*, which personal name meant 'bright-headed'. The personal name could be male or female, however it was more common as a male name. A sept of Uí Mhaine, a branch of the Oirghialla of Ulster, they were a most powerful family in Connacht and ruled over an extensive territory in Galway and Roscommon. A sept who were lords of Breagh, an extensive district comprising a large part of Meath and north Dublin, they were a branch of the southern Uí Néill. A sept of Cineál Eachach in the barony of Loughinsholin now part of Derry. A sept of Leighe now Lea in Laois. A sept of Magh Drúchtain in Laois. A sept of Gallen in Laois. A sept of Uí Théigh in the north of the present Wicklow. A sept of Ard ó gCeallaigh in the parish of Templeboy in Sligo. A sept of Corcu Lóighdhe in south-west Cork. In 1890 Kelly was the second most numerous name in Ireland; the estimated number of bearers was 55,900, and it was the most numerous surname in Galway, Kildare, Offaly and Leitrim. In that year the surname was found in every County in Ireland. It was chiefly found in Dublin, Galway, Mayo, Roscommon and Cork. In the United States Kelly is the 74th most numerous surname with an estimated 280,500 bearers, Kelley is the 198th most numerous surname wth an estimated 143,000 bearers, and O'Kelley is the 7,187th most numerous surname with an estimated 5,500 bearers. It is numerous in the state of New York. In England and Wales in 1996 Kelly was the 52nd most numerous surname. In Scotland in 1995 Kelly was the 38th most numerous surname.

MacKenna, Mac Cionaoith
A Gaelic surname meaning son of *Cionaodh*, which personal name
meant 'fire-sprung'. A sept of the southern Uí Neill, who were chiefs
of the barony of Trough in the north of Monaghan. A sept in
Roscommon who were followers of ó Conchobhair. The name is
corrupted to *Mag Cineáith* in Kerry Cork and Limerick. In 1890
McKenna was the eighty-eight most numerous surname and the
estimated number of bearers was 9,000. In that year the surname was
chiefly found in Antrim, Monaghan, Tyrone, Kerry, Armagh, Dublin
and Louth. Kenna was principally found in Dublin and Tipperary
(estimated bearers 940). In the United States it is the 1,603rd most
numerous surname with an estimated 22,000 bearers.

Kennelly, Kenneally, Quinnelly, ó Cinnfhaolaidh
A Gaelic surname derived from *Ceannfhaoladh* meaning 'wolf-head,
or learned man'. A sept of the Ui Fidhgheinte, who were seated in Ui
Conaill Gabhra, now the baronies of Upper and Lower Connello in
Limerick, until dispossessed by the Camro-Normans. See also
Conneelly. In 1890 the surname was principally found in Cork,
Waterford and Tipperary, and the estimated number of bearers was
1,610.

O'Kennedy, ó Cinnéide
A Gaelic surname meaning descendant of *Cinnéide*. The personal
name *Cinnéide*, means 'rough-headed, helmeted-head'. In early
Ireland this name was found in the south. It was borne by the father of
Brian Boru. A sept of the Dál gCais, who derive their name and
descent from Cinnéide, son of Donnchuán a brother of Brian Boru.
They were originally seated at Glenomra, co-extensive with the present
parish of Killokennedy in east Clare. They were driven by the *ó
Briain* and *MacConmara* out of Clare and settled in north Tipperary,
in the baronies of Upper and Lower Ormond and became lords of
Ormond (Ur Mhumhan). They divided into three sub-septs ;
ó Cinnéide Fionn (the Fair), *ó Cinneide Donn* (the Brown), *ó
Cinneide Ruadh* (the Red). A sept of the Clann Cearnaigh, a branch of
the Uí Mhaine in Galway. Kennedy is also a Scottish name, which was
found in Galloway from the twelfth century. The name would have
spread to east Ulster both during and prior to the Plantation.
O'Kennedy was the sixteenth most numerous name in Ireland in
1890, the estimated number of bearers was 19,900, and the surname
was to be found in every county in Ireland. The largest numbers were
to be found in Tipperary, Dublin and Antrim. In the United States
Kennedy is the 137th most numerous surname with an estimated
184,250 bearers. In England and Wales in 1996 it was the 168th most
numerous surname. In Scotland in 1995 it was the 58th most
numerous surname.

Kenny, ó Cionaoith
A Gaelic surname meaning descendant of *Cionaodh*, which personal
name perhaps meant 'fire-sprung'. A sept of the southern Uí Neill

who were chiefs of the barony of Trough in Monaghan. A sept of Uí Mhaine who were followers of *ó Conchobhair*. Kenny was the seventy-sixth most numerous name in 1890, the estimated number of bearers was 9,600 and the surname was chiefly found in Dublin, Galway and Roscommon. In the United States it is the 1,799th most numerous surname with an estimated 19,250 bearers. Kenney is numerous in the states of Massachusetts.

(Mac)Keogh, Kehoe, MacEochadha, Mac Eochaidh,
A Gaelic surname meaning son of *Eochaidh* meaning perhaps 'horse rider or fighter on horseback'. *Mac Eothach* son of Eochaidh is a variant. A sept of Leinster who were hereditary bards to the O'Byrnes. A sept who were chiefs of Moyfinn in the barony of Athlone, Roscommon, they were a branch of the O'Kellys of Uí Maine. A sept who were anciently chiefs of Moylurg, now the barony of Boyle in Roscommon, they were dispossessed by the MacDermotts. A sept who were anciently chiefs of Owney in Tipperary, they were dispossessed by the O'Mulryans. In 1890 Kehoe was principally found in Wexford and the estimated number of bearers was 2,284; Keogh was principally found in Dublin and the estimated number of bearers was 4,300.

McKeown, McKeon, McKeone, Mac Eoghain, Mac Eóin
A Gaelic surname meaning son of *Eoghan* (born of the yew). A sept of Sligo. In its anglicised form difficult to distinguish from *Mac Eóin*, meaning son of John. A surname adopted by a branch of the Scottish Bissett who settled in the Glens of Antrim during the thirteenth century. Also see Owens. In 1890 McKeown was principally to be found in Antrim, Armagh, Down, Derry and Louth, and the estimated number of bearers was 5,300. McKeon and McKeone was principally to be found in Leitrim and Louth, and the estimated number of bearers was 1,800 and 500. A total of 7,840 bearers including variants. Keon and Keown was principally found in Donegal, Down and Fermanagh (estimated bearers 806). In the United States Keown is the 9,435th most numerous surname with an estimated 2,750 bearers.

Kerr
A Scottish Border surname of local or territorial origin. The Lothian branch spells the name Kerr, and the Roxburgh branch Ker. Sometimes spelt as Carr (of which see above). In 1863 Kerr was the thirty-seventh most numerous surname in Scotland and the estimated number of bearers was 11,700. In 1890 Kerr was numerous in Antrim, it was also to be found in Down and Tyrone. The estimated number of bearers was 6,361. In the United States Kerr is the 721st most numerous surname with an estimated 44,000 bearers. In England and Wales in 1996 Kerr was the 403rd most numerous surname. In Scotland in 1995 Kerr was the 31st most numerous surname.

Kerrigan, ó Ciaragáin
A Gaelic surname meaning descendant of *Ciaragán* (diminutive of

ciar meaning 'black'). A sept of the Ui Fiachrach, formerly seated at Baile Ui Chiaragain (Ballykerrigan) in the parish of Balla in Mayo. In north Galway it is often translated as Comber and Comer, from its supposed connection with *cíor* meaning a 'comb'. In 1890 the surname was principally found in Mayo and Donegal, and the estimated number of bearers was 1,840. In the United States it is the 6,433rd most numerous surname with an estimated 5,500 bearers.

Keys, Keyes, Mac an Chaoich
May be of English, Irish, or Scottish origin. The Gaelic surname derived from *caoch* for 'a blind man'. A sept who were a branch of the O'Reillys of Cavan. Also see MacKay, and MacKee. In 1890 Keys was principally found in Fermanagh and Antrim, and Keyes was principally found in Tipperary and Wexford, and the estimated number of bearers was 1,430. In the United States Keys is the 1,333rd most numerous surname with an estimated 24,750 bearers, and Keyes was the 1,991st most numerous surname with an estimated 16,500 bearers.

Kiely, Keely, Kealy, Keily, Keeley
The anglicisation of a number of distinct septs : *ó Cadhla*, meaning descendant of Cadhla meaning 'beautiful, comely. graceful'. A sept of Connacht who were Chiefs in Connemara. A sept of Thomond who were Chiefs of Tuath Luimnigh near Limerick. *MacCaochlaoich*, meaning son of the blind hero. A sept of west Cork, translated as Keily, Kelly and Coakley (see above). *ó Caollaidhe*, meaning descendant of *Caollaidhe*, also written *ó Caollaighe*. A sept, who were Chiefs of Ui Bearchon in the present barony of Ida in Kilkenny. A sept of Laois who were Chiefs of Crioch O mBuidhe, in the present barony of Ballyadams. A sept of Tipperary who were Chiefs of Aolmhagh. In 1890 Kiely and Keily was principally found in Cork, Limerick and Waterford, Keely and Keeley was principally found in Dublin, Wicklow and Galway, and Kealy in Kilkenny. The estimated number of bearers for all variants was 4,920. In the United States Kiley is the 8,127th most numerous surname with an estimated 2,750 bearers.

Kiernan, Kieran, ó Ciaráin,
A Gaelic surname meaning descendant of *Ciarán* diminutive of *ciar* meaning 'black'. A sept who were lords of Fearmhaigh, Tir Connell, Donegal. A sept who were originally seated in the barony of Imokilly in Cork. Also see Mac Tiernan. In 1890 Kiernan was numerous in Longford, it was also to be found in Cavan, Dublin and Leitrim. The estimated number of bearers was 3,136 (including varients).

Killeen, Killen, ó Cillín
A Gaelic surname meaning descendant of Cillín (according to Woulfe a diminutive of *Ceallach* meaning 'war'). Little definitive information available on this surname. In 1890 Killeen was principally found in Clare, Mayo and Offaly, and the estimated number of bearers was

1,790. Killen was principally found in Antrim and the estimated number of bearers was 630. In the United States Killen is the 8,561st most numerous surname with an estimated 2,750 bearers.

King, ó Cingeadh, ó Cionga
A Gaelic surname meaning descendant of *Cingeadh* meaning 'valiant'. According to Woulfe this surname belonged to Westmeath, Offaly, Galway and Clare. A variant of the surname is *ó Cingeadh*. An English surname derived from a nickname indicating the possession of kingly qualities or appearance, or a pageant name, one who had acted as king in a play or pageant. In 1853 King was the thirty-sixth most common surname in England and Wales, with an estimated 42,300 bearers. In Ireland in 1890 King was the eighty-sixth most numerous surname and the estimated number of bearers was 9,000. In that year the surname was chiefly found in Galway, Dublin, Antrim, Mayo and Limerick. In the United States it is the 30th most numerous surname with an estimated 522,500 bearers. In England and Wales in 1996 it was the 36th most numerous surname. In Scotland in 1995 it was the 74th most numerous surname.

Kingston,
A surname of English origin derived from a placename. A family of this surname established itself in west Cork in the aftermath of the Cromwellian plantations. In 1890 the surname was principally found in Cork and Dublin, and the estimated number of bearers was 1,790.

Kinsella, Cinnsealach
A Gaelic surname, one of the few without the prefix ó or Mac, being taken from the clan name Uí Ceinnsealaigh which was a territory covering much of north Wexford and parts of southern Carlow and Wicklow. Cinnsealach from *ceann salach* meaning 'unclean head'. The sept took their name from Eanna Ceinnsealaigh fourth in descent from Cathair Mor, High-King of Ireland in the fourth century, they are descended from *Enna Cinnsealach* son of *Diarmaid* MacMurchadha, the King of Leinster who invited the Cambro-Normans to Ireland. In 1890 Kinsella was principally found in Dublin, Wexford, Wicklow and Kildare, and the estimated number of bearers was 3,620. In the United States Kinsella is the 7,966th most numerous surname with an estimated 2,750 bearers.

Kirby, ó Ciarmhaic, Mac Geirble
A Gaelic surname derived from *Ciarmhac* meaning 'black-son'. A sept who were anciently chiefs of Eoghanacht Aine, the district lying around Knockany in East Limerick until the time of the Cambro-Norman Invasion. In Mayo *Mac Geirble* from whom the townland of Carrowkeribly in the Parish of Attymas, is so called. In Connacht *ó Coirbín* may be so translated. In 1890 Kirby was principally found in Mayo, Kerry and Limerick, and the estimated number of bearers was 1,480.

Kirk
A Scottish surname of local origin, from residence near a church. Also see Quirke. In 1890 Kirk was principally found in Antrim and Louth, and the estimated number of bearers was 1,700. In the United States Kirk is the 526th most numerous surname with an estimated 60,500 bearers. In England and Wales in 1996 it was the 36th most numerous surname. In Scotland in 1995 it was the 74th most numerous surname.

Kirwan, Ó Ciardhubháin
A Gaelic surname meaning descendant of *Ciardubhán*, diminutive of *Ciardubh* meaning 'jet-black'. A sept of who were anciently erenaghs of Louth. A sept of Clare. One of the 'Tribes of Galway', they appear to have settled in Galway in the reign of Henry VI and from that time they made an important contribution to the city. In 1890 Kirwan was principally found in Dublin, Wexford and Tipperary, and the estimated number of bearers was 2,640. In the United States it is the 8,723rd most numerous surname with an estimated 2,750 bearers.

Kyne, see **Coyne**

Lacey, de Lacy, Leacy, Ó Laitheasa
A surname of Anglo-Norman origin. Families of this name were granted territory in Meath and in Limerick. The Gaelic sept *Ó Flaitheasa*, derived from *Flaith* meaning 'prince', subsequently *Ó Laitheasa* of Wexford is so anglicised. In 1890 Lacey was principally found in Wexford, Dublin and Galway, and the estimated number of bearers was 2,240 (all variants). In the United States Lacy is the 1,263rd most numerous surname with an estimated 27,500 bearers, and Lacey is the 1,682nd most numerous surname with an estimated 19,250 bearers.

Lally, Mullally, Ó Maolalaidh
A Gaelic surname meaning descendant of *Maolaladh* (speckled chief according to Woulfe). A sept of th Uí Mhaine, whose territory comprised the plain of Maonmhagh, lying around Loughrea. At the time of the Cambro-Norman invasion they were dispossessed by the Burkes, and settled at Tulach na dála (Tullaghnadaly, or Tolendal), four miles north of the town of Tuam in Galway. In 1890 Lally was principally found in Mayo and Galway, and the estimated number of bearers was 1,520. The estimated number of bearers for Mullally was 630. In the United States Lally is the 6,858th most numerous surname with an estimated 5,500 bearers.

Lamb, Lambe
An English surname from a nickname for the animal (meaning a meek and inoffensive person), or a shortened form of Lambert. In 1890 the surname was principally found in Dublin, and the estimated number of bearers was 2,240 (including variants). In the United States Lamb is the 477th most numerous surname with an estimated 66,000

In England and Wales in 1996 it was the 309th most numerous surname.

Lambert

An English surname from the Old French and Old German meaning 'land bright', a popular name from the twelfth century introduced from Flanders where St. Lambert of Maestricht was venerated. In 1890 Lambert was principally found in Wexford and Dublin, and the estimated number of bearers was 985. In the United States it is the 292nd most numerous surname with an estimated 101,750 bearers. In England and Wales in 1996 it was the 245th most numerous surname.

Lane, see Lyons

Larkin, ó Lorcáin

A Gaelic surname derived from *lorc* meaning 'fierce'. A sept of Leinster who were seated in the Barony of Forth in Wexford, until dispossessed by the Normans. A sept of Oriel, who were described at different times as lord of Ui Niallain, Farney, and West Ui Breasail. A sept of the Ui Mhaine in Galway. A sept of Meath who were anciently lords of Caille Follamain. A sept of Tipperary who were erenagh of Lorrha. A sept of the Cineál Eoghain in Donegal. In 1890 Larkin was principally found in Dublin, Armagh, Galway and Tipperary, and the estimated number of bearers was 3,810. In the United States it is the 1,421st most numerous surname with an estimated 24,750 bearers.

MacLaughlin, Mac Lochlainn

A Gaelic surname meaning descendant of *Lochlainn*, which personal name probably meant 'Viking'. The sept was named for *Lochlainn* of whom it is said was killed by his own people in 1023. The leading sept of the Cineál Eoghain and of the northern Uí Néill until displaced by *ó Neill*. Their territory was Inishowen, the original territory of the Cineál Eoghain. The *Mac Lochlainn* provided eleven Kings of the Cineál Eoghain and two High Kings of Ireland between 1061 and 1241. In 1090 *Domhnall* established himself as High King and in 1149 *Muirchertagh* assumed the High Kingship. The last *Mac Lochlainn* King of Tír Eoghain was Domhnall who was killed at the Battle of Cam Eirghe by the combined forces of the *ó Neill* and *ó Domhnaill*. After their defeat by *ó Neill* in 1241 their power fell into decline and they were displaced as lords of Inishowen by the *ó Dochartaigh* who were a Cineál Chonaill sept. They are most numerous in the Inishowen peninsula of Donegal and the City of Derry. A branch settled in Mayo in the seventeenth century. A sept appears to have existed in Leitrim, who were followers of *ó Ruairc* (O'Rourke). In 1890, MacLaughlin was the twenty-first most numerous surname and the estimated number of bearers was 17,500, and the surname was principally found in Antrim, Donegal and Derry. The surname McLoughlin was chiefly found in Dublin and scattered throughout Ireland. In the United States McLaughlin is the 440th most numerous surname with an estimated 71,500 bearers. It is numerous in the states of Delaware, New Jersey, and Pennsylvania.

Lavelle, ó Maolfábhail
A Gaelic surname derived from *Maolfábhail* meaning 'fond of travel', a sept of West Connacht. There was also a sept of the Cineál Eoghain, who were chiefs of Carraig Brachaidh (Carrickabraghy) in north-west Inishowen, in Donegal. In this case anglicised as MacFall. In 1890 Lavelle was principally found in Mayo and Galway, and the estimated number of bearers was 1,700. In the United States it is the 7,266th most numerous surname with an estimated 5,500 bearers.

Lavery, ó Labhradha
A Gaelic surname; descendant of *Labhraidh* meaning 'speaker'. A sept of Down, Who were based at Mag rath, now Moira in the Barony of Lower Iveagh. There were at three branches;-*bán* 'white;-*ruadh* 'red'; and-*tréan* 'strong'. Branches migrated to Kilkenny and Galway. Also see Armstrong, and Lavery. In 1890 Lavery was principally found in Armagh, Antrim and Down, and the estimated number of bearers was 2,285. In the United States it is the 8,820th most numerous surname with an estimated 2,750 bearers.

Lavin, Lavan, ó Láimhín
A Gaelic surname a corruption of *ó Flaithimhín* a sept who were followers of MacDermottRoe in Roscommon. It is sometimes anglicised Hand. 1890 the surname was principally found in Mayo and Roscommon, and the estimated number of bearers was 1,880.

Lawless, Laighléis
An English surname derived from the Middle English *laweles* meaning 'an outlaw'. A family who came to Ireland at the time of the Cambro-Norman Invasion. A branch settled in Tirawley in Mayo. In 1890 the surname was principally found in Dublin and Galway, and the estimated number of bearers was 1,880. In the United States it is the 3,825th most numerous surname with an estimated 8,250 bearers.

Lawlor, Lawlor, Lawler, Lalor, ó Leathlobhair
A Gaelic surname meaning meaning *leath* half; *lobhar* sick person. One of the seven septs of Laois. In 1890, the estimated number of persons bearing the surname was 6,400, and the surname was principally to be found in Dublin, Laois, Wicklow and Wexford. In the United States Lawler is the 2,213th most numerous surname with an estimated 16,500 bearers, and Lawlor is the 6,480th most numerous surname with an estimated 5,500 bearers.

Leahy, ó Laochdha
A Gaelic surname meaning descendant of *Laochdha*, meaning 'heroic'. In 1890 Leahy was principally found in Cork, Kerry, Limerick and Tipperary, and the estimated number of bearers was 4,700 (including variants). In the United States it is the 3,528th most numerous surname with an estimated 8,250 bearers.

McLean, McClean, MacGiollaEoin

A Scottish surname meaning son of the servant of St. John. The Macleans came to Ulster as galloglasses. In 1890 the surname was principally found in Antrim and Derry and the estimated number of bearers for McClean was 2,420, and for McLean was 1,920, and was 4,750 (including all variants).

O'Leary, Ó Laoghaire, Ó Laoire

A Gaelic surname meaning descendant of *Laoghaire*, which personal name meant 'calf-herd'. A sept of the Corcu Loíghdhe, who were originally chiefs of the area around Rosscarberry in west Cork. At the time of the Cambro-Norman invasion they moved to the parish of Inchigeelagh, where they became lords under Mac Carthaigh (MacCarthy) of the area between there and Macroom. The chief of the sept resided at Carrignacurra, a mile east of Inchigeelagh. In 1890, (O')Leary was the sixty-second most numerous surname and the estimated number of bearers was 11,000. In that year the surname was chiefly found in Cork (93 births), Kerry (38 births) and Wexford (21 births). In the United States O'Leary is the 1,836th most numerous surname with an estimated 19,250 bearers, and Leary is the 1,914th most numerous surname with an estimated 19,250 bearers. It is numerous in the state of Massachusetts.

Leavy, Levy, Mac Con Shlíbhe,

A Gaelic surname meaning 'son of the hound of the mountains'. A sept of Anaghaile (Annaly). In 1890 Leavy was numerous in Westmeath, it was also to be found in Longford. The estimated number of bearers for was 1,388 (including variants). In the United States Levy is the 872nd most numerous surname with an estimated 38,500 bearers.

MacLeavy, see Livingston(e)

Lee, Ó Laoidhigh

A Gaelic surname meaning descendant of *Laoidheach* meaning 'songful, poetical'. A sept of Connacht who were chiefs of Ui Briuin Eola, they were erenaghs of Annadown, and hereditary physicians to the O'Flahertys. An English surname, a varient of Lea (also Leigh) from the many places so named meaning 'dweller by the wood or clearing'. In 1890 Lee was chiefly found in Antrim, Dublin, Galway and Limerick, and the estimated number of bearers was 5,370. In the United States it is the 24th most numerous surname with an estimated 605,000 bearers. In England and Wales in 1996 it was the 35th most numerous surname.

Leech

An English and an Irish surname. Derived from the Middle English *leche* for 'physician'. A similar derivation from the Gaelic *liaigh*. In Galway *ó Laoghógh* (more usually Logue) is so translated. In 1890 Leech was principally found in Dublin, and the estimated number of bearers was 1,570. In the United States Leach is the 686th most numerous surname with an estimated 46,750 bearers. In England and Wales in 1996 Leach was the 404th most numerous surname.

Lehane, ó Liatháin
A Gaelic surname derived from *liath* meaning 'grey'. The principal sept of the name was seated in Cork. In 1890 Lehane was principally found in Cork and the estimated number of bearers was 1,340.

Lennon, ó Luinín
This anglicised form may be the translation of a number of Gaelic surnames. An important sept of which was *ó Luinín* meaning descendant of *Luinín*, diminutive of *Lon*, meaning 'a blackbird'. A sept of Fermanagh who were erenaghs of Derryvullen. In 1890 Lennon was principally found in Dublin and Armagh and the estimated number of bearers was 4,610.

Leonard, Mac Giolla Fhinnéin, ó Leannáin
A Gaelic surname meaning son of *Giolla Fhinnín* meaning servant of St Finnian. A sept of the Cineál Chonaill, being descended from Giolla Finnein O'Muldory. Their territory was Muinntear Feodachain, on the borders of Fermanagh and Donegal, and their chief was sometimes styled Lord of Loch Erne. The anglicisation of this surname disguises its origin. Also *ó Leannáin* a Gaelic surname meaning descendant of *Leannán* (diminutive of *Leann*, a cloak or mantle). A surname adopted by a number of distinct septs:
A sept of Fermanagh who were an ecclesiastical family and erenaghs of Lisgoole near Enniskillen. A sept of Mayo who were a branch of the Uí Fiachrach from near Killala. A sept of Galway who were a branch of the Uí Mhaine. Also an English surname from the Old German *Leonhard* meaning 'lion bold'. St Leonard is the patron saint of captives, Richard the lion heart was captive of the Holy Roman Emperor. In 1890 Leonard was numerous in Sligo, it was also to be found in Dublin and Cork. The estimated number of bearers was 4,435. In the United States Leonard is the 324th most numerous surname with an estimated 93,500 bearers. In England and Wales in 1996 Leonard was the 500th most numerous surname.

Lewis
An English and Welsh surname, from the French *Louis*. In 1890 Lewis was principally found in Dublin, Antrim, Cork and Tipperary, and the estimated number of bearers was 2,285. In the United States it is the 23rd most numerous surname with an estimated 621,000 bearers. In England and Wales in 1996 it was the 21st most numerous surname.

Lindsay, Lindesay
An English surname from a place name, Lindsey in Lincs.. In 1890 Lindsay was chiefly found in Antrim, and the estimated number of bearers was 1,700. In the United States Lindsey is the 411th most numerous surname with an estimated 74,250 bearers, and Lindsay is

the 974th most numerous surname with an estimated 33,000 bearers.

Linehan, Lenaghan, Lenihan
A Gaelic surname septs of which include: *ó Léanacheain*, meaning descendant of *Léanacháin*, diminuative of *Léanach* meaning 'cloaked'. A sept of Roscommon. In 1890 Linehan was principally found in Cork, Lenaghan was principally found in Antrim, and Lenihan was principally found in Limerick. The estimated number of bearers for all variants was 4,660.

Little, Lyttle
An English surname from the Old English for 'little'. Also a Scottish surname, they occupied the lower part of Upper Eskdale and a portion of Ewesdale, in Dumfriesshire. The Gaelic *ó Beagáin* and *ó Bigin*, has been so anglicised (usually Beggan(e) in Monaghan, and Biggins in Mayo). In 1890 the surname was principally found in Antrim, Dublin and Fermanagh, and the estimated number of bearers was 2,645. In the United States Little is the 226th most numerous surname with an estimated 126,500 bearers. In England and Wales in 1996 it was the 356th most numerous surname.

Livingston, Livingstone, Levingston.
A Scottish surname of territorial origin from the parish in West Lothian. The MacLeavys, a small sept of the Stewarts of Appin sometimes so anglicised their surname. In 1890 the surname was principally found in Armagh, Antrim and Down, and the estimated number of bearers was 1,925. In the United States Livingston is the 715th most numerous surname with an estimated 46,750 bearers.

Loftus, ó Lachtnáin, ó Lachtna
This Gaelic surname derived from *lachtna* meaning 'grey'. A sept who were chiefs of the district called the Two Bacs and of Glen Nephin in the Barony of Tirawley in Mayo. To be distinguished from the English surname and similar translations. In 1890 Loftus was principally found in Mayo, and the estimated number of bearers was 1,520. In the United States it is the 4,850th most numerous surname with an estimated 5,500 bearers.

Logan
A Scottish surname derived from the placname Logan in Ayrshire. May also be the anglicisation of the Gaelic *ó Leocháin* a sept of Meath who were chiefs of Gailenga Móra and Luighne, now the Baronies of Morgallion and Lune, who were dispossessed about the time of the Cambro-Norman invasion. In 1890 Logan was principally found in Antrim, and the estimated number of bearers was 2,465.

Logue, see Leech

Lonergan, Londrigan, ó Longargáin
A Gaelic surname meaning descendant of *Longargán*, diminutive of

Lonn garg, meaning 'strong fierce'. A sept of the Dál gCais who were chiefs in the east of Thuas Mhumhan (Thomond) until after 1318, when they were driven out by the O'Brien and MacNamaras, and settled in Tipperary. The sept produced a number of distinguished ecclesiastics. In 1890 Lonergan was numerous in Tipperary, it was also to be found in Waterford, Kilkenny and Cork. The estimated number of bearers for Lonergan was 2,195, and for Londrigan was 224. In the United States Lonergan is the 9,537th most numerous surname with an estimated 2,750 bearers.

Long, ó Longaigh

The Gaelic surname *ó Longaigh*, derived from *long* for 'a ship, a camp'. A sept of Muskerry, they were an erenagh family based in the parish of Cannaway in Cork. An English surname either descriptive, or a nickname. Also of Norman origin: *de Long*. In 1890 Long was principally found in Cork, Dublin, Limerick, Kerry and Donegal, and the estimated number of bearers was 4,070. In the United States it is the 86th most numerous surname with an estimated 253,000 bearers.

Loughran, ó Luchráin

A Gaelic surname meaning descendant of *Luchaireán* (diminutive of *luchair* meaning 'bright, glittering'). An ecclesiastical sept in the diocese of Armagh. In 1890 the surname was principally found in Tyrone, Antrim and Armagh, and the estimated number of bearers was 1,840.

MacLoughlin, O'Loughlin, ó Maoilsheachlainn

A Gaelic surname meaning descendant of *Maolsheachlainn* (servant of St. Secundinus), the Ard-Rí who was dethroned by Brian Boru. A sept of Clann Cholmain who were Kings of Meath prior to the Cambro-Norman invasion. The sept described as the *O'Melaghlens* were confined to the barony of Clonlonan in Westmeath. In its anglicised form of MacLoughlin difficult to distinguish from MacLaughlin. Sometimes an anglicisation of *ó Lachtnáin*. In 1890 McLoughlin was numerous in Sligo, Leitrim and Fermanagh, it was also to be found in Dublin. The estimated number of bearers was 7,616. In 1890 Loughlin was principally found in Leitrim, Dublin, and Kilkenny, and the estimated number of bearers was 1,750. Laughlin was principally found in Tyrone and Antrim, and the estimated number of bearers was 630. In the United States McLoughlin is the 7,523rd most numerous surname with an estimated 2,750 bearers.

Lowry

A Scottish surname derived from Laurance. See also Lavery above. In 1890 Lowry was principally found in Dublin, Antrim and Down, and the estimated number of bearers was 3,180 (including variants). In the United States Lowery is the 659th most numerous surname with an estimated 49,500 bearers.

134

Lucas
An English surname from the name Luke, as in the bible. In 1890 Lucas was principally found in Tyrone and Cavan, and the estimated number of bearers was 985. In the United States it is the 286th most numerous surname with an estimated 104,500 bearers. In England and Wales in 1996 it was the 289th most numerous surname.

Lydon, ó Lodáin
A Gaelic surname meaning descendant of *Lodán*, or *Loidéan*. In 1890 Lydon was principally found in Galway and Mayo, and the estimated number of bearers was 3,180 (including variants).

Lynch, ó Loingsigh, de Leach
A Gaelic surname meaning descendant of *Loingseach*, which personal name meant 'seafarer, exile'. A sept who were Chiefs of Dál Riada (Antrim and Down), they were dispossessed at the time of the Cambro-Norman invasion. A sept of Owney who were Chiefs of Uaithne Thíre, now the barony of Owney in Tipperary. Sometime after the Cambro-Norman invasion they were dispossessed by the ó Maolriain. A sept of Breifne, who were Chiefs of Cineál Bhacaid. A sept of the Dál gCais in Thuas Mhumhan (Thomond). A sept of the Corcu Lóighdhe, who were originally seated in west Cork. A sept of the Uí Fiachrach, who were settled in Sligo. A sept of Meath. Also *de Lench* of Cambro-Norman origin one of the 'Tribes of Galway'. In 1890 Lynch was the seventeenth most numerous name in Ireland, the estimated number of bearers was 19,800, and it was the most numerous surname in Westmeath The surname was to be found in nearly every county in Ireland and it was chiefly to be found in Cork, Cavan, Dublin, Kerry, Limerick, Clare, Meath and Derry. In the United States Lynch is the 235th most numerous surname with an estimated 123,750 bearers. It is numerous in the states of Connecticut, Delaware, and New Jersey. In England and Wales in 1996 it was the 249th most numerous surname.

Lyons, Lane, ó Laighin
A Gaelic surname meaning descendant of *Laighean* meaning 'lance, spear'. A sept in the barony of Kilconnell in Galway. A sept formerly seated near Kill in Kildare. *ó Liatháin*, is often anglicised as Lyons in Cork. Which means descendant of *Liathán*, which is a diminutive of *Liath* meaning 'grey'. *de Lyons* a surname of Norman origin, possibly of Lyons-la-Foret (Eure) the place-name in France. A family of the name settled in Meath and spread throughout the Pale. In 1890 Lyons was the eightieth most numerous surname, an estimated 9,400 persons bore the name and it was principally found in Mayo, Cork, Galway, Dublin, Kerry and Limerick. In 1890 Lane was principally found in Cork and Limerick and the estimated number of bearers was 3,000. In the United States Lyons is the 326th most numerous surname with an estimated 90,750 bearers. In England and Wales in 1996 it was the 426th most numerous surname.

Macken, Mackin, ó Maicín, ó Macáin
A Gaelic surname derived from *mac* meaning 'a son or youth'. There may have been a sept in Connacht and another in Oriel. According to Woulfe there was a Donegal sept *Mac Maicín*. In 1890 Macken was principally found in Mayo, Louth and Dublin, and Mackin was principally found in Monaghan, and the estimated number of bearers was 1,700.

Madden, ó Madáin
A Gaelic surname meaning descendant of *Madadhán*, diminutive of *Madadh*, meaning 'a dog'. A sept of the Uí Mhaine, whose territory consisted of the barony of Longford in Galway and the parish of Lusnagh in Offaly. *ó Maddegane* in Antrim were a separate family. In 1890 Madden was principally found in Galway, Cork, Dublin and Antrim, and the estimated number of bearers was 4,790. In the United States it is the 943rd most numerous surname with an estimated 35,750 bearers.

Magee, McGee, Mag Aoidh,
A Gaelic surname meaning descendant of *Aodh*, which personal name meant 'fire'. It may be of either Irish, or Scottish origin. Many of the surname in east Ulster would be of Scottish origin. A sept who were chiefs of Muinntear Tlámáin in Westmeath. According to Woulfe; Magee may be *ó Maolghaoithe*, descendant of *Maolghaoithe* meaning 'chief of the wind'. A sept of Tír Conaill; parish of Clondavaddog, Donegal. Also see Wynne. In 1890 Magee was the ninety-third most numerous surname and the estimated number of bearers was 8,600. In that year the surname was chiefly found in Antrim, Armagh and Down as Magee; and in Donegal and Tyrone as McGee. In the United States McGee is the 356th most numerous surname with an estimated 85,250 bearers, and Magee is the 1,097th most numerous surname with an estimated 30,250 bearers.

Magill, McGill
A Scottish surname *Mac an ghoill* meaning "son of the Lowlander or stranger". Macgill is a surname of Galloway. There were also Macgills in Jura, where they were known as *Clann a' ghoill*. It may also be an abbreviation of the many surnames begining *Mac Giolla*, either Irish or Scots. In 1890 Magill was principally found in Antrim, Armagh and Down, McGill was found in Donegal and Tyrone, and the estimated number of bearers was 3,765 (including variants).

Magrath, see **MacGrath**

MacGuire, Maguire, Mag Uidhir,
A Gaelic surname meaning son of *Odhar* genative of *uidhir dun* coloured perhaps the early name of the otter used as a personal name, also anglicised as Maguire and MacGuire. The leading sept of Fermanagh from the thirteenth century. They were dispossessed at the time of the Plantation of Ulster. In 1890 Maguire was the most

numerous surname in Fermanagh, it was the thirty-ninth most numerous surname in Ireland, and the estimated number of bearers was 14,400. The surname was principally to be found in Fermanagh, Dublin, Cavan and Donegal and it was found as McGuire in Roscommon and Mayo. In the United States Maguire is the 2,407th most numerous surname with an estimated 13,750 bearers, and it is numerous in the state of Massachusetts.

Maher, Meagher, ó Meachair,

A Gaelic surname meaning descendant of *Meachar*, which personal name meant 'fine, majestic'. This sept were lords of Uí Cairín, now the barony of Ikerrin in north Tipperary. They were related to the ó Cearbhaill of Eile. They resided at Druim Sailech, where now stands the castle of Moydrum, about five miles south of Roscrea. With the Cambro-Norman invasion they became subject to the Earls of Ormond. In 1890 Maher was the eighty-seventh most numerous surname, the estimated number of bearers was 9,000 and was chiefly found in Tipperary, Dublin and Kilkenny. In the United States Maher is the 1,798th most numerous surname with an estimated 19,250 bearers.

MacMahon, MacMathghamhna, Mac Mathúna

A Gaelic surname meaning son of *Mathghamhna*, which personal name meant 'bear-calf'. A sept of Thuas Mhumhan (Thomond), they derive their descent from Mahon, son of Murtagh More ó Briain, High King (1094-1119). Their territory was Corcu Baiscinn, which comprised the baronies of Moyarta and Clonderalaw in south-west Clare. A sept of Orghialla (Oriel), who replaced the ó Cearbhaill (O'Carroll) in the thirteenth century as lords of Orghialla. They remained lords of Orghialla down to the reign of Elizabeth I and were powerful in Monaghan until the time of Cromwell. Also see Mathews. In 1890, MacMahon was the sixty-fourth most numerous surname, the estimated number of bearers was 10,700 and was the most common surname in Clare. In that year the surname was chiefly found in Clare, Monaghan, Limerick and Dublin. In the United States McMahon is the 990th most numerous surname with an estimated 33,000 bearers, and McMahan is the 2,493rd most numerous surname with an estimated 13,750 bearers, and it is numerous in the state of Connecticut.

Mahon, Mohan, ó Mócháin

Sometimes an abbreviation of MacMahon (above). Also an anglicisation of ó *Mocháin*; descendant of *Mochán* (a pet form of some name commencing with *Moch-*, early) of which there were two septs in Connacht. A sept of the Cinel Ianna, in the diocese of Kilmacduagh in Galway. An ecclesiastical sept a branch of the Ui Fiachrach in Sligo, who were erenaghs of Killaraght, in the barony of Coolavin, and keepers of the cross of St. Attracta In 1890 Mahon was principally found in Dublin and Galway, and the estimated number of bearers was 3,900.

Mahoney, ó Mathghamhána, ó Mathúna

A Gaelic surname meaning descendant of *Mathghamhain*, which personal name means 'bear-calf'. Mathgamhain, a brother of Brian Boru was king of Cashel. A sept who were chiefs of Cineál mBéice, now the barony of Kinelmeaky, along the river bandon in Cork. They later established themselves in the district of Fonn Iartharach in southwest Cork. In 1890, Mahoney was the forty-sixth most numerous surname, the estimated number of bearers was 13,500, the surname was principally to be found in Cork (182 births), and it was also to be found in Kerry and Limerick. In the United States Mahoney is the 1,071st most numerous surname with an estimated 30,250 bearers. It is numerous in the state of Massachusetts.

O'Malley, ó Máille

A Gaelic surname meaning descendant of *Máille* (perhaps Old Celtic *Maglios*, according to Woulfe). A sept of Connacht who were chiefs of the two Umhalls, now the baronies of Burrishoole and Murresk in west Mayo. They were celebrated as naval commanders, being called the Manannans, or sea-gods of the western ocean, and having a considerable fleet under their command. A sept of Thuas Mhumhan (Thomond) who were chiefs of Tuath Luimnigh, a district in the neighbourhood of the city of Limerick. In its anglicised form sometimes difficult to distinguish from *ó Maoilaodha*, more usually anglicised as Molloy (see below). In 1890 Malley was numerous in Mayo, it was also to be found in Galway. The estimated number of bearers was 3,808 (including variants). In the United States O'Malley is the 2,845th most numerous surname with an estimated 11,000 bearers, and Maley is the 7,893rd most numerous surname with an estimated 2,750 bearers. O'Malley is numerous in the state of Massachusetts.

Mallon, Mellon, ó Mealláin

A Gaelic surname derived from *meall* meaning 'pleasant'. An ecclesiastical sept of the Cineál Eoghain who were hereditary keepers of the Bell of St. Patrick. They were seated in the parish of Donaghmore, near Dungannon in Tyrone. Also see Mulholland. In 1890 Mallon was principally found in Armagh, Antrim, and Tyrone, and the estimated number of bearers was 2,150. Mellon was principally found in Tyrone and the estimated number of bearers was 540. In the United States Mallon is the 8,093rd most numerous surname with an estimated 2,750 bearers.

Malone, ó Maoileoin

A Gaelic surname meaning descendant of devotee of St. John. An ecclesiastical sept of Clonmacnoise. In 1890 Malone was principally found in Dublin, Wexford and Clare, and the estimated number of bearers was 4,480. In the United States Malone is the 397th most numerous surname with an estimated 77,000 bearers.

138

Mangan, Mongan, Ó Mongáin
A Gaelic surname, derived from *Mong* "a head of long and abundant hair". A sept in north Connacht. A sept of Thomand, there are townlands called Ballymongaun in the Parishes of Cloncrew and Dromcolliher in Limerick, and in the Parish of Kilnamona in Clare. An erenagh sept of the Cineál Eoghain from the Parish of Termonamongan (in which there is a townland called Ballymongan), in Tyrone. In 1890 Mangan was principally found in Dublin, Limerick, Kerry, and Mayo, and the estimated number of bearers was 2,330. In the United States Mangan is the 7,819th most numerous surname with an estimated 2,750 bearers.

Manning
An English surname, perhaps derived from the Old French *manier* meaning 'to work'. In 1890 Manning was principally found in Cork and Dublin, and the estimated number of bearers was 2,420. In the United States it is the 362nd most numerous surname with an estimated 82,500 bearers. In England and Wales in 1996 it was the 385th most numerous surname.

Mannion, Ó Mainnín, Mannion
A Gaelic surname meaning descendant of *Mainnín*. A sept of Galway who were formerly chiefs of Sodhan, a district nearly co-extensive with the Barony of Tiaquin. In 1890 Mannion was numerous in Galway, it was also to be found in Roscommon. The estimated number of bearers was 4,076 (including variants). In the United States Manion is the 7,077th most numerous surname with an estimated 5,500 bearers.

Marron, Marren, Ó Mearáin
A Gaelic surname derived from *Mearán* (diminutive of *mear* meaning 'lively'). According to Woulfe there was a *Mac Mhearáin* sept of Westmeath. In 1890 Marron was principally found in Monaghan and Marren was principally found in Sligo, and the estimated number of bearers was 1,390. In the United States Marron is the 9,424th most numerous surname with an estimated 2,750 bearers.

MacManus, MacMaghnuis
A Gaelic surname meaning son of *Manus* (from Latin *Magnus*, great). A sept who were a branch of the Maguires, descenant of *Maghnus*, son of Donn Maguire, chief of Fermanagh who died in 1302. The chief of the sept lived at Senadh Mic Maghnusa now Belle Isle, in Lough Erne. In 1890 McManus was numerous in Fermanagh. The estimated number of bearers was 6,182. In the United States McManus is the 1,478th most numerous surname with an estimated 22,000 bearers.

Marshall
An English and a Scottish surname from the Old French *mareschal* "one who tends horses, especially one who treats their diseases; a shoeing smith, a farrier" Earlier surnames may refer to a high office

of state (the Earl Marshal). In 1890 Marshall was principally found in Antrim, Derry, Down and Dublin, and the estimated number of bearers was 2,645. In the United States it is the 119th most numerous surname with an estimated 206,250 bearers. In England and Wales in 1996 it was the 65th most numerous surname. In Scotland in 1995 it was the 51st most numerous surname.

Martin, Gil(l)martin, Mac Giolla Mhairtín, Mac Máirtín, ó Mártain
A surname of Irish, Scottish and English origin. A Gaelic surname *Mac Giolla Mhairtín* meaning 'son of the devotee of Saint Martin'. Also anglicised as MacGillmartins. A sept of the Cineál Eoghain who were chiefs of Cenél Feradaigh, which embraced the barony of Clogher in Tyrone. A sept in Fermanagh who were a branch of the MacGuires. *Mac Máirtín* in Tyrone a branch of the *ó Neill*. Martyn one of the 'Tribes of Galway'. In Scotland there are three sources of the surname: One of the three main branches of the Clan Cameron, *Clan Mhic Mhartin* of Letterfinlay. A family in East Lothian. Mac Martin, clerk to chancellor William the Lion. In St. Andrews in the fifteenth and sixteenth centuries. Martin of Marshadden descendent of Martin eldest son of Aonghas na Gaoithe (Clan Donald). In Ulster the surname would be of Scottish origin. The English surname is from the mediaeval Latin *Martinus*, a diminutive of *Martius*, from Mars the god of war. Martius was an early personal name. There is also a Manx surname *Mac Giolla Mhairtin*, which may have spread to the east coast of Ireland. In 1890, Martin was the thirty-eight most numerous surname, the estimated number of bearers was 14,600, and the surname was to be found all over Ireland, principally in Antrim, Down, Dublin and Monaghan. In 1890 Gilmartin was numerous in Sligo, it was also to be found in Leitrim. The estimated number of bearers was 1,075. In the United States Martin is the 16th most numerous surname with an estimated 750,750 bearers. In England and Wales in 1996 it was the 28th most numerous surname. In Scotland in 1995 it was the 33rd most numerous surname.

Masterson, Mac an Máighistir
An English surname meaning son of the Master (a reference to a cleric). There is also a Scottish surname of similar derivation, from Dumfries and Wigstown. *Mac an Mháighistir* a sept of Breffny, who originated in Cavan has been so anglicised. In 1890 the surname was principally found in Dublin, Longford and Cavan, and the estimated number of bearers was 2,100.

Mathews, Matthews
Both an English and a Scottish surname from the personal name Mathew, of biblical origin from the Hebrew male name *Matityahu* meaning 'gift of God'. The name was introduced to Britain by the Normans. The surname most likely meant 'son of Matthew'. According to MacLysaght a synonym of MacMahon (*MacMathghamhna*) in Louth. In 1890 Mathews was numerous in Louth, it was also to be found in Dublin, Antrim and Down. The

estimated number of bearers for Mathews was 2,284, and for Matthews was 1,164. In the United States Matthews is the 169th most numerous surname with an estimated 154,000 bearers, and Mathews is the 552nd most numerous surname with an estimated 57,750 bearers. In England and Wales in 1996 Matthews was the 84th most numerous surname.

Maxwell
A Scottish surname, *Macus* a Saxon Lord was granted land (now called Springwood) on the Tweed in the reign of David I. The lands were called Maccus's Wiel (from the Old English *wael*, a pool, whirlpool). In 1890 Maxwell was principally found in Antrim, Down and Dublin, and the estimated number of bearers was 3,050. In the United States it is the 404th most numerous surname with an estimated 77,000 bearers.

Meany, ó Maonaigh
See Mooney below. Difficult to distinguish from *ó Maine*, a sept of the Dál gCais in Thomond. In 1890 Meany was principally found in Kilkenny and Clare, and the estimated number of bearers was 1,520.

Meara, Mara, ó Meadhra
A Gaelic surname, from *Meadhair* (mirth). A sept of the Dál gCais who were chiefs of a district called Rosarguid, in the Barony of Upper Ormond in Tipperary, their territory centered upon Toomyvara (*Tuaim Uí Mheadhra*). In 1890 Meara was principally found in Tipperary, and the estimated number of bearers was 2,420 (all variants). In the United States Marra is the 4,928th most numerous surname with an estimated 5,500 bearers.

Meehan
The anglicisation of the surname of a number of Gaelic septs.: *ó Mithidhín*, meaning descendant of *Mithidhín* (born in June): a sept of Uí Maine who were co-arbs of Clontuskert near Ballinasloe in Galway; a sept who were co-arbs of St. Molaise at Ballaghmeehin in the parish of Rossinver in Leitrim. *ó Maotháin*, meaning descendant of *Maothán* (diminutive of *maoth*, soft), a surname found in Schrule in Mayo. In 1890 Meehan was principally found in Galway, Sligo, Donegal, Dublin and Clare, and the estimated number of bearers was 5,600 (including variants).

MacMenamin, Mac Meanman
A Gaelic surname derived from *Meanma* meaning 'courage, high spirits'. A sept of the Cineál Conaill, In 1890 McMenamin was principally found in Donegal and Tyrone, and the estimated number of bearers was 1,610.

Millar, Miller
Both an English and a Scottish surname. Millar is the more common Scottish form. It is derived from the occupation of a miller, from the Middle English *millere*. In Scotland in 1863 Miller (including

variants) was the eleventh most numerous surname, and the estimated number of bearers was 21,400. In 1890 the surname was principally found in Antrim (30%), Derry and Dublin, and the estimated number of bearers was 3,898 (Millar) and 3,539 (Miller). In the United States Miller is the 7th most numerous surname with an estimated 1,166,000 bearers. In England and Wales in 1996 Miller was the 61st most numerous surname. In Scotland in 1995 Miller was the 22nd most numerous surname, and Millar was the 77th most numerous surname.

Milligan, Milliken, ó Maoileagáin
Perhaps a Gaelic sept of west Ulster. In 1890 the surname was principally found in Antrim, Derry and Dublin, and the estimated number of bearers was 1,790.

Mills
An English surname. It is most likely derived from 'dweller by the mills', or perhaps a patronymic, from *Miles* or *Mill*. In 1890 Mills was principally found in Antrim, and the estimated number of bearers was 2,640. In the United States it is the 152nd most numerous surname with an estimated 167,750 bearers. In England and Wales in 1996 it was the 88th most numerous surname.

Mitchell, Mistéil
An English and a Scottish surname, from the Hebrew name *Michael*. *Mac Gille Mhicheil* anglicised as MacMicheil was to be found in Bute. *Mac Giolla Mhichil* a Gaelic surname meaning servant of St. Michael. A sept who were chiefs of Clann Chonghaile in Fermanagh, but were dispossessed by the Maguires in the fifteenth century. In Scotland in 1863 Mitchell was the twenty-fourth most numerous surname and the estimated number of bearers was 16,100. In 1890 Mitchell was principally found in Antrim, Galway and Dublin, and the estimated number of bearers was 5,700 (including variants). In the United States it is the 41st most numerous surname with an estimated 440,000 bearers. In England and Wales in 1996 it was the 51st most numerous surname. In Scotland in 1995 it was the 15th most numerous surname.

Moffatt, Moffat, Moffett, Moffet, Moffitt, Moffit
A Scottish surname of local origin from the town of Moffat in Annandale, Dumfriesshire. In the late seventeenth century the Moffettis of the West Marche were considered to be amongst the unruly Border clans. In 1890 the surname was principally found in Antrim, Sligo and Tyrone, and the estimated number of bearers was 3,050 (all variants).

Molloy, ó Maolmhuaidh
A Gaelic surname meaning descendant of *Maol Mhuadh*, meaning 'noble, proud'. They were descendants of *Fiachra*, son of *Niall* of the Nine Hostages and were lords of Feara Ceall. This territory comprised the modern baronies of Fircall, Ballycowan and Ballyboy in Offaly.

Also a sept who were a branch of the Siol Mireadhaigh in Roscommon, known as Clann Taidhg na h-oidhche. In its anglicised form difficult to distinguish from ó Laoghóg, descendant of Laoghóg (diminutive of Laogh, 'a calf'). Chiefs of Caladh, co-extensive with the barony of Kilconnell in Galway. In Donegal may be a corruption of ó Maolmhaodhóg, 'servant of St. Maodhóg'. In Connacht ó Maoilaodha, a variant of ó Maolaodha. In 1890 Molloy was numerous in Offaly, it was also to be found in Dublin, Galway, Mayo and Donegal. The estimated number of bearers was 5,689. In the United States Molloy is the 6,165th most numerous surname with an estimated 5,500 bearers.

Moloney, ó Maoldomhnaigh
A Gaelic surname meaning descendant of Maoldomhnaigh, which personal name meant 'servant of the Church'. A sept of Dál gCais who were chiefs of a district in the barony of Tulla, Clare. ó Maolfhachtna meaning 'a servant of St Facthtna', a sept of Tipperary has been assimilated into Moloney. In 1890 Moloney was the ninety-seventh most numerous surname and the estimated number of bearers was 8,300. In that year the surname was chiefly found in Limerick, Clare, Tipperary and Waterford.

Monaghan, Monahan, ó Manacháin
A Gaelic surname meaning descendant of Manach, meaning 'a monk'. A sept of Connacht, who were chiefs of Ui Briuin na Sionna in the barony of Ballintober in Roscommon. In the year 1249 they were ousted by the O'Beirnes. In 1890 the surname was principally found in Galway, Mayo, Dublin and Fermanagh, and the estimated number of bearers for Monaghan was 4,300 and for Monahan was 1,880.

Montgomery
A Scottish surname of Norman origin, from the ancient castle of Sainte Foi de Montgomery in the diocese of Lisieux. In 1890 was principally found in Antrim and Down, and the estimated number of bearers was 4,972. In the United States it is the 211th most numerous surname with an estimated 134,750 bearers.

Mooney, ó Maonaigh
A Gaelic surname meaning descendant of Maonach, meaning 'wealthy' according to Woulfe. A sept who were chiefs of Clann Murthuile in Roscommon. A sept of the Uí Fiachrach, whose territory was south of Sligo bay in the barony of Tireragh. A sept of the Siol nAnmchadha, in the south east of Galway. In 1890 Mooney was numerous in Offaly, it was also to be found in Dublin and Antrim. The estimated number of bearers was 6,092. In the United States it is the 904th most numerous surname with an estimated 35,750 bearers.

Moore, ó Mórdha
A Gaelic surname meaning descendant of Mórdha, meaning

'majestic'. The leading sept of the seven septs of Laois. Their chief fortress was to be found at Dunamase near Portlaoise. In 1609, after being defeated by the English, the remants of the sept were transplanted to Kerry, where they settled in the neighbourhood of Tarbert. However many returned later to their native territory. Also an English surname. It may have been a local surname given to a man who lived near a moor or a nickname for physical characteristics from the Old French meaning 'swarthy'. In 1890 Moore was the twentieth most numerous name in Ireland, the estimated number of bearers was 17,700, and the surname was to be found in every county in Ireland. It was principally to be found in Antrim, Dublin, Derry, Cork, Kildare and Tyrone. In the United States Moore is the 9th most numerous surname with an estimated 858,000 bearers. In England and Wales in 1996 it was the 33rd most numerous surname. In Scotland in 1995 it was the 87th most numerous surname.

Moran, ó Moráin
A Gaelic surname meaning descendant of *Mórán*, diminutive of *mór* meaning 'tall, great'. A sept of Uí Fiachrach, who occupied an area on both sides of the river moy. The chief of the sept resided at Ardnaree, near Ballina, Mayo. To be distinguished from : *ó Mughróin* a Gaelic surname meaning descendant of *Mughrón*, meaning "lad of the seals". A sept of the Síl Muireadaigh, in the present Roscommon, who were chiefs of Clann Cathail. *ó Moghráin* a Gaelic surname meaning descendant of Mughrón, diminutive of mór meaning slave-seal. A sept of the Uí Mhaine in Galway, who were chiefs of Cruffon, a district comprising the barony of Killian and part of Ballymoe. In 1890 Moran was the fifty-sixth most numerous name in Ireland and the estimated number of bearers was 11,800. In that year the surname was nearly to be found in every, but was chiefly to be found in Mayo, Dublin, Galway, Roscommon, Leitrim and Kerry. In the United States it is the 444th most numerous surname with an estimated 71,500 bearers. It is numerous in the state of Connecticut, New Jersey, and New York. In England and Wales in 1996 it was the 392nd most numerous surname.

Morgan
Morgan is one of the oldest and most numerous Welsh surnames. Derived from the Old Welsh *Morcant*, the meaning of which is not settled. In Scotland Morgan was to be found in Aberdeenshire, and Clan Morgan was the designation of the Mackays of the Reay country in Sutherland. May be an anglicisation of several Irish Surnames. In 1853 Morgan was the thirty-seventh most numerous surname in England, the estimated number of bearers being 41,000. In Ireland in 1890 Morgan was numerous in Louth, the surname was also to be found in Antrim, Armagh, Down and Dublin. The estimated number of bearers was 5,913. In the United States it is the 57th most numerous surname with an estimated 324,500 bearers. In England and Wales in 1996 it was the 39th most numerous surname.

Moriarty, Murtagh, ó Muircheartaigh
A Gaelic surname meaning descendant of *Muircheartach*, meaning 'navigator'. A sept who were anciently chiefs of Aos Aisde, along the river Mang in Kerry. Anglicised as Moriarty. In 1890 Moriarty was numerous in Kerry (74 births). The estimated number of bearers was 3,718. A sept who were lords of Teffia (Westmeath Longford), anglicised as Murtagh. In the United States Moriarty is the 4,067th most numerous surname with an estimated 8,250 bearers.

Moroney, ó Morruanaidh, ó Maolruanaidh
The Gaelic surname *ó Maolruanaidh* meaning follower of *Ruanaidh* has been corrupted to *ó Morruanaidh* in Thomand. This is a sept of the Dál gCais. In 1890 the surname was principally found in Clare, Limerick and Tipperary, and the estimated number of bearers was 1,970.

Morris
Mac Murris, a surname of Cambro-Norman origin, meaning son of Maurice: a branch of the Geraldines in Kerry who were lord of Lixnaw, also borne by a branch of the Prendergasts in Mayo. Also *de Moiréis* from the French meaning 'of residence nearby a marsh'. Morris is one of the 'Tribes of Galway', being descendants of a family named Mares, which settled there in 1485. Also see Morrison and Morrissey. In 1890 Morris was principally found in Dublin, Mayo, Tyrone, and Monaghan, and the estimated number of bearers was 5,150 (including variants). In the United States it is the 53rd most numerous surname with an estimated 343,750 bearers. In England and Wales in 1996 it was the 32nd most numerous surname.

Morrison
Both an English and a Scottish surname meaning son of Maurice (from Latin *Mauricius*, moorish). Also see Morris. In 1890 Morrison was principally found in Antrim, Down and Dublin, and the estimated number of bearers was 4,970 (including variants). In the United States it is the 221st most numerous surname with an estimated 132,000 bearers. In England and Wales in 1996 it was the 297th most numerous surname. In Scotland in 1995 it was the 21st most numerous surname.

Morrissey, ó Muirgheasa
A Gaelic surname meaning descendant of *Muirgheas* (sea strength). A sept of the Uí Fiachrach who were formerly chiefs of a district on the southern shore of Sligo Bay, in the barony of Tireragh. In 1890 Morrissey was numerous in Waterford, it was also to be found in Limerick and Cork. The estimated number of bearers was 4,032 (including variants). In the United States Morrissey is the 2,524th most numerous surname with an estimated 13,750 bearers.

McMorrow, MacMuireadhaigh,
A Gaelic surname meaning son of *Muireadhach* (lord, master). A sept

145

of Breifne (Breifney). In 1890 McMorrow was numerous in Leitrim. The estimated number of bearers was 940.

Morrow
An English surname, sometimes an anglicisation of above. In 1890 Morrow was principally found in Antrim, Donegal, Armagh and Down, and the estimated number of bearers was 4,080. In the United States it is the 525th most numerous surname with an estimated 60,500 bearers.

Moynihan, ó Muimhneacháin
A sept of Munster meaning descendant of *Muimhneachán* (meaning Munsterman). In 1890 Moynihan was principally found in Kerry and Cork, and the estimated number of bearers was 2,960.

Mulcahy, ó Maolchatha
A sept of Munster meaning descendant of *Maolcatha* meaning 'battle-chief' or *Maolcathach* 'warlike-chief', or *Maolchathaigh* 'follower of *Cathach*, (warlike)'; according to Woulfe. In 1890 Mulcahy was principally found in Cok, Limerick, Waterford and Tipperary, and the estimated number of bearers was 3,405. In the United States it is the 5,814th most numerous surname with an estimated 5,500 bearers.

Mulcreevy, see Rice

Mulhall, ó Maolchathail
A Gaelic surname meaning descendant of *Maolchathail* meaning "servant of St. Cathal'. A sept of Laois/Offaly. In 1890 Mulhall was principally found in Dublin, Kilkenny, Carlow and Laois, and the estimated number of bearers was 1,480.

Mulholland, ó Maolchallann
A Gaelic sept 'son of the devotee of (St.) Calann'. They were an ecclesiastical family who were hereditary keepers of the Bell of St. Patrick, known as the Bell of the Testament, this they shared at one time with the *ó Meallain* (Mallons). Their territory was located in the Barony of Loughinsholin (now in County Derry but origionally part of Tir Eoghain), a branch of the family settled in Antrim. In 1890 Mulholland was principally found in Antrim, Down and Derry, and the estimated number of bearers was 3,270. In the United States it is the 5,437th most numerous surname with an estimated 5,500 bearers.

Mullally, see Lally

McMullan, Macmillan, MacMaoláin
A Scottish surname meaning 'son of the bald or tonsured one'. At one time the Clan Macmillan had possessions near Knap in Argyllshire. In 1890 McMullan was principally found in Antrim and Down, and the estimated number of bearers was 4,840 (including

variants). In Scotland in 1995 McMillan was the 67th most numerous surname.

Mullan, Mullen, Mullin, ó Maoláin,
A Gaelic surname meaning descendant of *Maolán*, which personal name meant 'bald'. It has been anglicised as Mullan, Mullen and Mullin. The surname was adopted by several unidentifiable septs. A leading sept of ó Catháin's country in Derry. In 1890 Mullan was the seventieth most numerous surname and the estimated number of bearers was 9,800. In that year the surname was chiefly found in Tyrone, Derry, Galway and Antrim. In the United States Mullins is the 330th most numerous surname with an estimated 90,750 bearers, and Mullen is the 869th most numerous surname with an estimated 38,500 bearers.

Mullane
The Munster form of Mullins (see below), see also Mullan (above). In 1890 Mullane was principally found in Cork and Limerick, and the estimated number of bearers was 1,390.

Mullany, ó Maoileanaigh
A Gaelic surname meaning descendant of *Maolsheanaigh* meaning 'servant of St. Seanach'. A sept of Connacht who were seated in the neighbourhood of Loch Cé. In 1890 Mullany was principally found in Roscommon, Mayo and Sligo, and the estimated number of bearers was 1,430.

Mulligan, ó Maolacháin
A Gaelic surname meaning descendant of *Maolachán*, from *maol*, 'bald'. It is difficult to distinguish any distinct septs. In 1890 Mulligan was principally found in Dublin, Mayo and Monaghan, and the estimated number of bearers was 4,700. In the United States it is the 2,892nd most numerous surname with an estimated 11,000 bearers.

Mullins, ó Maoláin
A Gaelic surname meaning descendant of *Maolám* (diminutive of *maol* meaning 'bald'). It is difficult to distinguish between it an similar sounding anglicisations. In 1890 the surname was principally found in Cork and Clare, and the estimated number of bearers was 2,110. In the United States it is the 330th most numerous surname with an estimated 90,750 bearers.

Mulrooney, see **Rooney**

Mulvey, ó Maoilmhiadhaigh
A Gaelic surname meaning descendant of *Maolmiadhach* meaning "honourable chief'. A sept of Anaghaile (Annaly). In 1890 Mulvey was numerous in Leitrim. The estimated number of bearers was 940.

Murphy, ó Murchadha, ó Murchú
A Gaelic surname and the most numerous surname in Ireland, meaning descendant of *Murchadh*. The male personal name *Murchadh* means 'sea-battler' and it was one of the more popular early Irish names. A sept of Muscraidhe (Muskerry) in Cork who were either of the Múscraighe Mitine, or of the Uí Chonaill Gabhra. A sept of Cineál Eoghain, who were chiefs of Síol Aodha, in the present Tyrone. A sept of the Uí Fiachrach who were chiefs of a district on the southern shore of Sligo Bay, now in the parishes of Skreen and Templeboy, these were displaced in the thirteenth century. A sept of the Uí Chinsealaigh in Wexford, who were chiefs of Uí Feilme, which comprised the barony of Ballaghkeen, in the east of that county. In addition there would have been other septs. In 1890, the estimated number of bearers was 62,600, and it was the most numerous surname in Armagh and Wexford. In that year the surname was distributed throughout the country, the largest number of births being found in Cork (500), Dublin and Wexford. In the United States Murphy is the 59th most numerous surname with an estimated 321,750 bearers, and Murphey is the 6,025th most numerous surname wiith an estimated 5,500 bearers. In England and Wales in 1996 it was the 60th most numerous surname. In Scotland in 1995 it was the 63rd most numerous surname.

Murray, ó Muireadhaigh, ó Muirí
A Gaelic surname meaning descendant of *Muireadhach*, which personal name may have meant 'a lord, a master', it was a popular early Irish name. A sept of the Uí Mhaine in Mayo and Roscommon, a great-great grandfather of mine was Patrick Murray a cobbler from Westport. A sept in Cork. A sept in Westmeath. *Mac Muireadhaigh* (MacMurray) of Donegal. Also a Scottish name, where in 1990 it was the twelfth most numerous name. Of territorial origin from the province of Moray. In east Ulster the name would be of Scottish origin. *MacMuireadhaigh*; which is Mac Murray of Galloway. The English surname may be from the Middle English *murie* meaning 'merry'. In Ireland in 1890 Murray was the eighteenth most numerous surname, the estimated number of bearers was 19,600, and it was to be found in every county. It was principally to be found in Dublin, Antrim, Cork, Down, Galway and Mayo. In the United States Murray is the 122nd most numerous surname with an estimated 203,500 bearers, and it is numerous in the state of Delaware, In England and Wales in 1996 it was the 98th most numerous surname. In Scotland in 1995 it was the 12th most numerous surname.

Murtagh, ó Muircheartaigh
A Gaelic surname, a sept of Meath, meaning descendant of *Muircheartach* meaning 'expert navigator'. In addition there were other septs. In 1890 Murtagh was numerous in Westmeath, it was also to be found in Dublin and Sligo. The estimated number of bearers was 2,956 (including variants).

148

Nagle, de Angulo

A surname of Norman origin, meaning 'at the angle or corner, from residence thereat'. *Gilbert de Angulo* was one of the earliest invadors. They were granted lands in Meath and became barons of Navan. Branches of the family settled elsewhere. Woulfe suggests that *Mac an óglaoic* (son of the soldier), a sept of Sligo who were erenaghs of the church of Killery, near Lough Gill, is so anglicised. In 1890 Nagle was principally found in Cork, and the estimated number of bearers was 1,750. In the United States it is the 2,931st most numerous surname with an estimated 11,000 bearers.

MacNamara, Mac Conmara

A Gaelic surname, son of *Cu Mara* meaning 'hound of the sea'. A sept of Dál gCais, who derive their descent from *Cairin* son of *Car*, the ancestor of the Dál gCais. They were next to the *ó Briain* in power. Their original territory was Uí Caisin, corresponding to the present deanery of Ogashin and comprising nine parishes in the east of Clare. In later times they ruled over Upper and Lower Tulla, which from their clan name was known as Clann Chuiléin. They were hereditary marshals to *ó Briain*, whom they inaugurated. In 1890 McNamara was the ninety-fourth most numerous surname and the estimated number of bearers was 8,600. In that year the surname was chiefly found in Clare, Limerick, Mayo, Dublin and Cork. In the United States it is the 1,599th most numerous surname with an estimated 22,000 bearers.

McNally, McAnally, Mac Con Ulaidh

A Gaelic surname being a sept of Orghialla, meaning 'son of the hound of Ulidia'. In 1890 McNally was principally found in Antrim, Armagh, Monaghan and Dublin. and the estimated number of bearers was 4,520 (including variants). In the United States McNally is the 1,795th most numerous surname with an estimated 19,250 bearers.

McNamee, MacConmidhe

A Gaelic surname meaning 'son of the hound of Meath (*Cú-Midhe*)'. A sept who were heriditary poets to the ó Neills of the Cineál Eoghain. In 1890 the surname was principally found in Derry and the estimated number of bearers was 1,790.

Naughton, ó Neachtáin

A Gaelic surname derived from the personal name *Neachtan* (or *Nechan*) meaning 'descendant of the waters'. A sept of the Dál gCais, of the same stock as Quinn and Hartigan. A sept of the Uí Mhaine who were chiefs of Maonmhagh, the plain lying around Loughrea (in Galway), until the Cambro-Norman invasion. when they removed to the Fews of Athlone. There is also a Scottish surname MacNauchtan. In 1890 Naughton was principally found in Galway, Mayo, Roscommon and Clare, and the estimated number of bearers was 3,180 (including variants). In the United States it is the 8,451st most numerous surname with an estimated 2,750 bearers.

Neary, ó Nárdhaigh

A Gaelic surname meaning descendant of *Náradhach* meaning 'good, noble'. A sept of Connacht. In 1890 the surname was principally found in Mayo, Roscommon, Dublin and Louth, and the estimated number of bearers was 1,930. In the United States it is the 6,898th most numerous surname with an estimated 5,500 bearers.

N(e)ilan, ó Nialláin

A Gaelic surname meaning descendant of *Niallán* (a diminutive of *Niall*). A sept of Thomond who spread to Connacht. In 1890 the surname was principally found in Galway, Roscommon and Sligo, and the estimated number of bearers was 1,610.

MacNeill

A surname of Scottish origin, the MacNeill's of Barra (an island of the Outer Hebrides), who were followers of the Lord of the Isles came to Ireland as galloglasses during the fourteenth century. The later became lords of Clandeboy. Subsequently MacNeill's came to north Antrim in the late sixteenth centuy. In 1890 McNeill was principally found in Antrim and Derry, and the estimated number of bearers was 2,600. In the United States McNeil is the 811th most numerous surname with an estimated 41,250 bearers, and McNiel is the 9,212th most numerous surname with an estimated 2,750 bearers.

O'Neill, ó Neill

A Gaelic surname meaning descendants of *Niall*. The meaning of the personal name *Niall* is uncertain. The most famous bearer of the name was *Niall Naígiallach* ('of the Nine Hostages'), ancestor of the Uí Néill. Adopted by several septs, the principal septs being located in Tír Eoghain (Tyrone). A sept of the Cineál Eoghain, who became Lords of Ulster after they defeated the Mac Lochlainn (McLaughlin). Their territory Tír Eoghain, comprised the present Tyrone and south Derry. A sub-sept the Clann Aodha Bhuidhe during the fourteenth Century settled in Antrim, in an area now known as Clandeboy. A sept in Thomond (Thuas Mhumhan) of Dál gCais origin, who were Chiefs of Clann Dealbhaoith in the barony of Bunratty in the present Clare. A sept in Leinster, whose territory was Magh-dá-chon now the parish of Moyacomb in the barony of Rathvilly in Carlow and extending into the barony of Shillelagh in Wicklow, also called Farren O'Neill. A sept of Déise which settled in the south of Tipperary. In 1890 O'Neill was the tenth most numerous surname in Ireland, the estimated number of bearers was 29,100, and the surname was found in nearly every county in Ireland. It was principally found in Dublin, Antrim, Cork and Tyrone. In the United States O'Neal is the 540th most numerous surname with anestimated 60,500 bearers, O'Neill is the 768th most numerous surname with an estimated 44,000 bearers, and O'Neil is the 978th most numerous surname with an estimated 33,000 bearers. It is numerous in the states of Connecticut, Delaware, Maryland, Massachusetts, New York, and Pennsylvania. In England and Wales in 1996 it was the 207th most numerous surname.

Nelson, Neilson
A Scottish surname, meaning son of Niall. The Neilsons of Craigcaffie
are said to trace their descent form Niall, Earl of Carrick, husband of
Margaret Stewart who died in 1256. Also an English surname. In
1890 Nelson was principally found in Antrim, Down, Derry and
Tyrone, and the estimated number of bearers was 3,225. In the United
States Nelson is the 39th most numerous surname with an estimated
445,500 bearers. In England and Wales in 1996 it was the 238th most
numerous surname.

Nesbitt
Both an English and a Scottish surname. In Scotland of local origin
from the old barony of Nesbit in the parish of Edrom in Berwickshire.
In England from Nesbitt in Durham and Northumberland. In 1890
Nesbitt was principally found in Antrim, Armagh and Dublin, and the
estimated number of bearers was 1,340.

Neville, ó Niadh
A Gaelic surname meaning descendant of *Nia* meaning 'champion'.
A sept who were originally seated in the neighbourhood of Tralee in
Kerry. In later times they were erenaghs of Knockpatrick, near Foynes
in Limerick. In west Galway the surname is sometimes anglicised
Needham. *ó Cnáimhín*, meaning descendant of *Cnáimhín* (diminutive
of *cnámh* meaning a bone), a sept of the Dál gCais is so anglicised in
west Clare. There is also an English surname of French origin. In
1890 Neville was principally found in Limerick and Cork, and the
estimated number of bearers was 1,750.

Nicholl,
Both an English and a Scottish surname derived from the personal
name Nicholas. Such introduced by the Normans and from the Greek
meaning 'victory-people'. In some instances it is of local origin being
a reference to Lincoln (called Nicol by the Normans), England. In
1890 the surname was principally found in Antrim and Derry, and the
estimated number of bearers was 2,200. In the United States Nichols is
the 153rd most numerous surname with an estimated 165,000 bearers.
In England and Wales in 1996 it was the 190th most numerous
surname.

Nicholson,
Both an English and a Scottish surname, see immediately above. In
Scotland the surname was to be found in the Lowlands, in Lasswade
and in Skye. In 1890 the surname was principally found in Antrim,
Sligo and Dublin, and the estimated number of bearers was 1,970. In
the United States it is the 522nd most numerous surname with an
estimated 60,500 bearers. In England and Wales in 1996 it was the
183rd most numerous surname.

Nixon,
Both an English and a Scottish surname, meaning son of Nick (a pet

form of Nicholos, see immediately above). In 1890 the surname was principally found in Antrim, Cavan and Fermanagh, and the estimated number of bearers was 2,110. In the United States it is the 661st most numerous surname with an estimated 49,500 bearers. In England and Wales in 1996 it was the 469th most numerous surname.

Nolan, Nowlan, ó Nualláin

A Gaelic surname meaning descendant of *Nuallan* a diminutive of *Nuall* meaning 'famous'. A sept who were known as Chiefs of Fothart Feadha i.e. barony of Forth in Carlow, this sept had the privilege of inaugurating MacMurrough as King of Leinster, a branch migrated to east Connacht and Longford. A sept of the Corcu Loíghdhe in south-west Cork. In Fermanagh it is an anglicised form of ó hUltacháin (Hultaghan). In Roscommon and Mayo is used synonymously with Holohan. In 1890 Nolan was the fortieth most numerous surname in Ireland, the estimated number of bearers was 14,300, and it was principally to be found in Dublin, Wexford, Carlow, Wicklow, Kildare, Kerry, Tipperary, Mayo and Galway. In the United States Nolan is the 741st most numerous surname with an estimated 44,000 bearers, Nolen is the 2,746th most numerous surname with an estimated 13,750 bearers, and Nolin is the 9,520th most numerous surname with an estimated 2,750 bearers. It is numerous in the state of Connecticut. In England and Wales in 1996 Nolan was the 425th most numerous surname.

Noonan, ó hIonmhaineáin, ó Nuanáin

A Gaelic surname derived from *Ionmhain* meaning 'beloved'. An ecclesiastical sept who were erenaghs of the church of St. Beretchert at Tullylease, in the Barony of Duhallow in Cork. In 1890 Noonan was principally found in Cork, Clare, Limerick and Tipperary, and the estimated number of bearers was 3,720 (including variants). In the United States Noonan is the 3,158th most numerous surname with an estimated 11,000 bearers.

Noone, ó Nuadhan

A Gaelic sept derived from *Nuadha* (the name of an ancient sea divinity), The sept anciently possessed the district of Callraighe Laithimh, nearly co-extensive with the present parish of Calry, near the town of Sligo. In 1890 Noone was principally found in Galway, Roscommon and Mayo, and the estimated number of bearers was 2,150.

de Nugent, Nugent, Gilsenan, MacGiollaSeanáin

A surname of Norman origin (from a place called Nogent in France). *Gilbert de Nugent* was made Baron of Devlin by Hugh de Lacy, and in 1621 Richard Nugent became Earl of Westmeath. An English family called Nugent from Winchester settled in Cork, they became the *Uinnseadún* (*Mag Uinseannáin*) sept whose chief lived at Aghavarten Castle near Carrigaline. The Gaelic sept *MacGiollSeanáin* of Meath and Cavan more often anglicised as Gilsenan has also been anglicised as Nugent. In 1890 Nugent was principally found in Armagh, Dublin, Cork, Tipperary and Tyrone, and the estimated number of bearers was 3,360. In the United States Nugent is the 2,233rd most numerous surname with an estimated 16,500 bearers.

MacNulty, Mac an Ultaigh, MacDuinnshléibhe, Dunleavy
A Gaelic surname meaning 'son of the Ulidian' (East Ulster). The *MacDuinnshléibhe* sept of Donegal were also known as *Mac an Ultaigh*. In Meath the surname was Nulty. In 1890 McNulty was principally found in Donegal and Mayo, and the estimated number of bearers was 3,090. In the United States McNulty is the 2,847th most numerous surname with an estimated 11,000 bearers.

Orr
A Scottish surname derived from the Gaelic *odhar* meaning 'of sallow complection'. The surname was to be found in the parish of Lochwinnoch in Renfrewshire (a sept of the Campbells), and in Campbeltown, Kintyre. In 1890 the surname was principally found in Antrim, Down, Derry and Tyrone, and the estimated number of bearers was 3,270. In the United States it is the 636th most numerous surname with an estimated 52,250 bearers.

Owens
A Welsh surname meaning son of Owen, in Gaelic Eoghan, and Eugene in English. Sometimes an anglicisation of *MacEóin* (MacEoin, MacKeon), or *ó hEoghain*. In 1890 Owens was found in 23 counties, but principally in Dublin, Roscommon and Cork, and the estimated number of bearers was 3,990. In the United States it is the 111th most numerous surname with an estimated 214,500 bearers. In England and Wales in 1996 it was the 406th most numerous surname.

Parker,
An English surname derived from the Old French *parquier* meaning 'one in charge of a park, park-keeper'. In 1890 the surname was principally found in Antrim and Cork, and the estimated number of bearers was 1,790. In the United States it is the 47th most numerous surname with an estimated 401,500 bearers. In England and Wales in 1996 it was the 46th most numerous surname.

MacParland, McPartlan, McPartlin, Mac Parthaláin, MacFarland
This Gaelic surname means 'son of Bartholomew'. Partholón in legend was the first invador of Ireland, 278 years after the death of Noah. A sept of Oriel whose territory was near Keady in Armagh. Also a Scottish surname of Galloway. In 1890 McPartland was principally found in Armagh, McPartlan and McPartlin in Leitrim, and the estimated number of bearers was 2,465 (all variants). McFarland was principally found in Tyrone and Armagh, and the estimated number of bearers was 2,060. In the United States McFarland is the 816th most numerous surname with an estimated 41,250 bearers.

153

Patterson
A Scottish surname meaning 'son of Patrick', from the Latin *patricius* meaning 'nobleman'. The native home of the Clan Pheadirean (Patersons) was on the north side of Lochfyne. MacPhadruig has been anglicised both as MacPatrick and Paterson. In 1863 Paterson was the nineteenth most numerous surname in Scotland. In 1890 Patterson was numerous in Down, it was also to be found in Antrim, Armagh, Derry and Tyrone. The estimated number of bearers was 6,854 (including variants). In the United States it is the 87th most numerous surname with an estimated 253,000 bearers. In England and Wales in 1996 it was the 354th most numerous surname. In Scotland in 1995 Paterson was the 18th most numerous surname.

Patton, Patten, ó Peatáin
An Irish, Scottish and English Surname. The English and Scottish surname Patton is derived from Patrick, which was a popular personal name prior to the Reformation. In Scotland the surname was to be found in Ayrshire. The English surname Patten is derived from the Middle English *paten* for 'patten, clog', being reference to 'a patten-maker'. The Gaelic *ó Peatáin* were a sept of the Cineál Eoghain, *Peatán* being a diminutive of Patrick. At one time they were seated in the barony of Raphoe in Donegal. In 1890 Patton was principally found in Antrim and Down, and Patten in Mayo, and the estimated number of bearers was 2,690 (including variants). In the United States it is the 382nd most numerous surname with an estimated 79,750 bearers.

Pearson
Both an English and a Scottish surname meaning son of *Pierre* or *Piers* (a form of Peter). In 1890 Pearson was principally found in Antrim and Dublin, and the estimated number of bearers was 1,390. In the United States it is the 255th most numerous surname with an estimated 115,500 bearers. In England and Wales in 1996 it was the 102nd most numerous surname.

Phelan, see **Whelan**

Philips, Phillips
An English surname derived from the name Philip from the Greek meaning 'lover of horses'. The Christian name was common in England during the Middle Ages. In 1890 the surname was chiefly found in Mayo, Antrim and Dublin, and the estimated number of persons bearing the surname was 3,450. In the United States Phillips is the 45th most numerous surname with an estimated 409,750 bearers. In England and Wales in 1996 Phillips was the 43rd most numerous surname.

Pierce
An English surname derived from the Old French *Pierre* for Peter. The Christian name was common in England during the Middle Ages.

In 1890 the surname was chiefly found in Dublin and Wexford, and the estimated number of persons bearing the surname was 1,700. In the United States it is the 167th most numerous surname with an estimated 154,000 bearers.

Plunkett, Pluinceid
A surname of Norman origin, a family of which settled in north Dublin. In 1890 the surname was chiefly found in Dublin, and the estimated number of persons bearing the surname was 1,250. In the United States Plunkett is the 3,480th most numerous surname with an estimated 11,000 bearers.

Pollock,
A Scottish surname of local origin, a Peter son of Fulbert, or Fulburt, had a grant of Upper Pollock in Renfrewshire from the High Steward, and took his surname from the lands. In 1890 the surname was principally found in Antrim and Tyrone, and the estimated number of bearers was 1,840.

Porter
An English and Scottish surname, drived from the Old French *portier* meaning 'door-keeper, gate-keeper'. The porter was an important official connected to a castle or monastic institution, land and privileges were attached to the office. In 1890 Porter was principally found in Antrim, Down, Derry and Armagh, and the estimated number of bearers was 3,270. In the United States it is the 129th most numerous surname with an estimated 189,750 bearers. In England and Wales in 1996 it was the 163rd most numerous surname.

Power, de/le Paor
A surname of Cambro-Norman origin from *le poer* meaning 'poor man' consequent upon a vow of poverty. A family of the surname first settled in Waterford and spread both east and west, subsequently they became completely hibernicized. In 1890 it was the fifty-fourth most numerous surname and the estimated number of bearers was 12,100. It was the most common name in Waterford. In that year the surname was chiefly found in Waterford, Cork, Dublin, Tipperary, Wexford, Kilkenny and Limerick. In the United States Powers is the 314th most numerous surname with an estimated 96,250 bearers, and Power is the 2,665th most numerous surname with an estimated 13,750 bearers. In England and Wales in 1996 Power was the 441st most numerous surname.

de Prendergast, de Priondragás
A surname of Cambro-Norman origin, derived from Prendergast, a parish in Pembrokeshire in Wales. *Maurice de Prendergast* accompanied Strongbow to Ireland. This family established themselves early in Wexford. Subsequently they established themselves in Connacht. Also see Morris. In 1890 Prendergast was principally found in Mayo, Dublin and Waterford, and the estimated

155

number of bearers was 2,330. In the United States Prendergast is the 6,733rd most numerous surname with an estimated 5,500 bearers.

Price
A Welsh surname *ap Rhys* 'son of Rhys'. An English surname derived from the Old French *pris* 'price' metonymic for fixer of prices. In 1890 the surname was chiefly found in Dublin and Antrim, and the estimated number of persons bearing the surname was 2,105. In the United States it is the 76th most numerous surname with an estimated 272,250 bearers. In England and Wales in 1996 it was the 47th most numerous surname.

Purcell, Puirsceil
A surname of Cambro-Norman origin derived from the French *pourcel* meaning 'little pig'. The family became completely hibernicized and were one of the most influential families of Ormond (Kilkenny and Tipperary). The head of the family had the title Baron of Loughmoe (near Thurles, County Tipperary). In 1890 the estimated number of persons bearing the surname was 3,539. In that year the surname was chiefly found in Kilkenny and Dublin in Leinster and Tipperary in Munster.

McQuaid, McQuade, Mac Uaid
A Gaelic surname meaning 'son of Wat (a pet form of Walter)'. A sept of Monaghan whose origin is obscure. Also see Watt. In 1890 McQuaid was principally found in Monaghan and Fermanagh, McQuade in Antrim, and the estimated number of bearers was 2,465 (all variants). In the United States McQuade is the 9.801st most numerous surname with an estimated 2,750 bearers.

Quigley, ó Coigligh
A Gaelic surname which according to Woulfe is derived from *coigeal* meaning 'an untidy person, with unkempt hair'. In 1890 Quigley was principally found in Derry, Dublin, Donegal, Galway, Louth and Sligo, and the estimated number of bearers was 3,990.

McQuillan, Mac Uidhilín
A surname of Cambro-Norman origin, meaning son of Hugelin. The de Mandeville's became Lords of the Route in Antrim and had their chief residence at Dunluce Castle. They also established themseles at Dufferin in Down. *Mac Coilín* of Tirconnell, may also have been so anglicised. Also see McWilliams. In 1890 it was principally found in Antrim and Monaghan. The estimated number of bearers was 1,480.

Quinlan, ó Caoindealbháin, ó Caoinleáin
A Gaelic surname derived from *Caoindealbhán* meaning 'gracefully shaped'.A sept of Meath who were chiefs of Cinel Laoghaire, near Trim until the Cambro-Norman invasion. A branch of the sept settled in north Tipperary. In 1890 Quinlan was principally found in Tipperary and Kerry, and the estimated number of bearers was 2,420.

Quinn, Quin, ó Cuinn

A Gaelic surname meaning descendant of *Conn*, which personal name may have meant 'wisdom', or 'chief' (head, sence, reason, intelligence; also a freeman, according to Woulfe). The most famous bearer of such personal name was *Conn Cétchathach* ('of the Hundred Battles') legendary ancestor of the Connachta Kings of Ireland. This surname was adopted by several distinct septs:

A sept of the Cineál Eoghain who established themselves in Clanndeboy in the present Antrim during the fourteenth century.

A sept of the Cineál Eoghain in Magh Itha, now comprised in the barony of North Raphoe in Donegal. O'Duggan writing in the early part of the fourteenth century referred to :

> "The men of Noble Magh Itha;
> who defend the confines;
> delightful their habits in every church; ...
> The brave ó Cuinn and ó Cionaths."

The confines mentioned in the poem may have meant the border with the Cineál Chonaill, *ó Cionath* may have become extinct or merged with *ó Cuinn* given the likeness of the two names. In the 1850's there were 176 Quinn households in Donegal; the largest concentration being in the parish of Donaghmore (35); followed by the parish of Inishkeel (23). My great-grandfather William Quin a scutcher of flax lived in Gobnascale, and his father Daniel died in nearby Callan.

A sept of the Cineál Eoghain, who inhabited that part of Tír Eoghain, in the barony of Loughshilon now in County Derry.

A sept who were chiefs of Magh Lughadh and Síol Chathasaigh in Antrim.

A sept of Thuas Mhumhan (Thomond), also found in Tipperary a branch of the Dál gCais, descended from Conn, lords of Muintir Iferainn, originally seated at Inchiquin.

A sept of Anghaile (Annaly), a branch of the Conmhaicne and of the same stock as *ó Fearghail* (O'Farrells), who were chiefs of Muintir Ghiollagáin, an extensive district in Longford until they were displaced by the ó Fearghail.

A sept known as the Clan Chuain of Uí Fiachrach (Sligo and north Mayo). During the twelfth century they transferred their allegiance to *Mac Diarmada* (MacDermott) of Moylurg.

A sept of Uí Fiachrach, who were chiefs of Cúil Chearnadha.

A sept of Tír Amhalgaidh, now the barony of Tirawley in Mayo, who were Chiefs of Dun Fine, now Dunfeeny, nine miles north-west of Killalla.

A sept of the race of Laeghaire, of the same stock as the *ó Moráin* (O'Moran) who were chiefs of an area around Ballycong, near Ballymore Lough in the parish of Attymas, in the barony of Gallen.

At the close of the fourteenth century an O'Neill took the name Quinn and his descendants settled in Galway. The surname has been in Dublin for the past four hundred years and amongst its bearers have been a tutor to the Scottish royal family, a Lord Mayor and a famous actor. The surname has been in County Wicklow since at least the seventeenth century and in 1854 there were 53 Quinn households.

Quinn was the nineteenth most numerous surname in 1890, the estimated number of bearers was 18,200, and it was the most numerous surname in Tyrone. In that year the name was to be found in every county in Ireland. It was principally to be found in Dublin, Tyrone, Antrim, Roscommon and Galway. In the United States, Quinn is the 402nd most numerous surname with an estimated 77,000 bearers, O'Quinn is the 6,426th most numerous surname with an estimated 5,500 bearers, and Quin is the 15,374th most numerous surname with an estimated 2,500 bearers. This gives an estimated total figure of 85,000 for Quinn including variants. It is numerous in the states of Connecticut, New Jersey, and New York. In England and Wales in 1996 it was the 255th most numerous surname.

Quirke, Ó Cuirc
A Gaelic surname meaning descendant of *Corc*, meaning 'heart', though it may have mean 'red, crimson'. *Corc mac Luighdech* was the legendary founder of the kingdom of Cashel and ancestor of many kings of Munster. A sept who were anciently chiefs of Muscraighe Breogain also called Muscraighe Cuirc, in the present Barony of Clanwilliam, in Tipperary. Also see Kirk. In 1890 the surname was principally found in Tipperary and Kerry, and the estimated number of bearers was 1,790.

Rabbit, see McAneny

Rafferty, Ó Raithbheartaigh
A Gaelic surname derived from *rath bheartach* meaning 'prosperity wielder'. A sept which originated in the Sligo Donegal area. In 1890 Rafferty was principally found in Antrim, Tyrone and Louth, and the estimated number of bearers was 2,464. In the United States it is the 4,018th most numerous surname with an estimated 8,250 bearers.

Rainey
A Scottish surname, derived from Reginald. There is a similar surname in England. In 1890 Rainey was principally found in Antrim and Down, and the estimated number of bearers was 1,750.

Rankin
A Scottish surname derived from Randolph, from Ayrshire. In 1890 Rankin was principally found in Derry and Donegal, and the estimated number of bearers was 1,610.

Rea,
Both an English and a Scottish surname. The English surname being of local origin from residence near a stream or low-lying land near a stream. In Scotland a form of MacRea. In 1890 the surname was principally found in Antrim and Down, and the estimated number of bearers was 2,200.

Reddy, ó Rodaigh
A Gaelic surname meaning descendant of *Rodach* (derived from *rod* meaning 'strong'). A sept of the Uí Mhaine in Galway. In 1890 Reddy was principally found in Dublin and Kilkenny, and the estimated number of bearers was 1,430. In the United States it is the 3,776th most numerous surname with an estimated 8,250 bearers.

Redmond
A surname of either Gaelic or Cambro-Norman origin. The Cambro-Norman surname derived from the French *Raimond*; Old German *Raginmunnd* compound of *ragan* 'counsel' 'might' and *mund* 'protection'. The ancestry of the Wexford Redmonds is traceable to Alexander FitzRedmond who was granted the Hook area in the first Norman settlement. The MacDavymore Branch of the MacMurrough adopted the surname Redmond in the seventeenth century. They occupied the North Wexford area. In 1890 the estimated numbers bearing the name was 3,539, and it was principally found in Wexford, Dublin and Wicklow. In the United States it is the 1,573rd most numerous surname with an estimated 22,000 bearers.

Regan, ó Riagáin, ó Réagáin
A Gaelic surname meaning descendant of *Riagáin*, which personal name meant 'little king'. A sept of Meath who were a branch of the southern Uí Néill and one of the four tribes of Tara. They were lords of south Breagh, but were dispossessed shortly after the Cambro-Norman invasion. A sept of Thuas Mhumhan (Thomond), said to be descended of *Riagán*, son of *Donncuan*, a brother of Brian Boru. In 1890 Regan was the sixty-sixth most numerous surname, the estimated number of bearers was 10,500 and the surname was chiefly found in Cork, Roscommon and Mayo. In the United States Reagan is the 2,000th most numerous surname with an estimated 16,500 bearers. It is numerous in the state of Massachusetts.

Reid
An English or Scottish surname meaning 'red haired' or 'ruddy complexioned'. Most likely of Scottish origin in Ireland. Reed was at one time numerous in Kyle. In 1890 Reid was the eighty-first most numerous surname, the estimated number of bearers was 9,200 and was chiefly found in Antrim, Dublin, Down, Tyrone and Armagh. In 1863 it was the thirteenth most common name in Scotland, with an estimated 19,700 bearers. In the United States it is the 232nd most numerous surname with an estimated 126,500 bearers. In England and Wales in 1996 it was the 159th most numerous surname. In Scotland in 1995 it was the 11th most numerous surname.

Reidy, ó Riada
A Gaelic surname meaning descendant of *Riada*. A sept of the Dál gCais. In 1890 Reidy was principally found in Kerry and Clare, and the estimated number of bearers was 2,200.

O'Reilly, Ó Raghallaigh
A Gaelic surname meaning descendant of *Raghallach*, which personal name was from the Old Norse and introduced by the Vikings. The principal sept of Brifne (Breffny), who are of the same stock as the *Ó Ruairc* (O'Rourke). They were Chiefs of Breffny-O'Reilly, which originally comprised the greater part of the present Cavan. In 1890 O'Reilly was the eleventh most numerous surname in Ireland, the estimated number of bearers was 29,000, and it was the most numerous surname in Cavan, Longford and Meath. In that year the surname was found in every county in Ireland. It was principally found in Cavan, Longford, Dublin, Meath, Mayo and Cork. In the United States Reilly is the 901st most numerous surname with an estimated 35,750 bearers, and O'Reilly is the 3,584th most numerous surname with an estimated 8,250 bearers. It is numerous in the states of Connecticut, New Jersey, New York, and Pennsylvania. In England and Wales in 1996 Riley was the 153rd most numerous surname. In Scotland in 1995 Reilly was the 98th most numerous surname.

Reynolds, Mac Raghnaill
A Gaelic surname meaning son of Reginald. A sept of Anghaile (Annaly) who were chiefs of Muinntear Eolais in south Leitrim. In its anglicised form difficult to distinguish from Reynolds, the name of an old Dublin family since the end of the thirteenth century. Also an English surname from the personal name first introduced to England by Scandinavian settlers in the Old Norse form *Rognvaldr*. In 1890 Reynolds was numerous in Leitrim, it was also to be found in Dublin, Antrim and Louth. The estimated number of bearers was 5,062. In the United States it is the 112th most numerous surname with an estimated 214,500 bearers. In England and Wales in 1996 it was the 112th most numerous surname.

Rice, Ó Maolchraoibhe
A Gaelic surname meaning descendant of *Maolchraoibhe* (chief of Craobh, a place-name). A sept of Orghialla (Oriel) who were originally located west of the Upper Bann, but afterwards settled in Clannaboy. At the begining of the seventeenth century they occupied the west side of Knockbreda near Belfast in Down. The name has been translated both as Mulcreevy and Rice. The common Welsh surname *Ap Rhys*, has been anglicised as Rice. This family settled in Limerick and Dingle in the fourteenth and fifteenth century, where they were wealthy merchants. In 1890 was numerous in Louth, it was also to be found in Antrim, Armagh and Dublin. The estimated number of bearers for was 4,435. In the United States it is the 146th most numerous surname with an estimated 176,000 bearers. In England and Wales in 1996 it was the 432nd most numerous surname.

Richardson
An English surname derived from the Old German *Ric(h)ard* meaning 'powerful, brave'. Richard was one of the most popular personal names introduced into England by the Normans. Also a

Scottish surname of the same derivation. In 1890 Richardson was principally found in Dublin and Antrim, and the estimated number of bearers was 2,420. In the United States it is the 63rd most numerous surname with an estimated 308,000 bearers. In England and Wales in 1996 it was the 55th most numerous surname.

O'Riordan, ó Ríoghbhardáin, ó Ríordáin,
A Gaelic surname meaning descendant of *Rígbardán*, meaning 'royal poet'. *Rígbardán mac Con Coirne*, King of Eile who was slain in 1058 at the battle of Sliabh gCrot was an ancestor of the sept. They later moved into Desmond, to west Cork and Muskerry in particular. They were followers of the MacCarthy's. In 1890 Riordan was numerous in Cork (94 births), it was also to be found in Kerry and Limerick. The estimated number of bearers was 7,123 (including variants). In the United States Reardon is the 2,372 most numerous surname with an estimated 13,750 bearers.

Roberts,
A Scottish surname meaning son of Robert. See immediately below. In 1890 the surname was distributed evenly throughout the country and the estimated number of bearers was 1,790. In the United States it is the 43rd most numerous surname with an estimated 420,750 bearers. In England and Wales in 1996 it was the 11th most numerous surname.

Robinson, Robertson
An English or Scottish surname meaning son of Robin. The more usual Scottish form is Robertson meaning son of Robert. It is likely that the Scottish Robertson has become anglicised as Robinson in Ulster. Furthermore there is confusion between Robertson and Roberton, which is of territorial origin from Roberton in Lanarkshire. The Robertsons's of Struan in Gaelic are called the Clann Donnacha, from the name of their first chief. There are also families of Lude and Straloch. In 1863 it was the fifth most common name in Scotland, with an estimated 31,200 bearers. In 1990 it was the eight most numerous surname. In 1853 it was the twelfth most common surname in England and Wales, with an estimated 66,700 bearers. In Ireland in 1890 Robinson was the seventy-third most numerous surname, the estimated number of bearers was 9,700 and the surname was chiefly found in Antrim, Down, Dublin, Armagh and Tyrone. In the United States Robinson is the 20th most numerous surname with an estimated 640,750 bearers. In England and Wales in 1996 Robinson was the 12th most numerous surname, and Robertson was the 164th most numerous surname. In Scotland in 1995 Robertson was the 5th most numerous surname.

Roche, de la Roche
Richard FitzGoderbert *de la Roche*, son of Godebert Flandrensis of Rhos in Pembrokeshire was one of the Norman barons that returned with Dermot MacMurragh in 1167. A brother Robert settled in

Shelmalier East, his sons David, Henry and Adam adopted the surname *de la Roche*. In 1890 it was principally found in Cork, Wexford, Dublin, Limerick and Mayo. The estimated number of bearers was 8,198 (including variants). In the United States it is the 2,053rd most numerous surname with an estimated 16,500 bearers.

Rogers, Rodgers, Mac Ruaidhí

An English surname derived from the Old German Ro(d)ger, meaning 'fame-spear'. The name was introduced to England by the Normans. The form Rodgers is more common in Scotland. Also the anglicisation of *Mac Ruaidhrí* a Gaelic surname meaning son of Ruaidhrí. A sept of the Cineál Eoghain who were chiefs of Tellach Ainbhith and Muinntear in Tyrone and erenaghs of Ballynascreen in Derry. Also the anglicisation of a galloglass family, a branch of the MacDonnells who came to Ireland in the fourteenth century. In 1890 the surname was principally to be found in Antrim, Down, Dublin and Roscommon, and the estimated number of bearers was 7,600. In the United States Rogers is the 54th most numerous surname with an estimated 338,250 bearers. In England and Wales in 1996 Rogers was the 77th most numerous surname.

Rooney, ó Ruanaidh, ó Rúnaighean

Rooney is an anglicisation of a number of different Gaelic septs. A Gaelic surname meaning descendant of *Ruanaidh* (hero). A sept of Down who were based in the parish of Ballyroney, north of Rathfriland. *ó Ruanaidhín*, descendant of Ruanaidhín (diminutive of Ruanaidh) of Donegal and north Leitrim. *ó Rúnaighean* of Sligo. *ó Maolruanaidh*, meaning a descendant of Maolruanaidh (follower of Ruanaidh). A sept who prior to the Maguires were lords of Fermanagh. This is usually anglicised as Mulrooney but sometimes as Rooney. In 1890 Rooney was numerous in Leitrim, it was also to be found in Dublin, Down, Antrim and Mayo. The estimated number of bearers was 5,331. In the United States Rooney is the 2,158th most numerous surname with an estimated 16,500 bearers, and Roney is the 3,683rd most numerous surname with an estimated 8,250 bearers.

Ross

Both an English and a Scottish surname of local origin. In Scotland the first record of the surname was in north Ayrshire, where a family of English origin (Yorkshire) was granted lands. In the north of Scotland the surname was derived from the district of Ross Also a descriptive surname from the Middle English *rous* meaning 'red-haired'. In England there were many place called Ross (Bedfordshire, Hereford, Kent, Lancs., Yorkshire). In 1890 Ross was principally found in Antrim, Derry, Cork and Down, and the estimated number of bearers was 3,270. In the United States it is the 80th most numerous surname with an estimated 26,400 bearers. In England and Wales in 1996 it was the 185th most numerous surname. In Scotland in 1995 it was the 16th most numerous surname.

O'Rourke, ó Ruairc

A Gaelic surname meaning descendant of *Ruarc*. The personal name *Ruadhrac* came from the Norse *Hrothrekr*. The leading sept of Breifne (Breffny). Three of their ancestors in the tenth and eleventh centuries were Kings of Connaught. As lords of Breifne (Breffny) their territory extended from Kells in Meath to Drumcliff in Sligo. In the twelfth Century their power declined, with ó *Raghallaigh* (O'Reilly) becoming lord of east Breffny. They took a leading part in the Elizabeth wars and were only dispossessed with the Cromwellian confiscations. A sept of Uí Mhaine in Galway. A sept of Lia Con in the Barony of Tireragh in Sligo. A sept who were erenagh of Termonn Feichin, at Ballysadare, Sligo. In 1890 O'Rourke was the ninety-eight most numerous surname and the estimated number of bearers was 8,300. In that year the surname was chiefly found in Dublin, Leitrim, Roscommon and Wexford. In the United States O'Rourke is the 2,393rd most numerous surname with an estimated 13,750 bearers, and Rourke was the 8,171st most numerous surname with an estimated 2,750 bearers.

Ruane, ó Ruadháin

A Gaelic surname meaning descendant of *Ruadhán* (diminutive of *ruadh* for 'red'). A sept of the Ui Fiachrach who possessed a district lying between Newbrook and Kileen, to the north of Ballinrobe in Mayo. A sept of the Uí Mhaine in Galway. During the twelfth and thirteenth centuries seven of the name were bishops in Connacht. In 1890 the surname was principally found in Mayo (1,300) and Galway, and the estimated number of bearers was 1,660.

Russell

Both an English and a Scottish surname, from the Old French *rous-el* a diminutive of *rous* 'red'. In Scotland in 1863 Russell was the forty-ninth most numerous surname and the estimated number of bearers was 9,500. In Ireland in 1890 Russell was principally found in Antrim, Dublin and Down, and the estimated number of bearers was 4,520. In the United States it is the 97th most numerous surname with an estimated 233,750 bearers. In England and Wales in 1996 it was the 93rd most numerous surname. In Scotland in 1995 it was the 47th most numerous surname.

Ryan, ó Maoilriain, ó Riain

A Gaelic surname meaning descendants of *Maolrian*. The personal name *Rian* is most likely a diminutive of *Rí* meaning a 'king'. A sept of Leinster origin who settled in the thirteenth or fourteenth century in Uaithne Tíre and Uaithne Cliach, now the baronies of Owney in Tipperary and Owneybeg in east Limerick. Should be distinguished from ó *Riain* meaning descendent of *Riaghan* or *Rian*. A sept in Carlow who were lords of Uí Dhróna, now the barony of Idrone. ó *Ruadháin*, meaning descendent of *Ruadhán*; a diminutive *Ruadh* meaning 'red haired'. Also anglicised as O'Ruane. A sept of the Uí Fiachrach in Mayo and also A sept of the Uí Mhaine in Galway. In

1890 Ryan was the eight most numerous surname in Ireland, the estimated number of bearers was 32,000, and it was the most numerous surname in Limerick and Tipperary. In that year the surname was also to be found in Dublin, Cork, Waterford, Kilkenny, Wexford, Clare and Galway. In the United States Ryan is the 203rd most numerous surname with an estimated 140,250 bearers. It is numerous in the states of Connecticut, New Jersey, and New York. In England and Wales in 1996 it was the 135th most numerous surname.

Savage, Mac an t-Sábhaisigh, ó Sabháin

A surname of Norman origin from the Old French *sauvage* meaning 'wild'. In 1177 William *le Savage* was granted territory in the Upper Ards in Down. The family became hibernicized from the fifteenth century onwards, and the surname was Gaelicised as *Mac an t-Sábhaisigh*. The Gaelic *ó Sabháin* sept of Munster has also being anglicised as Savage. In 1890 Savage was principally found in Antrim, Down, Dublin and Cork, and the estimated number of bearers was 2,730. In the United States it is the 582nd most numerous surname with an estimated 55,000 bearers. In England and Wales in 1996 it was the 344th most numerous surname.

Scanlon, ó Scannláin, ó Scannail

A Gaelic surname meaning descendant of *Scannlán* (diminutive of *Scannal*, meaning quarrel, contention). A sept of the southern Uí Fiachrach and of the same stock as the O'Shaughnessys and O'Heynes. A sept of Cork who were erenaghs of Cloyne. A sept of Fermanagh who were erenaghs of Devenish. Also the *ó Scannail* sept of the race of Cairbre, who were originally seated in the barony of Carbury, to the north of Sligo town. In 1890 Scanlon was numerous in Sligo, it was also to be found in Kerry, Clare, Limerick and Cork. The estimated number of bearers for Scanlon was 2,419, and for Scanlan was 1,881. In the United States Scanlon is the 3,257th most numerous surname with an estimated 11,000 bearers, and Scanlan was the 6,519th most numerous surname with an estimated 5,500 bearers.

Scannell, ó Scannláin

A Gaelic surname adopted by several septs. The personal name may be associatd with *scandal* meaning 'quarrel, contention'. A sept who were formerly erenaghs of Cloyne in Cork. In 1890 the surname was principally found in Cork and Kerry, and the estimated number of bearers was 1,880.

Scott

Both an English and Scottish surname. In England a border name from the Old English *Scott* originally 'an Irishman' later 'a Gael from Scotland'. The surname may have established itself in Scotland from Northumberland. They were a powerful clan on the English/Scottish border. In 1863 (and also in 1990) it was the tenth most numerous name in Scotland, with an estimated 22,400 bearers. In Ireland, in 1890 Scott was the ninetieth most numerous surname and the estimated number of bearers was 8,700. In that year the surname was chiefly found in Antrim, Down, Derry and Dublin. In the United States it is the 34th most numerous surname with an estimated 508,750 bearers. In England and Wales in 1996 it was the 42nd most numerous surname. In Scotland in 1995 it was the 10th most numerous surname.

Scully, ó Scolaidhe, ó Scolaighe
A Gaelic sept who were originally chiefs of West Devlin in Westmeatrh until dispersed early in the twelfth century. The surname is derived from *scolaige* meaning 'scholar, schoolman'. Subsequently they became erenaghs of the church of St. Ruan, at Lorrha in north Tipperary. There is a townland called Ballyscully in the Parish of Duniry, Barony of Leitrin, in Galway. In 1890 Scully was principally found in Cork, Dublin, Carlow and Ofally, and the estimated number of bearers was 2,910. In the United States Scully is the 4,238th most numerous surname with an estimated 8,250 bearers.

Sexton, ó Seasnáin
A Gaelic surname, a sept of the Dál gCais in Thomond. The anglicised form appeared early in the city of Limerick. There is also an English surname, being a reference to the officer in a church in charge of the sacred vessels and vestments. In 1890 the surname was principally found in Cork, Clare, Limerick and Cavan, and the estimated number of bearers was 1,930. In the United States Sexton is the 680th most numerous surname with an estimated 46,750 bearers.

Shanahan, ó Seanacháin
A Gaelic surname derived from *seanach* meaning 'old, wise'. A sept of the Dál gCais who were chiefs of Ui Rongaile (co-extensive with the parishes of Kilnoe and Killuran in Clare) in Thomond. In 1318 they were expelled by Torlough O'Brien and the MacNamaras. They settled firstly in Waterford, but subsequently scattered. In 1890 Shanahan was principally found in Cork, Kerry, Tipperary, Limerick and Waterford, and the estimated number of bearers was 2,910 (including variants). In the United States Shanahan is the 4,816th most numerous surname with an estimated 5,500 bearers.

Shannon,
It is difficult to be certain as to which Gaelic surname this is an anglicisation. *ó Seanáin* derived from a diminutive of *sean* meaning 'old, wise'. Also a Scottish surname of similar derivation, found in Galloway and Kintyre. See *ó Seanacháin* (also anglicised as Shanahan). In 1890 the surname was principally found in Antrim, Clare and Roscommon, and the estimated number of bearers was 3,225. In the United States Shannon is the 679th most numerous surname with an estimated 46,750 bearers.

Sharkey, ó Searcaigh
A Gaelic sept derived from *searcach* meaning 'loving'. A sept which

165

originated in Tir Eoghain, but spread to Donegal and Connacht. In 1890 Sharkey was principally found in Roscommon, Donegal, Tyrone, Dublin and Louth, and the estimated number of bearers was 2,600. In the United States Sharkey is the 4,216th most numerous surname with an estimated 8,250 bearers.

McShane, Mac Sagháin
A Gaelic surname meaning son of Sean (the Irish form of John). In Tyrone the sept was a branch of the *ó Neill*. In 1890 McShane was principally found in Donegal and Louth, and the estimated number of bearers was 1,520.

McSharry, Mac Searraigh
A Gaelic surname derived from *Searrach* meaning 'foal, flighty'. A sept of Breifney. Sometimes translated as Foley in Sligo. In 1890 McShary was numerous in Leitrim, it was also to be found in Donegal and Sligo. The estimated number of bearers was 1,299.

Shaughnessy, ó Seachnasaigh
A Gaelic surname meaning descendant of *Seachnasach*. A sept of the Ui Fiachrach Aidhne. On the decline of the O'Cahill in the thirteenth century, they became chiefs of Cinel Aodha (Kinelea, the district lying around Gort in Galway). In 1890 the surname was principally found in Galway (50%), and the estimated number of bearers was 1,840. In the United States Shaugnasessy is the 7,872nd most numerous surname with an estimated 2,750 bearers, and O'Shaughnessy is the 9,923rd most numerous surname with an estimated 2,750 bearers.

Shaw
An English surname from *Shaw* 'dweller by the wood', from the Old English *sceaga*. A Scottish Lowland surname of territorial origin. *Mac Sithech* a branch of the Clan Chattan of Aberdeenshire from *sithech* (son of) the wolf. In 1890 Shaw was principally found in Antrim, Down and Dublin, and the estimated number of bearers was 3,580. In the United States it is the 144th most numerous surname with an estimated 178,750 bearers. In England and Wales in 1996 it was the 59th most numerous surname. In Scotland in 1995 it was the 85th most numerous surname.

O'Shea, ó Séaghdha, ó Se
A Gaelic surname meaning descendant of *Seaghdha*, which personal name was a rare early Irish name meaning 'fine, stately'. A sept of the Corcu Dhuibhne in west Kerry, who were Lords of Uíbh Ráthach, now the barony of Iveragh, prior to the Cambro-Norman Invasion. A branch of this sept migrated to Kilkenny and Tipperary in the thirteenth century. A sept of the Uí Fiachrach, in the barony of Tirawley, Mayo. In 1890 O'Shea was the forty-ninth most numerous surname and the estimated number of bearers was 13,000, and the surname was principally to be found in Kerry (146 births), Cork, Kilkenny, Tipperary and Waterford. In the United States Shea is the

1,001st most numerous surname with an estimated 33,000 bearers, and O'Shea is the 4,326th most numerous surname with an estimated 8,250 bearers. It is numerous in the states of Connecticut, and Massachusetts.

Sheehan, Sheahan, ó Síodhacháin, ó Síocháin
A Gaelic surname meaning descendant of *Síodhachán*, which personal name was a diminutive of *Síodhách* meaning 'peaceful'. A sept of Dál gCais. A sept of Uí Mhaine, who were followers of ó Ceallaigh (O'Kelly). In 1890 Sheehan was the seventy-seventh most numerous surname and the estimated number of bearers was 9,600. In that year the surname was chiefly found in Cork, Kerry and Limerick. Half of the Munster entries were to be found in Cork (97 births). In the United States Sheehan is the 9,501st most numerous surname with an estimated 2,750 bearers. It is numerous in the states of Connecticut, and Massachusetts.

Sheehy, Mac Sithigh
According to MacLysaght a galloglass family from the Clan McDonald which settled in Munster. In 1890 Sheehy was principally found in Kerry, Limerick and Cork, and the estimated number of bearers was 2,464. In the United States Sheehy is the 9,501st most numerous surname with an estimated 2,750 bearers.

Sheeran, ó Síoráin, ó Sírín
A Gaelic sept of which there is no further information available. In 1890 Sheeran was principally found in Leinster and the estimated number of bearers was 1,340. In the United States Shearin is the 9,905th most numerous surname with an estimated 2,750 bearers.

Sheridan, ó Sirideáin
A Gaelic surname meaning descendant of *Sirideán*. A sept of Longford who were erenaghs of Granard, who afterwards moved to Cavan. A sept of the Síol Muireadhaigh in Connacht. In 1890 Sheridan was numerous in Cavan and Sligo, it was also to be found in Dublin and Mayo. The estimated number of bearers was 6,496 (including variants). In the United States it is the 1,572 most numerous surname with an estimated 22,000 bearers.

Shields, Sheilds
A Scottish surname, also spelt Shiel (see immediately below). Originally a border surname of local origin from the Middle English *schele* meaning ' shepherd's summer-hut', and later 'a small house'. An English surname derived from Old English *scild*, or *sceld* meaning 'shield' probably for a maker of shields. Also from the Old English meaning dweller 'by the shelter' or 'by the shallow place'. Difficult to distinguish from the surname below. In 1890 the surname was principally found in Antrim and Down, and the estimated number of bearers was 2,465 (including variants). In the United States Shields is the 580th most numerous surname with an estimated 55,000 bearers.

167

Shiels, Sheils, ó Siadhail
A Gaelic sept who were hereditary physicans in the north of Ireland, and may have originated in Inishowen in Donegal. Difficult to distinguish from the immmediatly preceeding surname. In 1890 the surname was principally found in Dublin, Donegal and Derry, and the estimated number of bearers was 2,510.

Simpson, Simson
A Scottish surname meaning 'son of Sim'. Simon was a popular personal name prior to the Reformation in England and Scotland. There is also an English surname of similar derivation, additionally there are three places called Simpson in Devon which gave rise to such surname. In 1863 Simpson was the forty-third most numerous surname in Scotland. In 1890 Simpson was principally found in Antrim, and the estimated number of bearers was 3,360. In the United States Simpson is the 126th most numerous surname with an estimated 192,500 bearers. In England and Wales in 1996 Simpson was the 67th most numerous surname. In Scotland in 1995 Simpson was the 32nd most numerous surname.

Sinnott, Synnott, Sinóid
A surname of English origin from the Old English meaning 'victory-bold'. They came to Ireland at the time of the Cambro-Norman invasion and settled principally in Wexford. In 1890 the surname was principally found in Wexford (Sinnott) and Dublin (Synnott), and the estimated number of bearers was 1,660.

Slattery, ó Slararra
A Gaelic surname derived from *Slatra* meaning 'bold, strong'. A sept of the Dál gCais formerly seated at Ballyslattery (also called Newgrove) in the Barony of Tulla Upper in Clare, who later dispersed throughout Munster. In 1890 Slattery was principally found in Tipperary, Kerry, Cork, Clare and Limerick, and the estimated number of bearers was 3,090. In the United States Slattery is the 4,410th most numerous surname with an estimated 8,250 bearers.

Sloan, Sloane, ó Sluaghadháin
Both an Irish and a Scottish surname derived from *Sluaghadhach* meaning 'fit for hoasting' (in the military sence). In Scotland a sept of Galloway. In Ireland a sept of Mayo. In 1890 Sloan was principally found in Antrim, and the estimated number of bearers was 2,730. In the United States Sloan is the 665th most numerous surname with an estimated 49,500 bearers.

Small
Both an English and a Scottish surname, being a reference to stature. In 1890 Small was principally found in Antrim, Armagh and Down, and the estimated number of bearers was 1,340. In the United States it is the 556th most numerous surname with an estimated 57,750 bearers.

Smith, Smyth, Smythe, Mac Gabhann, Mac Gowan
An Irish, English and Scottish surname. The Gaelic surname means 'son of the smith'. A sept that originated in Cavan. A sept of Clann an Ghobhann of Clare who were hereditary historians to the *ó Lochlainn* of Burren. A sept of Clann an Ghobhann of Tipperary who were hereditary historians to *ó Cinnéide* (O'Kennedy) of Ur Mhumhan (Ormond). An English surname of occupation. Smith was adopted by, and by the descendants of blacksmiths. Blacksmiths were to be found in every town or manor in England. A tenant often held his land on condition of performing such duties. The variation of spelling as between 'Smith' and 'Smyth(e)' was a result of the interchangeability of 'i' and 'y' in Old English. It is the most numerous surname in both England and Scotland. In 1890 Smith was the fifth most numerous surname in Ireland, the estimated number of bearers was 33,700, and it was the most numerous surname in Antrim. In that year the surname was found in every county. It was principally found in Antrim, Cavan and Dublin. In the United States Smith is the most numerous surname with an estimated 2,766,500 bearers. In England and Wales in 1996 it was the most numerous surname. In Scotland in 1995 it was the most numerous surname.

Somers
Both an English and a Scottish surname derived from the Old French *somier, sommier,* a sumpter applied to both men and horses. In 1890 Somers was princiipally found in Wexford and Dublin, and the estimated number of bearers was 1,700.

Speers
Both an English and a Scottish surname. In Scotland it may be *spyer* meaning 'a watchman'. In England it is most likely a reference to a spearman. In 1890 Speers was principally fund in Antrim and the estimated number of bearers was 1700. In the United States Spears is the 717th most numerous surname with an estimated 44,000 bearers.

Spelman, ó Spealáin
A Gaelic surname derived from speal meaning 'a sythe'. A sept of the Ui Fiachrach who were formerly seated in Coillin Aodha (now Culleen), in the parish of Kilglas in Sligo. In 1890 Spelman was principally found in Galway, Roscommon and Mayo, and the estimated number of bearers was 1,340.

Spence
Both an English and a Scottish surname derived from Middle English *spense, spence,* meaning 'larder' referring to one who worked at or was in charge of the buttery. In 1890 Spence was principally found in Antrim and Down, and the estimated number of bearers was 2,600. In the United States it is the 808th most numerous surname with an estimated 41,250 bearers.

Spillane, Ó Spealáin
A Gaelic surname meaning descendant of *Spealán* (diminutive of *speal* meaning 'a sythe'). A sept of the Dál gCais who were anciently chiefs of Ui Luighdheach or Ileagh in the present Barony of Eliogarty in Tipperary, but long since dispersed through Munster and Leinster. In 1890 the surname was principally found in Cork and Kerry, and the estimated number of bearers was 1,970.

Stack
The origin of this surname is English. The Stacks have been established in north Kerry since the late thirteenth century. They became thoroughly Irish from an early date. In 1890 Stack was principally found in Kerry, Cork, Limerick, Wexford and Dublin, and the estimated number of bearers was 2,420. In the United States it is the 3,474th most numerous surname with an estimated 11,000 bearers.

Staffard, de Stafford
A surname of Anglo-Norman origin, *de Staford* from the place so named (there are few in England). The family that settled in the Barony of Forth in Wexford came from Buckinghamshire. In 1890 Staffard was principally found in Wexfod and Dublin, and the estimated number of bearers was 1,480. In the United States Stafford is the 628th most numerous surname with an estimated 52,250 bearers.

Stanton, Staunton, de Stanton
A surname of Anglo-Norman origin, their ancestor was Milo *de* Stanton, there are many places so named in England. They settled in Dublin, Kildare, Kilkenny, Cork and Mayo. In Mayo they were followers of de Burgo and were granted lands in the barony of Carra. They took the surname *Mac an Mhíleadha* (son of the knight), which anglicised as MacEvilly. In 1890 Stanton was principally found in Mayo and Cork, Staunton was principally found in Mayo, Galway, Tipperary, Kilkenny, and the estimated number of bearers was 3,000.

Steel, Steele
A Scottish surname of local origin, there are places so named in Ayr, Berwick and Dumfries. Also an English surname referring to a person who was as reliable as steel. In 1890 Steel was principally found in Antrim and Derry, and the estimated number of bearers was 2,420. In the United States Steele is the 312th most numerous surname with an estimated 96,250 bearers. It is numerous in the states of Connecticut, Delaware, Maryland, Massachusetts, New Jersey, New York, Pennsylvania. In England and Wales in 1996 Steele was the 402nd most numerous surname.

Stenson
An English surname of territorial origin, from a place in Derbyshire. In 1890 Stenson was numerous in Sligo. The estimated number of bearers was 672.

170

Stephens
Most likely a surname adopted by the descendants of the Cambro-Norman invaders in Connacht: FitzStephens. In 1890 Stephens was principally found in Mayo, and the estimated number of bearers was 1,610. In the United States it is the 165th most numerous surname with an estimated 156,750 bearers. In England and Wales in 1996 it was the 246th most numerous surname.

Stevenson, Stephenson
Both an English and a Scottish surname, meaning son of Steven or Stephen. In 1890 was principally found in Antrim, Armagh and Down, and the estimated number of bearers was 4,750. In the United States Stevenson is the 345th most numerous surname with an estimated 85,250 bearers, and Stephenson is the 643rd most numerous surname with an estimated 49,500 bearers. In England and Wales in 1996 Stevenson was the 230th most numerous surname, and Stephenson was the 131st most numerous surname. In Scotland in 1995 Stevenson was the 52nd most numerous surname.

Stewart, Stuart
A Scottish surname, in Old English *stiward* meant 'one who looked after domestic animals'; hence by extension one who provide for his master's table. Stuart is a variant of Stewart. In Scotland by the eleventh century the steward was chief of the royal household. In 1863 it was the sixth most common surname in Scotland, with an estimated 30,600 bearing the surname. In Ireland in 1890 Stewart was the fifty-eight most numerous surname and the estimated number of bearers was 11,400. In that year the surname was chiefly found in Antrim, Down, Derry, Donegal and Tyrone. In the United States Stewart is the 51st most numerous surname with an estimated 365,750 bearers, and Stuart is the 917th most numerous surname with an estimated 35,750 bearers. In England and Wales in 1996 Stewart was the 110th most numerous surname. In Scotland in 1995 Stewart was the 7th most numerous surname.

O'Sullivan, Ó Súileabháin
A Gaelic surname meaning descendant of *Súildubhán*, which rare personal name meant 'dark-eyed'. A leading sept, which is said to have originated in Cnoc Rafann now Knockgraffon in the south of Tipperary along the river Suir and forced westwards by Cambro-Norman invaders. Their new home was in the west of Deas Mhumhan (Desmond), on the shores of the bays of Kenmare and Bantry. They divided into several sub-septs : *O'Súilleabháin More* in the barony of Dunkerron, a branch of this sept was at Cappanacushy. *O'Súilleabháin Beare* in the territory of Beare now the baronies of Beare and Bantry in Cork. *O'Súilleabháin Maol* (The leader of the sept was known as: Mac Finghin Dubh). A sept of the Clann Giolla Mochuda, who changed their name to Mac Gillycuddy of Kerry. In 1890, O'Sullivan was the third most numerous surname, the estimated number of bearers was 43,600, and it was the most common surname

in Counties Cork (373 births) and Kerry (295 births). In that year the surname was found in every county in Munster. It was also to be found in Dublin, Antrim and Galway. In the United States Sullivan is the 105th most numerous surname with an estimated 222,750 bearers, and O'Sullivan is the 3,853rd most numerous surname with an estimated 8,250 bearers. It is numerous in the state of Connecticut. In England and Wales in 1996 Sullivan was the 241st most numerous surname, and O'Sullivan was the 360th most numerous surname.

Sutton, de Suttoun
An English surname of territorial origin, a place name very common in England. From the Old English meaning the place (south of the village). This family established itself in Wexford until they were dispossessed during the Cromwellian period. In 1890 the name was principally found in Dublin, Wexford and Cork, and the estimated number of bearers was 1,210. In the United States Sutton is the 283rd most numerous surname with an estimated 104,500 bearers. In England and Wales in 1996 it was the 193rd most numerous surname.

MacSweeny, MacSwenney, Swenney, Swenny, Mac Suibhne
A Scottish Gaelic surname meaning son of *Suibhne*, which personal name meant 'pleasant'. They came to Donegal for the second time in the fourteenth century as Galloglass to the *ó Domhnaill* (O'Donnell). They divided into three septs. *Mac Suibhne Fánad*, who held Rathmullan Castle and territory in the north-east of the barony of Kilmacrenan, Donegal. *Mac Suibhne Boghaineach*, of Baghnagh, now the barony of Banagh, Donegal. *Mac Suibhne na dTuath* of Tuath Toraidhe, or the mainland opposite Tory Island in Donegal. A branch of *Mac Suibhne Fánad* settled in Desmond (Deas Mhumhan) as galloglass to *MacCarthaigh* (MacCarthy), they had several castles in the barony of Muskerry, Cork. In 1890 Sweeney was the fifth-first most numerous surname, the estimated number of bearers was 12,500 and the surname was chiefly found in Cork, Donegal, Mayo and Kerry. In the United States Sweeney is the 650th most numerous surname with an estimated 49,500 bearers, Sweeny is the 9,766th most numerous surname with an estimated 2,750 bearers, and McSweeney is the 9,800th most numerous surname with an estimated 2,750 bearers. Sweeney is numerous in the state of Pennsylvania.

Taggart, Mac Entaggart, Mac an tSagairt
A Gaelic surname meaning 'son of the priest'. A sept of Ulster. In 1890 Taggart was principally found in Antrim and the estimated number of bearers was 1,880.

Mac Taghlin, see Houston

Tate, Tait
Both an English and a Scottish surname derived from the Old Norse *teitr* meaning 'glad, cheerful'. In 1890 Tate was principally found in Antrim and Down, Tait in Derry, and the estimated number of bearers

was 1,610. In the United States Tate is the 348th most numerous surname with an estimated 85,250 bearers.

Taylor
An English occupational surname. In England in 1853 Taylor was the fourth most numerous surname and the estimated number of bearers was 124,400. In 1863 Taylor was the twenty-ninth most numerous surname in Scotland and the estimated number of bearers was 14,400. In Ireland in 1890 the surname was principally found in Antrim, Down, Derry and Dublin, and the estimated number of bearers was 6,720.

Thompson
An English and Scottish surname meaning son of Thom, in Ulster it is mostly of Scottish origin and spelt Thomson. In Scotland: A family possessed of Duddingston near Edinburgh, in Pertshire. A sept of Clan Campbell in Argyllshire, really Mac Tavishes by Mac Thomais Clan Tavish of Dunardarig descendent of Tavis Conn second illigimate son of Gillespick son of Callen Mor Maith. In 1890 Thompson was the forty-second most numerous surname and the estimated number of bearers was 14,200. It was the most common surname in Down and the surname was principally to be found in Antrim, Down, Armagh, Derry, Dublin, Fermanagh and Longford. In the United States Taylor is the 10th most numerous surname with an estimated 855,250 bearers. In England and Wales in 1996 it was the 4th most numerous surname. In Scotland in 1995 it was the 13th most numerous surname.

Thornton
An English surname of local origin. However Mac Giolla Domhnaigh states that in most parts of south Connacht and North Munster it is the anglicised form of *ó Draighneain*, a sept of south Galway. In 1890 Thornton was principally found in Gaway, Dublin and Mayo, and the estimated number of bearers was 2,420. In the United States it is the 354th most numerous surname with an estimated 85,250 bearers. In England and Wales in 1996 it was the 302nd most numerous surname.

MacTiernan, (Mac)Kiernan, Mac Tighearnáin
A Gaelic surname meaning son of *Tighearnán* (diminutive of *Tighearna*, meaning 'lord'). A sept of Breifney who were formerly chiefs of Tellach Dhunchadha, now the barony of Tullyhunco in the west of Cavan. A sept of Fermanagh of the same stock as the Maguires who were formerly chiefs of Clann Fearghaile. A sept who were a branch of the O'Connors in Roscommon, descended from *Tighearnán*, grandson of Turlough Mor O'Connor, Ard Rí. In its anglicised form difficult to distinguish from *ó Tighearnaigh*. In 1890 McTernan was numerous in Leitrim, and the estimated number of bearers was 896 (including variants), McKiernan was to be found in Ulster and the estimated number of bearers was 800.

Tierney, ó Tighearnaigh

A Gaelic surname derived from *Tighearnach* meaning 'lordly'. A sept of the Cineál Eoghain who were anciently chiefs of Fearnmaigh in the present Donegal. A sept of the Ui Fiachrach who were lords of Ceara, now the barony of Carra in Mayo. A sept of the southern Ui Néill in Westmeath. Note also the immediately preceding surname with which it is confused. In 1890 Tierney was principally found in Dublin, Tipperary and Galway, and the estimated number of bearers was 3,495. In the United States Tierney is the 3,411th most numerous surname with an estimated 11,000 bearers.

Tighe, ó Taidgh, Mac Taidhg

A Gaelic surname derived from *Tadhg* meaning 'poet, philosopher'. A sept who were of the same stock as the O'Connors and who were chiefs of their household. A sept of Leinster who were anciently chiefs of Ui Mail, now Imail in Wicklow. A sept of Ulster who were chiefs of Fir Li in Derry, A sept of Thomond. A 'Mac' sept were anciently chiefs of Muinntear Siorthachain in Westmeath. According to Woulfe *Mac Ceanglaigh* a rare surname in Meath and Cavan is translated as Kangley and Tighe. In 1890 Tighe was principally found in Mayo, and the estimated number of bearers was 1,480.

Tobin, de St. Aubyn, Tóibin

A surname of Norman origin, whose bearers became completely hibernicized. "*de St. Aubyn*" a town in Brittany, the scene of a battle between the French and Bretons aided by the English in 1488. The Tobins settled in Tipperary and Kilkenny, whence they spread into the neighbouring counties. In 1890 Tobin was numerous in Waterford, it was also to be found in Cork, Tippeary, Limerick, Dublin and Kilkenny. The estimated number of bearers was 4,390. In the United States Tobin is the 1,761st most numerous surname with an estimated 19,250 bearers.

Todd

Both an English and a Scottish surname, derived from the Middle English *tod(de)* meaning fox, In England chiefly Northern. In 1890 Todd was principally found in Antrim and Down, and the estimated number of bearers was 1,700. In the United States Todd is the 368th most numerous surname with an estimated 82,500 bearers. In England and Wales in 1996 it was the 286th most numerous surname.

Toner, ó Tomhnair

A Gaelic surname meaning descendant of *Tomhnar* (a Norse personal name). A sept of the Cineál Eoghain who were seated near Lough Swilly in Donegal, where they built the church called for them Cill ó dTomhnair, now anglicised Killodonnell. In 1890 the surname was principally found in Armagh, Derry and Antrim, and the estimated number of bearers was 1,880.

O'Toole, Ó Tuathail

A Gaelic surname meaning descendant of *Tuathal* (meaning, people mighty). One of the principle septs of Leinster, originally of Kildare they moved to Wicklow. In 1890, the estimated number of persons bearing the surname was 4,500, and the surname was principally to be found in Dublin, Galway, Wicklow and Kildare. In the United States Toole is the 5,470th most numerous surname with an estimated 5,500 bearers.

Towey, Ó Toghdha

A Gaelic surname meaning descendant of *Toghdha* (meaning 'chosen, elected'). A sept of the Uí Fiachrach who were chiefs of Bredagh, a district now in the barony of Tirawley, embracing the parish of Moygawnagh and part of the adjoining parish of Kilfian. In 1890 Towey was numerous in Roscommon, it was also to be found in Mayo. The estimated number of bearers was 1,344.

Travers, Trover, Ó Treabhair

A Gaelic surname derived from *treabhar* meaning 'prudent, wise, skilful'. A sept of Leitrim of the same stock as the Mac Clancys, who were erenaghs of Killarga, also translated as Trover. Also a surname of Norman origin *de Tryvers* of Treviers in Normandy, and old surname in Dublin and parts of the south. In 1890 Travers was principally found in Donegal, Dublin and Leitrim, and the estimated number of bearers was 1,700.

Traynor, Treanor, Trainor, Mac Thréinfhir

A Gaelic surname derived from *Tréanfhear* meaning 'strong-man'. A sept of Oriel In Scotland the surname has been recorded in Fife. There is an English surname Trainer derived from the Middle English *trayne* meaning to 'set a trap', a reference to a trapper. In 1890 Traynor was principally found in Dublin, Treanor and Trainor in Antrim, Armagh, Monaghan and Tyrone, and the estimated number of bearers was 3,450 (all variants). In the United States Traynor is the 8,158th most numerous surname with an estimated 2,750 bearers, and Trainor is the 5,141st most numerous surname with an estimated 5,500 bearers.

Treacy, Tracey, Tracy, Ó Treasaigh

A Gaelic surname derived from *Treasach* meaning 'warlike, fierce'. A sept of Leinster who were anciently lords of Uí Bairrche a district embracing the Barony of Slievemargy in Laois. A sept of Connacht of the same stock as the Madden's who were seated in south-east Galway. A sept of Fermanagh. In 1890 Treacy was principally found in Tipperary and Galway, Tracet and Tracy in Dublin, and the estimated number of bearers was 3,765 (all variants). In the United States Tracy is the 1,082nd most numerous surname with an estimated 30,200 bearers, and Tracey is the 4,790th most numerous surname with an estimated 5,500 bearers.

Troy, Ó Troighthigh
Both a Gaelic surname and a surname of Cambro-Norman origin. *de Troye*, of Troyes formerly the capital of Champagne in France. The sept name derived from *Troightheach* meaning a 'foot-soldier', their original territory was in or near Corcomroe in north-west Clare. However they dispersed to Offaly, North Tipperary, Limerick and Cork, and were know as O'Treahy. In 1890 Troy was principally found in Offaly, Cork and Tipperary, and the estimated number of bearers was 1,390.

Tully, Mac Maoltuile, Ó Maoltuile
A Gaelic surname meaning descendant of *Maoltuile* (devoted to the will, i.e. of God). A sept of Roscommon who were hereditary physicians to the O'Connors of Connacht and the O'Rourkes of Breifney. This has been shortened to MacTuile, and also corrupted to Mac an Tuile. Also translated as Flood, owing to *tuile* being 'flood'. In 1890 the surname was principally found in Galway, Dublin and Cavan, and the estimated number of bearers was 2,020. In the United States Tully is the 5,176th most numerous surname with an estimated 5,500 bearers.

Tuohy, Ó Tuathaigh
A Gaelic surname meaning descendant of *Tuathach* (rustic; also a lord). A sept of the Uí Mhaine who were originally seated at Aughrim in Galway. In 1890 the surname was principally found in Clare and Galway, and the estimated number of bearers was 1,790 (all nine varieties).

Turner
Both an English and a Scottish surname, with a number of possible derivations. From the Old French *le turner* which refered to 'one who turns or fashions objects of wood, metal, bone, etc., on a lathe'. It may be from the Old French *tournoieur* referring to one who takes part in a tournament. It may have been 'turn hare' a reference to one so fast that he could outstrip a hare. In Scotland the surname was to be found in New Abbey, Aberdeen and Cowal. In 1853 Turner was the twenty-third most unmerous surname in England, with an estimated 56,300 bearers. In 1890 Turner was principally found in Dublin, Antrim and Cork, and the estimated number of bearers was 3,000. In the United States it is the 44th most numerous surname with an estimated 418,000 bearers. In England and Wales in 1996 it was the 27th most numerous surname.

Twomey, Toomey, Ó Tuama
A Gaelic Surname derived from *Tuaim* a rare early personal name. A sept of the Dál gCais. In the census of 1659 it was numerous in the Barony of Barretts in Cork. In 1890 Twomey was principally found in Cork and Kerry, Toomey in Dublin and Limerick, and the estimated number of bearers was 3,585. In the United States Twomey is the 7,505th most numerous surname with an estimated 2,750 bearers.

Tyrrell
A surname of Norman origin. At the time of the Cambro-Norman Invasion Hugh Tyrrell received the Lordship of Castleknock. In Westmeath they possessed the barony of Fertullagh. In 1890 Tyrrell was principally found in Dublin, Kildare and Wicklow, and the estimated number of bearers was 1,340. In the United States Tyrrell is the 6,374th most numerous surname with an estimated 5,500 bearers.

Vaughan, ó Mocháin
The Gaelic surname *ó Mocháin* and its variant *ó Macháin* have been so translated in Munster. There is also a Welsh surname derived from *fychan* mutation of *bychan* meaning 'little, small of stature'. In 1890 Vaughan was principally found in Cork, Clare, Limerick, Antrim and Down, and the estimated number of bearers was 1,570. In the United States Vaughan is the 854th most numerous surname with an estimated 38,500 bearers. In England and Wales in 1996 Vaughan was the 322nd most numerous surname.

McVeigh, Mac an Bheatha
The Gaelic surname means 'son of life'. It is both Irish and Scottish and difficult to distinguish from translations of other surnames. In 1890 McVeigh was principally found in Antrim and Down, and the estimated number of bearers was 3,050 (including variants).

Waldron, de Bhaldraithe
A surname of Cambro-Norman origin, a branch of the Costelloes of Mayo. In 1890 the Waldron was principally found in Mayo, Roscommon and Dublin, and the estimated number of bearers was 1,930. In the United States it is the 1,904th most numerous surname with an estimated 19,250 bearers.

Walker
A surname of English or Scottish origin. The English surname is from the Old English *wealcere*, meaning 'a fuller of cloth'. The surname in this form originated in the west and north of England. In Lowland Scotland Walker was a trade name denoting the same as England, in the Highlands it was an anglicisation of *Mac an fhucadair*, meaning son of the smith or the stranger's son. In England and Wales in 1853 Walker was the eighteenth most numerous surname and the estimated number of bearers was 59,300. In Scotland in 1853 Walker was the twenty-eight most numerous surname and the estimated number of bearers was 14,600. In Ireland in 1890 Walker was principally found in Antrim, Dublin, Down and Derry, and the estimated number of bearers was 5,500. In the United States it is the 25th most numerous surname with an estimated 602,250 bearers. In England and Wales in 1996 it was the 15th most numerous surname. In Scotland in 1995 it was the 17th most numerous surname.

Wall, de Wale, de Vaal, de Bhál, Fáltach
A surname of Norman origin. It is scattered and their may have been

at least two septs in the west known as *Fálthach* (the adjectival form of
de Bhál). There is also an English surname derived from the Old
English *weall* from residence near some wall. In 1890 Wall was
principally found in Dublin, Waterford, Cork, Kilkenny, Limerick and
Tipperary, and the estimated number of bearers was 2,600. In the
United States Wall is the 555th most numerous surname with an
estimated 57,750 bearers. In England and Wales in 1996 it was the
341st most numerous surname.

Wallace, Bhailis
A surname of Camro-Norman, English or Scottish origin. In Scotland
Wallace most probably means a Strathclyde Briton and appeared in
Ayrshire, Renfrewshire and Strathclyde in the twelfth century. In
England Wallis and Wallace are a reference to Welshmen, and was to be
found in the border counties of Warwicks, Worcs. and Staffs. In
Ireland Woulfe describes *le Waleis*, meaning the Welshman as the
Norman equivalent of the Irish *Breathnach*. In 1890 Wallace was
principally found in Antrim, Galway, Cork, Limerick, Dublin, Down
and Derry, and the estimated number of bearers was 6,450. In the
United States Wallace is the 106th most numerous surname with an
estimated 222,750 bearers. In England and Wales in 1996 it was the
217th most numerous surname. In Scotland in 1995 it was the 49th
most numerous surname.

Walsh(e), Breathnach
A descriptive term applied generally to the early Cambro-Norman
Invaders, who had come from Wales (Welshman). It became
established as a surname in different parts of Ireland. In the barony of
Tirawley in Mayo, they are said to be descended from a Welshman
who came to Ireland in 1169. A sept of the name had established
themselves in east Cork by the fourteenth century, their ancestors had
been known as *le Waleys*. Also see Warren, and Welsh. In 1890 Walsh
was the forth most numerous surname in Ireland, the estimated
number of bearers was 41,700, and it was the most numerous surname
in Mayo. In that year the surname was found in large numbers in
nearly every county. It was principally found in Cork, Mayo,
Waterford, Galway, Dublin and Wexford. In the United States Walsh is
the 325th most numerous surname with an estimated 90,750 bearers.
In England and Wales in 1996 it was the 105th most numerous
surname.

Ward, Mac an Bhaird
A Gaelic surname meaning 'son of the bard'. A sept of Tír Connell,
who were bards to *ó Domhnaill* (O'Donnell) and who gave their name
to the parish of Lettermacaward (Leitir Mac an Bhaird) in the barony
of Boylagh. A sept of the Uí Mhaine who were bards to the ó
Ceallaigh (O'Kelly). They were seated at Muine Chasain and
Ballymacward. A sept of Oirgialla (Oriel), of which there is little
information. In England it is most likely from the Old English
wearde meaning 'watching, guarding'. In 1853 it was the thirtieth

most numerous surname in England and Wales, with an estimated 45,700 bearers. It is unlikely that the surname spread from England to Ireland. In 1890 Ward was the seventy-eight most numerous surname in Ireland and the estimated number of bearers was 9,700. In that year the surname was found in every county in Ireland, but was chiefly found in Donegal, Dublin and Galway. In the United States Ward is the 66th most numerous surname with an estimated 297,000 bearers. In England and Wales in 1996 it was the 31st most numerous surname.

Warren, ó Marannáin
A surname of Norman origin, *de Warenne, de Gwarenna*, from La Varenne, in Seine-Inferieure in France. In east Kerry it has been re-anglicised as Walsh. The Gaelic *ó Marannáin*; a corruption of *ó Manannnáin* derived from *Manannán* (the name of an ancient sea-god), has been so anglicised in the neighbourhood of Kenmare, in Kerry. In 1890 Warren was principally found in Kerry, Dublin and Cork, and the estimated number of bearers was 1,570. In the United States Warren is the 138th most numerous surname with an estimated 184,250 bearers. In England and Wales in 1996 it was the 189th most numerous surname.

Waters
A translation of several Gaelic surnames. *Mac Conuisce* meaning son of the water-hound (*Cu-uisce*), a sept of Monaghan which spread to Mayo; *ó Fuaruisce* a sept of Sligo and Donegal, also translated as Whor(r)iskey; *ó hUaruisce*, also translated as Ho(u)riskey and Ca/oldwell; *ó hUisce* a sept of Connacht, also translated as Hiskey; *ó Tuaruis*, a sept of Donegal, also translated as T(u)(oo)rish. In addition there is an English surname eithr from a reference to a 'dweller by a stream; or derived from the personal name Walter, which was so pronounced. In 1890 the surname was principally found in Sligo, Wexford and Monaghan, and the estimated number of bearers was 2,110. In the United States it is the 429th most numerous surname with an estimated 71,500 bearers. In England and Wales in 1996 it was the 359th most numerous surname.

Watson
An English or Scottish surname meaning 'son of Walter'. *Waldhar* from the Old German, compound of *vald* 'rule' and *harja* 'folk'. The personal name was introduced into Britain by the Normans. In the sixteenth and seventeenth centuries the surname was numerous throughout the Scottish Lowlands. In England in 1853 Watson was the 48th most numerous surname and the estimated number of bearers was 34,800. In Scotland in 1863 Watson was the 28th most numerous surname and the estimated number of bearers was 15,000 (by 1995 it was the 20th most numerous surname). In 1890 it was numerous in Armagh, it was also to be found in Antrim and Down. The estimated number of bearers was 5,376. In the United States it is the 72nd most numerous surname with an estimated 283,250 bearers. In England and Wales in 1996 it was the 44th most numerous surname.

179

Watt, Watts
Both an Englishand a Scottish surname derived from Wat a diminutive of Walter. There might be some connection to *Mac Uaid* (MacQuaid of Monaghan). In 1890 Watt was principally found in Antrim, and the estimated number of bearers was 1,480. In the United States Watts is the 294th most numerous surname with an estimated 101,750 bearers. In England and Wales in 1996 it was the 131st most numerous surname. In Scotland in 1995 it was the 66th most numerous surname.

Webb
An English surname derived from the Old English *web* for 'weaver'. In 1890 Webb was principally found in Dublin and Antrim, and the estimated number of bearers was 1,480. In the United States it is the 125th most numerous surname with an estimated 198,000 bearers. In England and Wales in 1996 it was the 76th most numerous surname.

Webster
An English surname of similar derivation to the above. In 1890 Webster was principally found in Antrim and Dublin, and the estimated number of bearers was 940. In the United States it is the 395th most numerous surname with an estimated 77,000 bearers. In England and Wales in 1996 it was the 146th most numerous surname.

Weir, Mac an Mhaoir
The Gaelic surname *Mac an Mhaoir* meant 'son of the steward'. There were septs in Armagh, Westmeath, Offaly and Roscommon. *ó Corra* has also been so translated. A Scottish surname of Norman origin from one or other of the places named Vere. There were families in Lanarkshire. In Dumbartonshire *Mac Amhaoir* meaning 'son of the officer' was translated into Weir. Also an English surname derived from the Old English *wer* meaning 'weir, dam, fish-trap' referring to a 'dweller by the dam'or 'the keeper of the fishing-weir'. In 1890 Weir was principally found in Antrim and Armagh, and the estimated number of bearers was 2,510.

Welsh
The Scottish form of Walsh derived from ther Middle English *walshe* for 'foreigner'. Also see Walsh. In 1890 Welsh was principally found in Antrim, and the estimated number of bearers was 1,430. In the United States Welch is the 240th most numerous surname with an estimated 121,000 bearers, and Welsh is the 1,205th most numerous surnamw with an estimated 27,500 bearers. In England and Wales in 1996 Welch was the 434th most numerous surname.

Whelan, Phelan, ó Faoláin
A Gaelic surname meaning descendant of *Faolán*, which personal name was a diminutive of *Faol* meaning 'wolf'. A sept who were lords of Déise (Decies) before the Cambro-Norman invasion, which is also anglicised as Phelan. A sept of Leinster who were anciently seated

at Magh Lacha, a plain in the barony of Kells, Kilkenny. *ó hAoláin* is a variant found in Laois Offaly. In 1890 Whelan was the seventy-ninth most numerous surname, the estimated number of bearers was 9,500 and in that year the surname was chiefly found in Dublin, Wexford, Waterford, Tipperary, Carlow and Laois. In 1890 Phelan was principally found in Waterford, Kilkenny, Laois and Tipperary, and the estimated number of person bearing the surname was 4,100. In the United States Whelan is the 4,144th most numerous surname with an estimated 8,250 bearers, and Phelan is the 2,914th most numerous surname with an estimated 11,000 bearers.

White, de Faoite
A surname of English, Scottish and Cambro-Norman origin. *Le Whyte* meaning 'of fair complexion'. As an Anglo-Norman name it came to Ireland in the fourteenth century. It has been Gaelicised as *de Faoite*. Also see Galligan. In 1890 White was the fiftieth most numerous surname in Ireland, the estimated number of bearers was 13,000, and the surname was to be found in every county in Ireland, chiefly in Antrim, Cork, Dublin and Wexford. In the United States it is the 14th most numerous surname with an estimated 767,250 bearers. In England and Wales in 1996 it was the 16th most numerous surname. In Scotland in 1995 it was the 61st most numerous surname.

Wilkinson
Both an English and a Scottish surname meaning son of Wilkin a diminutive of Will or William. In 1890 Wilkinson was principally found in Antrim and Armagh, and the estimated number of bearers was 1,480. In the United States it is the 631st most numerous surname with an estimated 52,250 bearers. In England and Wales in 1996 it was the 72nd most numerous surname.

Williams
An English surname. After the Norman Conquest William was the most popular personal name until it was later replaced by John. In this form it may also be Welsh. See also immediately below. In 1853 it was the third most numerour surname in England and Wales with an estimated 159,900 bearers. In 1890 Williams was principally found in Dublin, Cork, Limerick and Antrim, and the estimated number of bearers was 4,030. In the United States it is the 3rd most numerous surname with an estimated 1,922,250 bearers. In England and Wales in 1996 it was the 3rd most numerous surname.

McWilliams, Mac Uilleim
A Scottish surname. The Clan *Mac Mhic Uilleim* are descendant from William, son of William fifth chief of Macleod. They were a powerful Gaelic clan and claimants to the Scottish throne. The surname has also been used as a synonym for MacQuillan in Down. In 1890 the surname was principally found in Antrim and Derry, and the estimated number of bearers was 1,930.

Williamson
A Lowland Scottish surname of obvious meaning. In 1890 Williamson was principally found in Antrim, Armagh, Derry and Tyrone, and the estimated number of bearers was 2,555. In the United States it is the 213th most numerous surname with an estimated 134,750 bearers. In England and Wales in 1996 it was the 169th most numerous surname. In Scotland in 1995 it was the 80th most numerous surname.

Willis
Both an English and a Scottish surname derived from William. In 1890 Willis was principally found in Antrim and Down, and the estimated number of bearers was 1,480. In the United States it is the 172nd most numerous surname with an estimated 151,250 bearers. In England and Wales in 1996 it was the 226th most numerous surname.

Wilson, Mac Liam
A surname of English origin meaning son of Will, i.e. William, a common personal name in England after 1066. It has been Gaelicised as *Mac Liam*. Also a Scottish surname meaning descendant of William, very numerous in Ulster. A sept of Clan Gunn of Caithness and Sutherland. In 1890 Wilson was the twenty-sixth most numerous surname in Ireland, the estimated number of bearers was 16,300, and the surname was principally to be found in Antrim, Armagh, Down, Tyrone, Dublin, Derry and Fermanagh. In the United States it is the 8th most numerous surname with an estimated 932,250 bearers. In England and Wales in 1996 it was the 8th most numerous surname. In Scotland in 1995 it was the 3rd most numerous surname.

Woods, Wood
An English surname denoting residence in or near a wood. In 1853 Wood was the fourteenth most numerous surname in England. In 1890 Woods was numerous in Monaghan, it was also to be found in Antrim, Armagh, Down, Tyrone, Dublin, Louth and Cork. The estimated number of bearers was 6,137. In the United States it is the 107th most numerous surname with an estimated 220,000 bearers. In England and Wales in 1996 Wood was the 26th most numerous surname, and Woods was the 155th most numerous surname. In Scotland in 1995 Wood was the 53rd most numerous surname.

Wright
Both an English and a Scottish surname, from the Old English *wyrhta*, or, *wryhta* 'carpenter, joiner'. A surname common to the Lowlands of Scotland and the North of England. In 1890 Wright was principally found in Antrim, Down, Dublin and Armagh, and the estimated number of bearers was 4,610. In the United States it is the 31st most numerous surname with an estimated 519,750 bearers. In England and Wales in 1996 it was the 14th most numerous surname. In Scotland in 1995 it was the 56th most numerous surname.

Wylie, Wiley
This Scottish surname is a diminutive of William. In England the surname is of local origin from many and varied placenames. In 1890 Wylie was principally found in Antrim, and the estimated number of bearers was 2,285 (including variants).

Wynne, Ó Maolghaoithe
A Gaelic surname meaning descendant of *Maolghaoithe* (chief of the wind). A sept of Tirconnell who were originally seated in the parish of Clondavaddock, who apppear to have moved south to Connacht. Also takes the form of Magee. *Mac Gaoithe* another sept of Donegal has been so translated. An *ó Gaoithín* (similar derivation) sept of Connacht. There is also a Welsh surname from *gwyn* meaning 'white, fair'. In 1890 the surname was principally found in Dublin and Sligo, and the estimated number of bearers was 2,110. In the United States Wynn is the 909th most numerous surname with an estimated 35,750 bearers, and Wynne is the 3,674th most numerous surname with an estimated 8,250 bearers.

Young
An English surname from the Old English *geong* 'young' meaning a young man. In 1863 Young was the twentieth most numerous surname in Scotland and the estimated number of bearers was 17,600. In 1890 Young was principally found in Antrim, Tyrone, Dublin, Cork, Down and Derry, and the estimated number of bearers was 5,860. In the United States it is the 28th most numerous surname with an estimated 530,750 bearers. In England and Wales in 1996 it was the 49th most numerous surname. In Scotland in 1995 it was the 19th most numerous surname.

----

www.irishsurnames.net

www.irishgenealogyhomepage.com

seanequinn@ireland.com